The Lesbian South

The Lesbian South

Southern Feminists,
the Women in Print Movement,
and the Queer Literary Canon

· ·

JAIME HARKER

The University of North Carolina Press Chapel Hill

This book was published with the assistance of the Fred W. Morrison Fund of the University of North Carolina Press.

Set in Charis and Lato by Westchester Publishing Services
Manufactured in the United States of America

The University of North Carolina Press has been a member of the
Green Press Initiative since 2003.

Library of Congress Cataloging-in-Publication Data
Names: Harker, Jaime, author.
Title: The lesbian South : southern feminists, the women in print movement,
    and the queer literary canon / Jaime Harker.
Description: Chapel Hill : University of North Carolina Press, [2018] |
    Includes bibliographical references and index.
Identifiers: LCCN 2018004679| ISBN 9781469643342 (cloth : alk. paper) |
    ISBN 9781469643359 (pbk : alk. paper) | ISBN 9781469643366 (ebook)
Subjects: LCSH: Lesbian authors—Southern States. | American Literature—
    Southern States—History and criticism. | Lesbians—Southern States—
    Social life and customs. | Feminism and literature—Southern States.
Classification: LCC PS153.L46 H37 2018 | DDC 810.9/9206643—dc23
    LC record available at https://lccn.loc.gov/2018004679

Cover illustration: Untitled pictorial map of the South by Sue Sneddon,
from an issue of *Feminary: A Feminist Periodical for the South, Emphasizing
the Lesbian Vision*. Courtesy of Sue Sneddon.

For Dixie Grimes,

my lesbian feminist hero

Contents

Introduction, 1
Southern, Feminist, Queer: The Archive of Southern Lesbian Feminism

1 Creating a Southern Lesbian Feminist Culture, 17
The Women in Print Movement and the Battle of the Literary

2 The Radical South, 58
Politics and the Lesbian Feminist Imaginary

3 Queer Sexuality and the Lesbian Feminist South, 99

4 Women's Space, Queer Space, 140
*Communes, Landykes, and Queer Contact Zones in the
Lesbian Feminist South*

Conclusion, 189
Lesfic: Alternative Publishing, Activism, and Queer Women Writers

Acknowledgments, 197

The Lesbian South Timeline, 199

Notes, 203

Bibliography, 215

For Further Research, 229

Index, 233

A gallery of illustrations follows page 98

The Lesbian South

Introduction

Southern, Feminist, Queer:
The Archive of Southern Lesbian Feminism

. . . .

The genesis for *The Lesbian South* came in 2009, when I was reading a book of essays by Jane Rule. Rule explained why she moved from mainstream presses to feminist presses: "They have a growing network of bookstores all over North America, . . . they often sell large numbers of books through direct mail order, and their customers are people for whom books are important sources of nourishment."[1] Fed up with mainstream publishers, Rule decided to publish with "Naiad, a lesbian/feminist press in the States, run by Barbara Grier, whom I've known for twenty years."[2] Despite the press's challenges, including amateurish book covers, Rule felt comfortable with Naiad because they were committed to selling books over time and making "a living for themselves and their writers."[3]

Naiad books were a ubiquitous presence in gay bookstores when I came out. I still own the movie tie-in edition of Jane Rule's *Desert of the Heart*—a subtle novel adapted into a spectacularly trashy movie in the 1980s. I had never thought about Naiad Press in any sustained way, other than with slight embarrassment, but it suddenly occurred to me: Naiad Press had been based in Tallahassee, Florida. This meant that the largest lesbian press in the United States had been located in the South. No one, as far as I could tell, had ever remarked on the press's location, however. Making sense of that fact led, circuitously, to this book.

In some sense, though, I have been preparing to write this book for decades. My parents moved to Atlanta in 1989. I wandered into Charis Books, one of the oldest feminist bookstores in the country, by accident; my parents lived close by. Just one look at the Naiad paperbacks and crystals let me know that I had hit the jackpot. Whenever I visited Atlanta from then on, I would go to Charis. I was something of a gay bookstore connoisseur, so I noticed that Charis had books I had never seen anywhere else. Southern gay culture, I was learning, was both distinctive and fascinating. That early exposure to gay southern culture was excellent preparation for my campus visit to the University of Mississippi in 2003. Oxford, Mississippi felt right to me from my very first visit; I still remember having lunch at the now-defunct Downtown Grill (whose executive chef would become my partner twelve years later), looking out at the courthouse, and suddenly realizing *that* was where Benjy went the wrong way around the Square (in Faulkner's *The Sound and the Fury*). And I was hooked. Despite my friends' surprise, I was all in, ready to immerse myself in southern gay culture.

During my first semester, which was unsettling at best, I read John Howard's *Men Like That* and discovered a vast, hidden network of queer southerners in places ranging from state rest stops to gay bars in Jackson, Mississippi. Howard queered the entire landscape of my new home, showing me gay Mississippi authors (including Hubert Creekmore from Water Valley, where I currently reside), ancient murder scandals, and a Mississippi Civil Rights leader caught red-handed in a gay bar. He gave me language to understand the strange "open secret" of queer acceptance in Mississippi: a tolerance for gay family members and friends that far surpassed that of the Mormon culture from which I sprang, a code of silence preventing anyone from actually calling those friends and family "gay," and a total disconnect between the kind behavior of individuals and the homophobic voting patterns of the state as a whole (Mississippi, for example, passed its anti–gay marriage constitutional amendment in 2004 with an 88 percent majority). Howard made the point that what mattered in Mississippi was not if you were gay but if you were *known*. In small local communities, gay Mississippians, embedded in webs of kinship and friendship, lived quite comfortably, in a completely different pattern from the out gay neighborhoods of urban queers. National gay magazines frame queer life as a binary: out, liberated gays in urban areas in the North and West and oppressed, closeted queers in a homophobic South. But there is often a third way, one that Howard first articulated for me: "They were aware but rather *chose to ignore*."[4] I have lived in John Howard's Mississippi ever since, and it has been as charming and welcoming as the man himself.

Naiad Press got me thinking differently about gay southern culture, however. Naiad Press marketed itself as "the biggest lesbian press in the world"; it was *out*, in the classic gay liberation sense of the word. Was this an aberration or a larger movement? That question led me to memoirs and bibliographies, used bookstores and interlibrary loans, archives and periodicals and unpublished dissertations, as I discovered a network of southern lesbian feminists who created a radical literary tradition. Southern lesbian feminist writers worked within a revolution in print culture known as the women in print (WIP) movement. Anchored in small feminist presses, feminist periodicals, and feminist bookstores, WIP distrusted mainstream publishing and felt that only an autonomous publishing system could allow women to build an authentic women's culture. Feminist reading and writing communities welcomed and nurtured lesbian writers in unprecedented ways by providing a broader base of readership and promotion.

Southern writers, editors, and publishers were key players in this movement. Adopted southerner Barbara Grier ran Naiad Press. Daughters, Inc., one of the most prestigious women's presses, was founded by Texan June Arnold and published Rita Mae Brown, Blanche McCrary Boyd, and Bertha Harris (from Florida, South Carolina, and North Carolina, respectively). Feminist collectives published numerous periodicals in the South, notably Charlotte's *Sinister Wisdom* and Durham's *Feminary*. These print venues nurtured southern lesbian feminist writers including Minnie Bruce Pratt, Ann Allen Shockley, Alice Walker, Mab Segrest, and Cris South. These writers published not only in southern outlets but also in national feminist publications and presses like *off our backs*, *Ms.* magazine, and Firebrand Books; they also attended national conferences and participated in feminist retreats across the country. Even southern lesbian writers only tenuously connected to the feminist movement, like Fannie Flagg, or overtly hostile to it, like Florence King, participated in and benefitted from the publishing possibilities that emerged from WIP. The emergence of a Dorothy Allison would have been impossible without the feminist print culture that nurtured her.

The Lesbian South constructs a genealogy of southern lesbian feminism, from its origins in pre-Stonewall lesbian publishing, through lesbian feminist print culture, to its legacies and aftermaths. It explores the archive of southern lesbian feminism, one deeply engaged with radical politics, queer sexuality, and liberatory space. In its analysis, *The Lesbian South* intervenes in three key critical traditions: southern studies, feminist history and theory, and queer theory. Recognizing the network of southern lesbian feminist writers challenges the narrative and theoretical concerns of each scholarly movement. Below, I discuss the relationship of *The Lesbian South* with southern studies, feminist history, lesbian feminism, and queer theory to frame the arguments and conversations of this book.

Southern Literature and the Lure of Southern Essentialism

Southern literature has always been a fraught specialty. The idea of southern exceptionalism was essential to the Confederacy's defense of slavery, and that legacy haunts most invocations of "southern," in literature as elsewhere. Michael Kreyling argues that southern literature was a politically inflected canon that disavowed its own investment in politics. The Southern Agrarians touted the South's "organic integrity,"[5] grounded in "a few universal, transcendent propositions: community, tradition, nature, and God woven over time into a 'metaphysical dream.'"[6] This idyllic construction of the community and honor of the South depended on a willful ignorance of the specifics of the real violence, rape, theft, and terrorism inherent in the plantation system, and the transmutation of that system into Jim Crow and the tenant farming system.

Whatever complexities the Southern Agrarians brought to political discourse (Martyn Bone, for example, argues that the Southern Agrarians offered a more complicated version of the South than the nostalgic "moonlight and magnolia" version of nineteenth-century regionalists[7]), southern literary critics preferred an "enhanced but essential South"[8] that obscured the material conditions and noxious racial politics of its creation. Kreyling explains that "asymmetrical shapes of historical experience were converted to myth."[9] African American writers were largely excluded from this mythic tradition, as were other writers of color, white women writers, and queer writers, whose "perverse" interests were seen as antithetical to the traditional, heterosexual community of the South. Joel Peckham argued in 2013, for example, that "[Minnie Bruce] Pratt's open lesbianism may have made her somewhat of a third rail to Southern scholars—not only because speaking about lesbianism in the context of Southern literature might be unsettling to traditional conceptions of the region, or because by being designated as lesbian she has been set apart, but also because openly lesbian Southern writers like Rita Mae Brown or Dorothy Allison seem a 'new' phenomenon, unprecedented, ahistorical."[10]

The particularly southern construction of the literary has undergone extensive critique over the last several decades. Most recently, that critique has coalesced under the "new southern studies," which, Leigh Anne Duck argues, seeks "more interesting ways to explore how region is produced, imagined and experienced and how cultural forms move, interact, and develop."[11] For Duck, the South is "a mutable space, with its unfixed, porous borders and widely diverse residents—many of whom maintain strong attachments to other places," rather than "a thickly meaningful and binding regional culture."[12] New southern studies is interdisciplinary, transnational, and deeply suspicious of fixed geographical or identity categories. Transnational work has been particularly important, framing qualities understood as uniquely southern within larger networks and traditions, including plantation culture. Annette Trefzer's and Kathryn McKee's special issue of *American Literature*, "The Global South," and Jon Smith and Deborah Cohn's edited collection *Look Away! The U.S. South in New World Studies* are two examples from transnational southern studies.[13]

Given the ideological roots of "the South" and southern literature's ability to incorporate African American and white women writers without transforming its essentialist paradigm,[14] some critics have argued that invoking "the South" at all is to embrace an irredeemable term of chauvinism.[15] In her essay "Southern Nonidentity," Duck notes that the particular history of racial segregation in conceptions of the southern regional identity raise a "concern as to whether the concept of 'Southern identity' might be inherently treacherous."[16] Of course, it is true, as Duck argues, that "in articulating identity, [scholars] uncover nonidentity: members of a purported or even self-proclaimed group who lack shared characteristics, individuals who do not identify with the beliefs and behaviors they reveal to the public, and even persons with identical belief systems signifying diametrically opposed psychological dynamics."[17] And it is also true that cultural others sometimes accessed political power by forging coalitions with white supremacists.

Avoiding *southern* as a term of analysis, however, doesn't prevent it from functioning as a disciplinary tool. Scholars have been contesting the meaning of southernness, notably in recent investigations of black southern identity. The notion of diaspora allows a broader investigation of southernness by including expatriate black southerners, and their descendants, as an essential part of the southern African American experience. Thadious Davis's 2011 *Southscapes*, for example, investigates "the South" with African American experience at the center without eliding the realities of racial apartheid and racial terror.[18] This broad interest in the particularities of black southern identity is apparent in the work of other scholars as well.[19] Critiquing the ideological problems of *the South* as a raced and classed term doesn't prevent these scholars from redefining and using the term in their own analyses.

Similarly, queer studies scholars construct subversive versions of the South. Books by Gary Richards, Michael Bibler, Scott Herring, E. Patrick Johnson, and Mary Gray[20] challenge the metronormativity of queer studies in its oversight of southern and rural experience. That focus continues to complicate the popular view of the South as a site of abjection for racial and sexual minorities, detailing histories of resistance and reconstruction.

As part of this larger revisionist body of work, I have made *southern* a key term of analysis in *The Lesbian South*. That doesn't mean, however, that the particular writers I investigate all had the same understanding of or investment in southernness. Florence King and Blanche McCrary Boyd had a conservative, nostalgic notion of the South; even self-proclaimed radical Rita Mae Brown often shows evidence of the lure of concepts like honor and community as unchanging southern virtues. Some identified the South with political radicalism, not political conservatism (as I discuss in chapter 2). Alice Walker identifies only with black southern culture, rejecting the white South. For some, being southern inspired their radicalism and their lesbianism; for others, southernnness was an obstacle to both. Fannie Flagg and Dorothy Allison made southern identity primary to their personas, and for others, it was secondary. Some performed stereotypic southernness for cultural cachet; Rita Mae Brown, for example, used her southernness to buttress her poor, working-class credentials. For Dorothy Allison, southernness communicated her cultural outsiderness and allowed her to embody non-assimilation. To complicate things even further, some writers in this study embody contradictory relationships to southernness simultaneously.

These differences make a coherent definition of the South impossible to posit. Rather than adjudicating between these multiple positions, I represent each writer's perspective as I discuss her work, without taking sides about the "right" way to do southern identity or southern literature. Chapters 2, 3, and 4, however, articulate how the archive of southern lesbian feminism challenges and reimagines three common claims about the "essential South." Where the Fugitives positived a conservative, traditional South, southern lesbian feminists created a radical South; where the Fugitives embraced a normative view of family, southern lesbian feminists embraced transgressive sexuality; where the Fugitives celebrated a "sense of place"—a mystical connection to an unchanging landscape—southern lesbian feminists viewed space as malleable and changeable. The themes of chapters 2, 3, and 4—radical politics, queer sexuality, queer space—point to a distinctive recalibration of southern letters and southern identity that the archive of southern lesbian feminism accomplished. That collective synthesis is *The Lesbian South*'s contribution to the larger scholarly conversation about the meaning of the South. In *The Lesbian South*, "southern" includes expatriates, carpetbaggers, scalawags, outside agitators, race traitors, queers, and the nonwhite southerners who are so consistently erased from prescriptive notions of southern identity. Diasporic southerners are part of the story, as are immigrant southerners, whether they come from the Midwest, New

York, or California; Barbara Grier's role in shaping popular notions of lesbian literature, especially through the Tallahassee-based Naiad Press, makes her an essential part of the story of *The Lesbian South*. One can be southern and many other things—Latina, African American, Midwestern, queer, radical—and the subjects of *The Lesbian South* complicate southern identity in multiple ways. Yet for most of the writers discussed in this book, southern identity remained an important term of self-identification, one which they used to connect with each other. Struggling against the implicit racism, classism, and small-mindedness of their southern inheritance was a quixotic and generative gesture; the archive of southern lesbian feminism was invested in creating a South that was radical, queer, and free, even as some of its writers were simultaneously drawn to its reactionary pull. Such contradictions made this literary movement dynamic, flawed, and interesting.

The southern lesbian feminists of this study understood that simply dropping the term *southern*, or absenting oneself from the South, doesn't erase its ideological power. Deconstructing it doesn't take away its affective power, either, as Scott Romine argues.[21] Instead, the archive of southern lesbian feminism created alternative myths to counteract the "enhanced but essential South" of an emerging southern literature. The creation of a South grounded in different ideologies and notions of power, one in which "radical," "queer," and "southern" are not mutually exclusive, is the most lasting legacy of southern lesbian feminist writers, in their explorations of radical politics, transgressive sexuality, and queer space.

Women's Liberation and the Historicizing of Feminist History

Like *southern*, *feminist* is a term fraught with ideological weight. Unlike *southern*, *feminist* is generally not used with nostalgia and longing. How we have historicized women's liberation, and how that narrative continues to inform, and misinform, our understanding of it, is a story of competing narratives and self-interested selection. Clare Hemmings's *Why Stories Matter* is an excellent dissection of the three mutually exclusive narratives we share about feminism: progress (away from essentialism and toward deconstruction), return (to the politically invested feminism of old), or loss (of the commitment and unity of early feminism).[22] Of these, the progress narrative is by far the most common: women's liberation was middle-class, essentialist, and ignorant of race and class issues, and only later did larger questions of diversity—most recently, trans identity—become important in feminism. Only the rise of critiques of lesbians and women of color, and then critiques of the nature of identity itself, saved feminism from its own racist and essentialist origins.

Hemmings analyzes *how* these narratives of feminism make their own perspective logical and the rest unsupportable. She also suggests the consequences of such metanarratives—they oversimplify, erase, and sometimes falsify the complex and multiple movements all competing under the moniker "women's liberation": "Implicitly or explicitly, too, each decade is understood to house particular schools of thought and particular theorists, irrespective of whether or not their work spans much longer periods. . . . Whether positively or negatively inflected, the chronology remains the same, the decades overburdened yet curiously flattened, despite each story's unique truth claims."[23] The full complexity of women's liberation, then, is elided in all these narratives.

The problem of seeing feminism as dominated by discrete "waves" is a problem of "generational logic," as Jack Halberstam defines it. When Susan Faludi used a mother-daughter metaphor to describe the relationships of older and younger feminists (and the young's lack of respect for their foremothers), Halberstam questioned this insistence on placing feminism in discrete generations. "Faludi," Halberstam argued, "ignored the many challenges made to generational logics within a recent wave of queer theory on temporality. . . . Theorists . . . have elaborated more mobile notions of intergenerational exchange, arguing that the old does not always have to give way for the new, the new does not have to completely break with the old, and that these waves of influence need not be thought of always and only as parental."[24] It is a testament to the lure of such generational narratives, however, that Halberstam, on the very next page, branded Faludi "out of date"[25] compared to her own version of "gaga" feminism that was, she maintained, more fun and relevant to the young folks at the conference.

I thoroughly agree with both Hemmings and Halberstam that we need to complicate our temporal narratives of progress and remember that gender variance, pop culture interventions, "what if" musings, and deconstructionist performativity were a strand of women's liberation from its earliest incarnations. Hemmings's insistence on complexity and simultaneity came through an encounter with the archive:

> My own entry into this project arose partly from the experience of disjuncture between the linear stories told about the recent past of Western feminist theory and my encounters with multiple feminisms and feminist debates through this forty-to-fifty-year period.

I still remember my surprise when I first visited a feminist archive, perused newsletters and magazines from activist groups, and realized that discussions about sadomasochism in the lesbian community had been raging long before the sex wars and that black feminist and transnational critique had been a consistent component of feminist theory, rather than one initiated in the late 1970s or 1980s.[26]

Any trip to the archive, any perusal of a periodical from the time itself (as opposed to books *about* a particular era) yields similar complications and surprises. Many topics we consider contemporary concerns in feminism—such as intersectionality, polyamory, and transnationalism—were debated from the earliest days of the movement. Women's liberation was a combative, simultaneous, and complicated braid of multiple conversations, movements, and manifestos.

Poet Minnie Bruce Pratt expressed something similar in an oral history interview:

I think it's important, again, that Southern experiences of things not being so split up. So, for instance, when I went to the great Southeast Lesbian Conference in Atlanta in 1975, . . . we went to one of the theaters in the Little Five Points area—don't remember which one. There were about 300 lesbians in this theater.

Before the entertainment started, we were all singing, "I've been cheated, been mistreated, when will I be loved." And then the entertainment was the Dykes of the American Revolution, the DAR. They identified themselves as a socialist feminist group, right? And the people in this group did a drag show. . . . It was a lesbian feminist drag show with a butch and a femme. . . . Um, the concept of butch and femme was floating around. I knew, for instance, when I got together with Cris, that I was getting together with a butch, you know. She was all butch, comb in her back pocket.[27]

The simultaneity of this scene violates all the decade-based logic of histories of feminism. The essentialism of an emerging lesbian feminism coexists with "older" butch-femme roles and "anticipatory" work on the performativity of gender—lesbian feminist drag. Camp and humor coexist with serious political critique. The portrait Pratt paints here gets even more complex when you realize that Cris, the butch with a comb in her back pocket, would later come out as a bottom in sadomasochistic (S/M) culture. None of the paradigms Hemmings deconstructs so thoroughly can make sense of the simultaneity of this scene from 1975.

So what is the solution? Hemmings resists writing a counternarrative that "corrects" the oversimplifications, because, as she writes, "I have been persuaded by feminist historiographers' insistence that which story one tells about the past is always motivated by the position one occupies or wishes to occupy in the present. Since fullness in representations of the past can never be reached, a corrective approach will always be likely to erase the conditions of its own construction, particularly if it purports to be the final word."[28] But what if one doesn't "erase the conditions of its own construction," and doesn't purport to be the final word? Such complicated narratives, carefully delineated and framed, have been emerging over the last decade, along with memoirs and reprints that begin to provide a more nuanced understanding of women's liberation. Essay collections like *Feminist Coalitions* and *No Permanent Waves* emphasize the continuities between our "histories" of feminism and the fact that feminist activism has multiple genealogies, including disarmament and peace activism and other work that isn't just "women's issues."[29] Anne M. Valk's *Radical Sisters* investigates the many sites of feminist activism in one bounded geographic place in Washington, D.C., including radical feminist groups like the Furies and African American community activism.[30] Numerous studies of feminist activism across the South further complicate these simplistic narratives of feminism's failures.[31]

The Lesbian South contributes to this larger project of feminist history and genealogy. Through autobiographical framing and contemporary ruminations on the queer South, I make visible the position I occupy, to account for the conditions of this particular historical revision. And, like Hemmings, I make my own disruptive encounter with archives central to my narrative of southern lesbian feminist writers. The "archive" has become a productive site of analysis in queer scholarship, from Ann Cvetcovitch's *An Archive of Feeling* to Amy Stone and Jaime Cantrell's *Out of the Closets, into the Archives*.[32] Scholars' attempts to broaden what counts as an archive for queer investigation, to include, for example, oral histories, are laudable; they have influenced my decision to call this collective writing tradition the "archive" of southern lesbian feminism. Immersing myself in printed material from the 1970s and 1980s—periodicals, book jacket copy, original book publications, and especially letters, unfinished manuscripts, and other collected material from author archives—helped me to encounter a historical moment in all its complexity, without the mediations of subsequent conventional wisdom or movement history. Book history allowed me to access writers' understanding of movements and events when women's liberation wasn't fixed but was still, in a very real sense, being invented. In *The Lesbian South*, I try to recapture the sense of experimental possibility in early women's liberation, its sense of unfixity, possibility, and futurity.

As part of this attempt to immerse myself in that moment of becoming, I decided not to do contemporary interviews with the surviving writers discussed in this study. This is not to say that such interviews cannot be illuminating, as the work of Julie Enszer on *Conditions* and feminist presses shows.[33] Sometimes, however, with the passage of time and subjects' political evolutions, assessments of their experience and careers *now* differ significantly from their experience *as it happened*.[34] I wanted to encounter their experience as far from the "settled" narratives of feminist history as possible.

This decision imposed limitations on this study, but it also meant that I discovered networks, alliances, and friendships that I never could have anticipated—not only relationships between the subjects of *The Lesbian South*, but also connections to other figures and movements that are often seen as totally separate. I looked at their novels, essays, and poetry, read oral histories by Dorothy Allison and Minnie Bruce Pratt, and went through the considerable archival holdings of Naiad Press, Dorothy Allison, Minnie Bruce Pratt, Blanche McCrary Boyd, Mab Segrest, and Catherine Nicholson. I discovered friendships and alliances between many of the figures in this book; southern lesbian feminists, it seems, kept tabs on each other. I also discovered alliances between the archive of southern lesbian feminism and other movements often studied in isolation. As I discuss in chapters 2 and 3, many key figures in what we now call "women of color feminism," for example, including Barbara Smith and Cherríe Moraga, were closely aligned with southern lesbian feminists like Dorothy Allison and Minnie Bruce Pratt; Moraga was also part of the Barnard Sex Conference that became such a flash point for the lesbian sex wars, even though we usually don't include women of color in that particular fight. Smith and Moraga were, for a time, a couple, and other feminists of color were also lesbians, enmeshing ethnicity and sexuality in complicated ways that we also simplify in our narratives. *The Lesbian South* suggests many such intertwining strands between schools of thought and feminist groups that we tend to consider in isolation. While *The Lesbian South* creates its own limits (with its southern focus and its methodological choices), I hope to gesture toward more complicated webs and more porous boundaries in my own narrative.

Lesbian Feminism and Queer History

In *The Lesbian South*, I use both *lesbian feminist* and *queer* to describe the writers I analyze. Lesbian feminism is a movement with a terrible reputation. Many contemporary feminist historians blame lesbian feminism, and the "women's culture" it fostered, for the "failure" of feminism.[35] Feminists of color criticized lesbian feminists for their separatism and their inadequate attention to issues of race.[36] The "sex wars" of the 1980s further destroyed the reputation of lesbian feminists, who rejected butch/femme and S/M lesbians for their "male-identified" and "violent" sexuality; in turn, the activists cast out of the movement criticized prescriptive notions of "women's sexuality."[37] Queer theorists have rejected lesbian feminism as frumpy, sexphobic, transphobic, and essentialist, the foil to queer theory's antinormative, radical, and cool rebellion.

I didn't set out to investigate lesbian feminism, but it was an unavoidable element of the women's liberation scene when the women in the book were writing and publishing; whether embracing, tolerating, or resisting lesbian feminism, the southern lesbian feminist writers of *The Lesbian South* produced their work under its shadow. Lesbian feminism informed their publication venues, their themes, their sense of audience, and their sense of identity and purpose. It was the reading and writing community that made them. To understand and reclaim these southern writers, I had to come to terms with lesbian feminism.

When I was coming out in the early 1990s, lesbian feminism was already a throwback, a place where earnest, unfunny politicos lectured you about eating meat and howled at the moon on the winter solstice. I thought I knew what lesbian feminism was. I had read Adrienne Rich's "Compulsory Heterosexuality and Lesbian Existence"; I had checked out Mary Daly's *Beyond God the Father*, which was kept in a locked box at Brigham Young University's library (and had to be liberated by a disapproving librarian with a secret key); I had browsed Clarissa Pinkola Estés's *Women Who Run with the Wolves* at my local lesbian bookstore, before buying Jeannette Winterson's *Written on the Body* (featuring a first-person protagonist whose gender is unknown but whose lust for women is lyrical). I wasn't hostile to lesbian feminism, but I thought it was essentialist and old-fashioned.

When I read Bertha Harris's introduction to the 1993 reprint of *Lover*, however, I discovered that there was more to lesbian feminism. Harris mentions many women who influenced her, including Jill Johnston, a dance critic for the *Village Voice* who came out in the late 1960s and was known as a hilarious provocateur. Nothing in Audre Lorde's and Adrienne Rich's beautiful, serious writing prepared me for Johnston's performance in *Town Bloody Hall*, a documentary about Norman Mailer's town hall on feminism in 1971. Johnston was funny and irreverent, reading a stream-of-consciousness manifesto that delighted the audience. And when she ran over time and Mailer tried to muscle her off the stage, she neither acquiesced nor ranted. She laughed at him. Then she rolled around on the stage with two friends and hugged one suggestively right next to the podium, where Mailer tried to introduce the next speaker. I laugh every time I watch that clip of her speech and Mailer's blustery attempts to regain control of "his" forum. The irreverence of Johnston's lesbian feminism surprised me.

Lesbian feminism was also intensely sexual. Lesbian feminists were always contrasted negatively with the "sex-positive" feminists of the 1980s and 1990s, which made them, by default, "sex-negative." But that first generation of lesbian feminists were committed nonmonogamists, perceived as hypersexual, even predatory. As I discuss in chapter 3, transgressive sexuality of all kinds erupts continually in the archive of southern lesbian feminism; it is a discourse that lesbian feminism initially fostered and then could not contain. The term *lesbian*, in the earliest days of women's liberation, functioned much as *queer* functions today—as a radical, disruptive force that claimed a "universalist" critique of existing social structures like the family, and even constructions of gender themselves. As Victoria Hesford suggests in her discussion of Kate Millet, "Lesbianism, for Millett and for others in the early years of the women's liberation movement, as we have seen, was not necessarily an identity to be celebrated as a thing in itself, nor was it simply an 'issue' among others within the larger political project of feminism. . . . Rather, it was something closer to what we now call *queer*—a practice of subverting existing social identities and of anticipating future forms of social and sexual life."[38] The "lesbian" in early women's liberation was a perverse, hypersexualized figure who disrupted the mainstreaming of feminism. Indeed, the lesbian was a nonassimilationist queer before that term even existed. In an age when, as Bonnie Morris argues, the term *lesbian* seems to be disappearing (as those who in a previous generation might have identified as lesbian are more likely to identify as bisexual, or genderqueer, or transgendered),[39] remembering the connection of lesbian to radical political critique, sexual nonconformity, and utopian myth making is more important than ever.

In *The Lesbian South*, I look at a diverse group of writers for whom lesbian feminism was important to their identities as southern lesbians and to their development as writers. Southerners made a significant contribution to lesbian feminist discourse in the development of the women in print movement (chapter 1) and in the creation of a literary archive involving radical politics (chapter 2), queer sexuality (chapter 3), and the queering of space (chapter 4). Lesbian feminism had a generative role in the distinctively out and queer southern literary tradition investigated in this book. *The Lesbian South* thus contributes to a more nuanced understanding of lesbian feminism, one that acknowledges its influence on queer theory, recognizes its possibilities as well as its failures, and investigates particular reading and writing communities within lesbian feminism.

Queer genealogical narratives tend to scapegoat lesbian feminism, seeing it as an inferior discourse that gave way to the more sophisticated, transgressive, and transformative potential of queer theory. It is easy to see how destructive and unnecessary those lesbian feminist battles were; it is harder to see how similar infighting continues to circulate in queer theory today. Battles over pinkwashing, homonormativity, and queer history rage at conferences, in print, and in social media.[40] Michael Warner, one of the early scholars of queer theory, critiqued this infighting in an op-ed retrospective on queer theory for the *Chronicle of Higher Education*: "Queer theory in this broader sense now has so many branches, and has developed in so many disciplines, that it resists synthesis. The differences have often enough become bitter, sometimes occasioning the kind of queerer-than-thou competitiveness that is the telltale sign of scarcity in resources and recognition. . . . And given queer theory's strong suspicion of any politics of purity, it is ironic that queer theorists can often strike postures of righteous purity in denouncing one another."[41] Obviously, queer theory is more diverse than a few gatekeepers or well-publicized skirmishes. So, too, was lesbian feminism more than its well-documented failures. Moving beyond "queerer-than-thou" dismissals opens up more nuanced considerations of a host of cultural and literary phenomena, including the legacy of lesbian feminism itself. Using *lesbian feminist* as a descriptive term emphasizes continuities between the lesbian feminist and the queer and complicates, I hope, our more simplistic histories of the movement.

The Lesbian South is informed by the complex field of queer studies, as my subsequent chapters on radical politics, queer sexuality, and queer space demonstrate. It will, I hope, make a contribution to queer studies, grounded as it is in literary criticism, in the particularities of lesbian feminist print culture, and in the diverse range and variety of southern lesbian feminist literary experiments.

The Queer South and the Archive of
Southern Lesbian Feminism

What follows is an exploration of the archive of southern lesbian feminism. In chapter 1, "Creating a Southern Lesbian Feminist Culture," I introduce the main players of this literary movement and their relationship with feminist print culture. The *Ladder* was an important precursor, as was the rise of pulp paperbacks, which democratized access to literature through alternative distribution systems. The chapter traces the rise of book publishers, periodicals, bookstores, writers, and readers in a print culture network, with a focus on publishers Barbara Grier (the *Ladder* and Naiad Press) and June Arnold (Daughters, Inc.), the periodicals *Amazon Quarterly*, *Sinister Wisdom*, and *Feminary*, and a host of southern lesbian feminist writers including Bertha Harris, Rita Mae Brown, and Dorothy Allison. It chronicles the invention of a southern lesbian feminist culture through a battle of the literary between the experimental, led by June Arnold, who believed feminist (and lesbian) writing should be dramatically different from the status quo, and the popular, led by Barbara Grier, who embraced feminist and lesbian characters within familiar, accessible forms. The avant-garde/popular debate inspired the diverse literary production of southern lesbian feminists. By telling the story of the women in print movement through a genealogy of southern lesbian feminism, I set up the theoretical and literary investigations of *The Lesbian South*.

In the next three chapters I consider how this literary tradition engages radicalism, sexuality, and utopian spaces. In chapter 2, "The Radical South," I explore the engagement of southern lesbian feminists in radical politics and southern identity, with particular attention to the antiracist coalitions that emerged in the 1980s. The South has a long tradition of radical social movements, from Reconstruction to civil rights, but somehow the notion of an innately conservative South never goes away. Southern lesbian feminists were invested in recovering a radical history and creating their own radical legacies. This chapter analyzes the evolving approach to radical politics in the archive of southern lesbian feminism, from the radical poetic experiments of Rita Mae Brown and Pat Parker to intersectional antiracist coalitions like the collectives Conditions (which included Dorothy Allison) and Feminary (which included Cris South, Mab Segrest, and Minnie Bruce Pratt). The chapter analyzes how the archive of southern lesbian feminism created alternative narratives to make the South a hotbed of social and political change.

In chapter 3, "Queer Sexuality and the Lesbian Feminist South," I explore the central role of transgressive sexuality in the literary creations of southern lesbian feminists—both their embrace of grotesque sexual southernness and their critiques of the intersection of sexuality and power. The South has long been associated with deviant sexuality, most notably with the rise of the southern gothic and its inescapable queerness. This creates an unexpected bridge between the South and queer theory, for which deviance is a site of resistance against the normative. Most southern lesbian feminist writers in this study embraced the southern grotesque as a way to explore a wide range of hitherto unspeakable sexual practices. This chapter investigates the many nonnormative sexualities in the archive of Southern lesbian-feminism, including polyandry, incest, intergenerational sex, and rape.

In chapter 4, "Women's Space, Queer Space," I explore the spatial re-imaginations of southern lesbian feminists, from communes to queer contact zones. "Sense of place" has often been a traditional way of understanding the distinctiveness of the South, but feminist and queer geographers have shown how space is anything but natural; the organization and imagination of space is deeply implicated in existing power structures and ideologies. This chapter uses geography to reassess the "landyke" movement and its appearance in the archive of southern lesbian feminism, through utopian novels, novels specifically about lesbian communes, and novels that explore reconstructions of space within a larger hegemonic system.

The conclusion considers some of the legacies of this literary and political movement. The rise of megabookstores and ebooks transformed the feminist bookstore–led ecology of the women in print movement, but lesbian writers continue to write. Absent the productive tension of literary, popular, and political within a small-press system, the contemporary scene features underground lesbian presses, self-published lesbian writers, and queer book festivals to create a new system of distribution, one less linked to radical political movements but no less effective as an underground network of the queer South.

In *The Lesbian South*, I construct a literary history of a group of writers who, when remembered at all, tend to be approached in isolation. These sassy, talented, resourceful, and often hilarious southern lesbian feminists deserve to be remembered as the remarkable tribe they were. I hope I have done them justice in this book. It is part memoir, part literary history and criticism, but it is, finally, a love letter to the South—*my* South, going on fifteen years now, full of sexual deviants and political radicals, scalawags and carpetbaggers, potheads and drunkards, embracing racial mixing, excess, and unadulterated kindness.

1 Creating a Southern Lesbian Feminist Culture

The Women in Print Movement and the Battle of the Literary

. . . .

Women's liberation was obsessed with print. Feminists believed that an independent media was essential to a political and cultural revolution, and so produced a diverse array of publications: newspapers, stapled newsletters, bound journals, glossy slicks, poetry chapbooks, bound paperbacks. These publications cropped up across the nation in big cities, small college towns, communes, and suburbs, and in every state. Feminists read each other's publications, reprinted articles, passed on announcements for journals, conferences, and meetings, and constructed, in the absence of the Internet, what would become known as the women in print (WIP) movement. The complete history of this movement has yet to be written, but a number of scholars have begun to excavate it,[1] and participants in the movement have written memoirs.[2] My narrative below contributes to this body of scholarship. I view the larger movement through a small cohort of southern lesbian feminists; many knew each other, but all engaged with queerness and southernness in consequential ways. They contributed to an ongoing debate about the role of literature in the creation of a distinctly lesbian feminist culture.

Two figures will help me frame the key debates of the WIP movement. Barbara Grier and June Arnold were older than most women's liberationists, and they could not have been more different in background or tactics. Texas native Arnold came from wealth and privilege; after graduating from Rice University and marrying, she moved to Greenwich Village with her four children, and eventually became a novelist and publisher of Daughters, Inc., a press that embodied a highbrow aesthetic. Grier, by contrast, was a self-taught literary critic and bibliophile who never attended college, and worked as a secretary and a bill collector. After decades of involvement with the lesbian publication the *Ladder*, she founded Naiad Press, which began in Reno, Nevada, moved to Kansas City, Missouri, and entered its most lucrative phase on its final move to Tallahassee, Florida. Arnold and Grier shared a fierce commitment to lesbian literature and a tenacity that others sometimes found grating.

These disparate figures challenged traditional notions of the literary, from above and below. For Arnold, the exclusion of women in general, and lesbians in particular, from the literary canon led her to theorize a specifically lesbian feminist version of the literary, marked by experimentation and by feminist politics. I call this the "feminist avant-garde." For Grier, the elitism of the literary was problematic; she was drawn to accessible narratives and valued the popular for the cultural work it performed, especially for lesbian readers. I call this the "popular" or "pulp" (strictly speaking, pulp refers to mass-produced small paperbacks, but it also suggests a popular intervention that is denigrated or dismissed by cultural gatekeepers). Both approaches are emblematic of larger trends in women's liberation, and thus construct accessible guideposts in my history of the WIP movement.

Both Arnold and Grier were important midwives to the emergence of southern lesbian feminist writers; consequently, they serve as useful introductions to the writers whose books will become my central focus in the next three chapters. Most of the writers in *The Lesbian South* had relationships with Arnold and/or Grier. These were not always warm relationships, but because both Arnold and Grier had strong personalities, vast networks, and dreams of world domination, they had a surprising number of encounters with southern lesbian feminist writers, which makes them excellent mechanisms for placing the writers of *The Lesbian South* within the feminist print culture of their early careers. What follows is an abbreviated history of the WIP movement, with an emphasis on southern lesbian writers.

Though I discuss Arnold and Grier as antagonists, they were coconspirators as well. Both believed that literature could change the world and that feminist literature would not only create new ways to understand gender but also liberate women from patriarchy. Despite personal proclivities, all feminist bookwomen embraced a wide range of literary forms, from the experimental to the pulpy. As Cecilia Konchar Farr and I argue, "The multiplicity of feminist literary practices marked the Women's Liberation Movement as a whole, resulting in a number of genres and formal styles. Feminist literary culture . . . produced texts that ranged freely across cultural hierarchies."[3] Avant-garde and popular books were produced by the same presses, sold in the same bookstores, and reviewed in the same feminist periodicals. It was the tension between these two poles that made early feminist print culture so inventive and so vibrant. The absolutist rhetoric of both Arnold and Grier often obscures the ways that their projects were mutually constitutive. Could feminist literature value the difficult and still embrace the accessible? Could writing be feminist *and* "literary"? This was the quixotic dream that drove many WIP participants and informed the archive of southern lesbian feminism that would emerge from it.

Lesbiana and the Creation of a Lesbian Literary Tradition

Long before women's liberation emerged in the late 1960s, Barbara Grier made her reputation as an obsessive lesbian bibliophile. Her mentor, librarian Jeannette Foster (who collected the first comprehensive bibliography of lesbian writing),[4] introduced her to the *Ladder* (*TL*), a small, subscription-only magazine for lesbians published by the Daughters of Bilitis, an organization advocating for the rights of gay women. The organization often emphasized "mainstreaming" and encouraged butch women to dress to pass; it also provided an outlet for lesbians to claim rights and imagine a national lesbian community. Though it would be seen as too conservative by the early 1970s, in the late 1950s it was a lifeline for the many women who embraced it.[5]

Barbara Grier's interest was less political and more literary. She cared about books, as she had from the age of thirteen when she marched up to the librarian and "requested books about homosexuals."[6] She wanted novels about lesbians and she wanted them when they were not easy to find, except, perhaps, in the wire racks at the local drugstore. Self-taught as a book collector (with help from her librarian partners and Foster), Grier tracked down any book with lesbian content and wrote reviews of them in *TL* under the pseudonym Gene Damon. By 1966, she had become the book review editor for *TL*, in a wide-ranging column titled *Lesbiana*.

Foster's *Sex Variant Women* provided a lesbian literary history, but *Lesbiana* created an up-to-date contemporary lesbian literary culture. Grier's tradition was free of the restrictive Cold War aesthetics that informed her college-educated *TL* peers; her literary tradition included every text that had lesbian content, no matter where it might fall in a cultural hierarchy. This included what we now refer to as "lesbian pulp," and what *TL* editor Barbara Gittings dismissed as "trash."[7] Grier, significantly, called these novels "paperback originals," a descriptive term that avoided the negative connotations of "pulp" and "trash," even though she considered many of the paperback originals to be trash. She once defined their plots with devastating brevity: "The old familiar round of girl meets girl, falls in love, leaves girl temporarily for another girl, and ends up back in the arms of the first girl friend. It has the actual number of obligatory sex scenes, and the happy ending which used to indicate a fair evening waster."[8] But for Grier, paperback originals were not *necessarily* badly written. Indeed, she lamented the decline of paperback originals at the end of the 1960s. Following the spoof above, she wrote,

> There are no really good paperback originals around anymore. I can't help wondering what happened to Valerie Taylor, Paula Christian, Ann Bannon, etc. Rumors circulate and say that Ann Bannon has given up writing. Valerie Taylor and Paula Christian seem to feel there is no publishing market for their kind of book, and Artemis Smith has left the field in favor of working toward hardback publication in esoteric fiction (which hasn't actually happened yet). It is, to put it bluntly, a damned shame, because the audience who bought their books by the thousands of copies still exists, still lives in isolated towns throughout the United States and still needs this vicarious involvement with a world they cannot or do not share personally.[9]

Grier articulated a vision of the "cultural work" of lesbian pulps that academics in the 1990s and 2000s would elaborate in greater detail.[10] For Grier, paperback originals were important because they created a virtual community for lesbians in "isolated towns," providing "vicarious involvement" and a sense of belonging. Whether she personally valued these books as literature was less important than the desires of the "audience who bought their books by the thousands." She may have marked these books with a *T* (for "trash") in her published bibliography,[11] but she refused to ignore or denounce them. As biographer Joanne Passet argued, "Barbara was contesting the power of mainstream literary critics. As she knew from personal experience and from the many women who wrote to her, any book that helped a lesbian recognize herself in print was worthy of recognition and preservation."[12]

Grier didn't review only lesbian pulps, however. Note her mention of Artemis Smith's turn to "hardback publication in esoteric fiction." *Paperback originals* is a carefully neutral term; *esoteric*, defined in the dictionary as "understood by or meant for only the select few who have special knowledge or interest," may have been intended to be neutral, but it suggests elitism—*experimental*, for example, doesn't have the exclusive implication. Esoteric fiction in the 1960s embraced experimental aesthetics, on the one hand, and transgressive sexuality, including queer sexuality, on the other. As I argue in *Middlebrow Queer*, 1960s style embraced the antihero. The outsider became the most truly American, and misfits of all sorts—murderers, radicals, sociopaths—became fashionable. This opened up space for other kinds of alternatives to the "white straight male" protagonist who had become the representative American in the 1940s and 1950s.[13] Racial, gender, and sexual diversity became the norm. In the early 1960s John Rechy's *City of Night*, an experimental novel featuring a male hustler as its narrator, was published by highbrow Grove Press; James Baldwin's *Another Country*, which used transgressive sexuality to explore American racism, was published as a paperback original.[14] Both June Arnold and Bertha Harris took advantage of this publishing trend to publish their first novels in the 1960s (*Applesauce* in 1966 and *Catching Saradove* in 1969, respectively).

It is not a compliment, of course, that "homosexuals" were included in the same category as hustlers, prostitutes, thieves, and other criminals, which may have been why "esoteric" fiction did not inspire Barbara Grier. Her review of *Therese and Isabelle* demonstrates her reservations. "Miss Leduc," she argued, "is not a good writer. She is far, far too concerned with making poetic images out of garbage scenes. Her delicate preoccupation with scatological imagery is more nauseating than Henry Miller's blunt interpretations of the same sort of material. Spraying fecal matter with flower scented phrases does not alter the composition of the material."[15] Grier's disgust with the "scatological" betrays both age and her suspicion of a "liberation" that uses lesbian images to both titillate and disgust; indeed, she felt that the novel was destructive to lesbians in their quest for full equality. Her critique of the "poetic" embrace of "garbage material" suggests that the merging of explicit sexual material with experimental writing, so common in the 1960s from Hunter S. Thompson to Ishmael Reed, continued to frame lesbianism as innately transgressive and antiestablishment. Grier may have feared that these transgressive descriptions of lesbian sex precluded the depiction of lesbians' full humanity. Politically, she seemed to find these depictions damaging. And yet, Grier argued that "despite all I have said, the book must be read, if only to see what the current literary image of Lesbianism is like, in the field of esoteric fiction."[16] Esoteric fiction, like paperback originals, had a place in the lesbian literary tradition.

Grier was also not a fan of the explicitly sexual descriptions that were becoming more common in the 1960s literary scene. Grove Press's 1961 reissue of Henry Miller's *Tropic of Cancer* prompted one of many literary obscenity trials in the 1960s that extended the terms of what was acceptable in explicitly sexual literature. Esoteric writers were influenced by a host of popular genres, including sex paperbacks sold in adult bookstores in the 1960s. Heterosexual pornographic paperback houses published gay pulps to reach homosexual readers; gay pulps like Richard Amory's *The Song of the Loon* and Victor Banis's spy spoof *The Man from C.A.M.P.*, along with many other varieties of erotica, were distributed in drugstores, by direct mail, and in the newly emergent "adult bookstore." Only recently have scholars begun to investigate this phenomenon,[17] but Grier, who published articles in gay publications like *ONE* magazine,[18] was well aware of this gay publishing trend.

She was not, however, a fan of what she called "the blow-by-blow technicolor things which often pass these days as 'romance.'"[19] Indeed, she found much of this trend badly done, especially by women, because "women do not, by and large, do well as pornographers, or even pseudopornographers. They are either florid and asinine (Violette Leduc, for example) or falsely clinical, as in this title."[20] And yet, she didn't dismiss the "new pseudopornography," for despite her use of this disapproving term, she also believed that it had a place: "There is no question that some of these are literature, and some have serious social value. There is also little question that many of them don't have value of any kind. But it is necessary and good that they be published. It is necessary that *everything* and *anything* can be published, and after that the individual can decide what she wants to read or wishes to ignore."[21] Her construction of a lesbian literature is guided by individual choice and personal freedom, not prescriptive rules about the "right" way to do it. She wants to publish "everything and anything," plotting a lesbian literary tradition that is inclusive and leaves individual readers the right to decide which version best suits their needs.

Grier herself preferred the middle ground—well-written narratives with rounded characters and believable plots. "Popular ladies' author Gladys Tabor" was an ideal for Grier: "There is so little common sense in today's world, so much anger and so much bloodshed, it is a real delight to read this gracious lady's books."[22] Grace and common sense were not lauded qualities in the 1960s. Grier described her own ideal in her overview of books in 1967: "The most important achievement is that there have been *several dozen valid, literate studies* published in just that short time. The entire span of literature before these last eleven years has provided a lesser quality. . . . Those mainstream novels that have included Lesbians as perfectly acceptable ordinary members of society at large have done a good deal to make the world a better place for all of us: a place where being a Lesbian doesn't begin to carry even half the stigma it did some fifteen years ago."[23] Although there weren't as many of these novels about "perfectly acceptable ordinary" lesbians as she would like, Grier was delighted to find them within a broad array of lesbian literature. Grier preferred accessible, realistic fiction, but she didn't think it was her job to tell other readers what they should like. As a "self-appointed expert" of "Lesbian Literature and History,"[24] Grier embraced a diverse lesbian literary culture. And yet the only place she could publish this open-minded survey of lesbian literature was in a small alternative monthly magazine with a secret mailing list. There simply wasn't the public space for the kinds of fiction she preferred.

At least, not until gay liberation and women's liberation created new venues for publication. No longer were lesbians at the mercy of whatever books mainstream publishers or paperback companies thought would sell or what writers could afford to self-publish or distribute. There would be an explosion of print, enough that a new generation of self-taught literary critics could prescribe what lesbian literature should be, instead of simply describing what scraps they could find.

"A Dyke with a Book in Her Hand": Women's Presses and the Literary Lesbian

After Barbara Grier became editor of *TL* in 1968, she decided to transform it from a magazine for "gay women" to an explicitly feminist journal. To do so, she and the executive director of the Daughters of Bilitis, Rita Laporte, removed the confidential *TL* mailing list (a single printed copy, hidden so the FBI could not obtain the membership list, as it had tried to do on more than one occasion) and took it to Nevada to Laporte's residence. Then they declared their independence from the national organization, severing *TL* from the Daughters of Bilitis.[25] Members of the national organization, who had been about to oust Laporte, believed that Grier had stolen the magazine. *TL* became a feminist magazine for the last two years of its existence, independent of the Daughters of Bilitis and open to all women, not just lesbians. Former editor Barbara Gittings never forgave Grier for this theft.

What on earth had gotten into Barbara Grier? She had always been imperious, but the specific impetus behind this power grab was women's liberation. Grier started attending Kansas City's women's liberation meetings and invited the women to help with *TL*.[26] Her shift of *TL* to an explicit feminism led to new correspondences with lesbian feminists from around the country who discovered *TL* and wrote to educate her about the burgeoning feminist movement. As Grier's biographer notes, Grier "received tutorials on leather culture from University of Michigan graduate student Gayle Rubin, on the Feminist Economic Network from Martha Shelley, and on the Gay Liberation Front and Radicalesbians from Karla Jay."[27] Younger lesbian feminists, including Rita Mae Brown, Kate Millet, and Judy Grahn, began publishing in the journal. And though Grier's grand experiment with *TL* failed (it went bankrupt in 1972), the possibilities that bid for freedom unleashed and the contacts she gained through *TL* made Naiad Press's later success possible.

Barbara Grier was not the only bookish lesbian for whom women's liberation and gay liberation were an awakening. Women's liberation was a pop culture phenomenon, a national debate, and a good time in the late 1960s. It was a national movement, with consciousness-raising groups cropping up in cities, universities, and suburban homes. Its scope was broad, its tactics varied, and its ambition audacious. Radical feminism in particular was an outrageous carnival, full of manifestos, shifting alliances, strong personalities, and performance art political actions. All of the writers in this study were marked by the era, and most were explicitly involved in feminist activism and action.

In 1960 June Arnold left her abusive husband and moved with her four children to New York City to pursue her long-deferred dreams of becoming a writer. She moved in literary circles, took creative writing classes at The New School,[28] and eventually published an experimental novel in 1966. But it would take the women's movement to inspire her prose and transform her into a publisher and a literary organizer. She started, as so many women's liberationists did, with a consciousness-raising group,[29] but she quickly moved to more direct political action, participating in one of the most famous feminist actions in 1970, the takeover of the Fifth Street Women's Building. Nearly forty women's liberation groups, after trying to negotiate with the city for an abandoned property to use as a women's shelter, occupied the building without permission, fixed it up, and turned it into an all-purpose women's resource center providing child care, employment services, and spaces for consciousness-raising groups. The women held the building for fourteen days before they were forcibly removed by the police and arrested.[30] One of the lawyers who got them released, Parke Bowman, became Arnold's partner and cofounded Daughters, Inc. with her. Though the city succeeded in removing the women from the building (and later razing it to build a parking lot), it was unsuccessful in prosecuting many of the women responsible. During the action, Arnold had encouraged the women to turn their backs on the police photographers; this made it difficult for the police to identify the perpetrators, so they were released without being charged.[31] The novel Arnold wrote about this experience, *The Cook and the Carpenter*, would lead, inadvertently, to another revolution—this one in print.

Bertha Harris arrived in New York around the same time as Arnold. A scholarship student at the Woman's College of the University of North Carolina (now the University of North Carolina at Greensboro), Harris had edited her college literary magazine and become close friends with instructor Kate Millett,[32] later the lauded author of *Sexual Politics*, whom she followed to New York. Details of that first sojourn are hazy, but Harris gave birth to a daughter and participated in Greenwich Village's avant-garde scene, including a performance of Yvonne Rainer's postmodern dance *Trio A* in 1966. By 1966, she was back in North Carolina, getting a master's degree at University of North Carolina at Charlotte and studying with Catherine Nicholson, a professor who would later launch the southern lesbian feminist periodical *Sinister Wisdom*. When Harris returned to New York as an English instructor in the 1970s, she found a transformed and improved landscape for lesbian artists.

Rita Mae Brown was younger than Harris and Arnold, a pin-up girl for women's liberation. Born in Pennsylvania, Brown moved with her family to Florida and attended the University of Florida. She was expelled for civil rights activism in 1966 and went to New York City, where she attended New York University (NYU), wrote for underground publications, published poetry, and got involved in NYU's gay liberation front and the National Organization for Women (NOW). She was a key conspirator in the notorious 1970 "Lavender Menace" action against NOW, when she and other activists turned out the lights at a NOW meeting, appeared on the stage wearing shirts that said "Lavender Menace," and staged a teach-in. That same year, she cowrote "The Woman-Identified Woman" with the Radicalesbians; the document defined a lesbian as "the rage of all women condensed to the point of explosion."[33] She then moved to Washington, D.C., where she joined the Furies collective, seduced married philosopher Charlotte Bunch, and produced an influential feminist newspaper.

In San Francisco, Texas native Pat Parker joined the women's movement; she and Judy Grahn did readings together, becoming the first poet superstars of the women's movement. They were the only poets to be featured by Olivia Records on the spoken-word album *Where Would I Be without You*. Parker's "nickname was 'the Preacher'"[34] and her early publications were standards of the women's liberation movement.

Hardly anyone included in this study was not involved in women's liberation. Tennessee native Maureen Brady went north from college and formed Spinsters Ink with her partner Judith McDaniel. In Tennessee, writer and librarian Ann Allen Shockley, seeing publication possibilities open up, published what is generally regarded as the first black lesbian novel, *Loving Her*; she would become friends with a number of southern lesbian feminists, including June Arnold. South Carolina native Blanche McCrary Boyd left her husband to join a commune in Vermont, where she had relationships with women and met June Arnold and her fledgling women's press. In Florida, Dorothy Allison joined a commune, started a women's center, worked at the women's bookstore, and otherwise embraced the emerging national community of lesbian feminism, culminating in attending the Sagaris Feminist Institute in Vermont and meeting Rita Mae Brown, Blanche McCrary Boyd, and most importantly for her life as a writer, Bertha Harris. In Durham, North Carolina, Mab Segrest and Minnie Bruce Pratt were attending graduate school, becoming involved in the women's movement, and coming out; for the married Pratt it was a particularly traumatic experience that led her to lose custody of her two sons. In Charlotte, North Carolina, Catherine Nicholson would become entranced with feminist periodicals and manifestos, quit her university job, run the women's center, and eventually start a feminist journal with her much younger lover, Harriet Desmoines. Georgia native Alice Walker would move from civil rights activism in Jackson, Mississippi to the women's movement in New York, writing for *Ms.* magazine and eventually publishing the iconic *The Color Purple* in 1982. In Los Angeles, Fannie Flagg was mainly outside radical feminism, but she did attend Equal Rights Amendment fundraisers, where she (fatefully) met the newly arrived Rita Mae Brown. Only self-proclaimed "royalist" Florence King would refuse any alliance with the women's movement—which didn't prevent her from taking advantage of the publishing opportunities women's liberation afforded her, including in *Ms.* magazine.

In addition to mainstream interest in feminist voices, the rise of independent media helped to fuel women's liberation. Trysh Travis defines the WIP movement as "an attempt by a group of allied practitioners to create an alternative communications circuit—a woman-centered network of readers and writers, editors, printers, publishers, distributors, and retailers through which ideas, objects, and practices flowed in a continuous and dynamic loop."[35] Activists were eager to create "a communications network free from patriarchal and capitalist control."[36] That network included newsletters and periodicals, which published manifestos, position papers, poetry, news, and book reviews; women's presses, which published a wide range of writers and genres; women's bookstores, which sold the periodicals and books produced by these alternative presses; women readers, who supported these venues and often joined in as bookstore owners, writers, or publishers; and even the distributors and operators of the physical presses themselves.

Feminist periodicals emerged across the country in just about every major urban area. Kathryn Adams notes that "between March, 1968, and August, 1973, over 560 new publications produced by feminists appeared in the United States, each one serving as a mailing address for the movement."[37] Feminists also created their own book publishing companies. Two of the earliest were Diana Press in Baltimore and the Women's Press Collective in Oakland, California. Poet Judy Grahn was a key member of this collective, which started with photocopied pamphlets stapled in the middle with industrial staplers by women who volunteered their time. They bought industrial printing machines and then had to teach themselves how to use them; Grahn tells the story of a male printer who promised to show them how to use the press if they would sleep with him—he was ousted, and they taught themselves.[38] The Women's Press Collective published some of the earliest poetry chapbooks of the women's movement, by Grahn and Pat Parker, which were distributed widely. Diana Press was another collective in which the editorial act of choosing texts and the physical act of printing them were housed in the same workplace. It published Barbara Grier's anthologies of *TL* in the 1970s and Rita Mae Brown's poetry collection *The Hand that Cradles the Rock*.

In the early days of both presses, poetry had a prominent place—as, indeed, it did in the early feminist movement. Kim Whitehead defines that poetry as "grounded in women's individual experiences, geared toward women's liberation from gender oppression, and therefore involving the need for both subjective and collective expression."[39] The importance of experience inspired early women's liberationists: "Women who might *never* have considered a traditionally prosodic poem as a means of expression flocked to poetry when they discovered that it could *emerge* from their experience."[40] The valuing of that experience—often violent, usually invisible—meant that the content of women's poetry was vitally important, focusing on violence, empowerment, and sexuality.

Poetry, and women's literary expression more generally, was often framed in democratic terms. All women's experience had value, and thus writing by all women, not just professional writers, was important. Or, in Dorothy Allison's dismissive formulation of the notion (written in 1990):

The whole feminist small press movement was created out of that failed belief and the hope of re-establishing some way to have Literature that we could believe in. All those magazines and presses—the ones I have worked with and supported even when I found most of the writing tedious or embarrassing—were begun in that spirit of rejecting the false god for a true one. . . . If Literature was a dishonest system by which the work of mediocre men and women could be praised for how it fit into a belief system that devalued women, queers, people of color and the poor, then how could I try to become part of it. Worse, how could I judge any piece of writing, how could I know what was good or bad, worthwhile or a waste of time? That's the ethical system that insists a Naiad press novel has the same worth as one from Knopf (better even since it is the product of a dissident mind)—that there is no good or bad: only politics.[41]

Leave aside Allison's disillusionment with this system (though that tension was always a part of the system) and you see some of the values inherent in the WIP movement. First, it emphasized independence and autonomy, because most feminists saw clearly how the mainstream literary establishment was male dominated and assessed works not on "literary merit" but on political and cultural acceptability. Second, it encouraged a radical revision of the very category of "literary," because so many writers were excluded from the club based on ideology or identity. The literary was an open debate, a site of reclamation.

Though for many people this movement may have ended up with "there is no good or bad, only politics," one committed group of lesbians believed they could have it all: good writing, expanded content, and experimental prose. For them, the lesbian and the literary were fused, necessarily. Many wanted to create a distinctive lesbian culture grounded in literature and the arts. Their first role models were modernist lesbian expatriates whose experiments in both lifestyle and form were seen as mutually sustaining. And their most enthusiastic advocate was Bertha Harris. For the 1973 *Amazon Expedition: A Lesbian Feminist Anthology* Harris wrote an essay on lesbian society in Paris in the 1920s, beginning with a quirky anecdote that may or may not be true (as with all of Harris's anecdotes):

Now I am 35 and have a penchant for old ladies; but then I was 21 and had a penchant for old ladies.

I was 21 and fresh out of The Woman's College of the University of North Carolina . . . then it was a woman's college and called itself one. . . . Among the native pop it was called a hotbed of lesbianism.

This rumor, thank god, was true.

I was fresh out of the arms of the hotbed of lesbianism and out of the clutches of the closet-sado ex-marine Dean and on the streets of New York: the summer of 1959. And when I was not at my $55.00 a week job I was hanging out on the corner of Patchin Place—not, under any circumstances, to catch a glimpse of e. e. cummings—but waiting for Djuna Barnes to take her afternoon walk and, with all discretion, follow her—moved the way she moved, turn the way she turned, hold my head like her head. As often as I could (and with discretion) I followed her and, trailing her, received the silent messages about my past I needed and she could give: and never once during our exchange did I encroach upon her lordly solitude to give her my name. The name she made up for me was my real name; and it was the name she used, when, in my fantasy, she would stop and take my hand to thank me for all the flowers I daily stuffed into her mailbox in Patchin Place and then tell me how it was to be a dyke in Paris, in the Twenties.[42]

Djuna Barnes has become a particularly important figure of queer modernism; *Nightwood*, published in 1937, featured gender and sexual outsiders, including a trans character, and was praised by mainstream figures like T. S. Eliot. She also wrote the privately published *Ladies Almanack* in 1928, a spoof of Natalie Barney's lesbian network that Harris had certainly read in her trips to the Rare Books Room at the New York Public Library. In her article, Harris names the members of this artistic network as her literary forebears: Colette, Gertrude Stein, Alice B. Toklas, Sylvia Beach, Una Troubridge, Radclyffe Hall, Romaine Brooks, Natalie Clifford Barney. Harris explains that these writers were ignored by her university teachers and introduced to her by the owner of "the Phoenix Bookshop on Cornelia Street" (78). Her conclusion merged literary ardor with lesbian feminist rebellion: "Like every other dyke with a book in her hand, I know that these are the women our fathers stole us from. . . . They were American and English and French but mostly American but with the father's nationality in effect wiped out by the more profound nationality of their lesbianism" (79). Harris's sketch of "the only available expressions of lesbian culture we have in the modern western world" (87) is now familiar—Natalie Barney's salon, around which brilliant writers, painters, and dancers clustered—but in 1973, these writers were just beginning to be uncovered and reprinted. Harris was by far the most intense lesbian expatriate devotee, but June Arnold was also invested; Virginia Woolf was Arnold's role model, and she would later model Daughters, Inc. on Hogarth Press. This move to claim lesbian modernists was widespread in early women's liberation; even Naiad Press was influenced by the lesbian expatriate trend, reprinting Renee Vivien and Gertrude Stein in its early years.

Even more important was Harris's aside: "the more profound nationality of their lesbianism." This early articulation of a "queer nation" was partly bluster, at least for Harris, but the concept was common in her group of lesbian provocateurs; Jill Johnston's *Lesbian Nation* was published the same year. "Our fathers" had stolen lesbian culture, but it could be rediscovered and, even more importantly, reinvented through art. This focus on the aesthetic was a small part of women's liberation, but it was a potent force, and one of particular import for southern lesbian feminist writers, who were major players in the articulation of the feminist avant-garde. Dykes with books in their hands were coming out of the library and into your lecture halls, your classrooms, your women's music festivals, and your homes.

The earliest journal to take up the cause of the lesbian literary was the 1972 *Amazon Quarterly,* a lesbian feminist journal that sought to invent an autonomous, distinctive lesbian culture through literature. Two English graduate students, Gina Covina and Laurel Galana, laid out their vision for the journal in their first editorial statement, "Frontiers":

We want to explore through the pages of *Amazon Quarterly* just what might be the female sensibility in the arts. Freed from male identification, lesbians are obviously in a very good position to be the ones to cross the frontier Doris Lessing has told us the "free woman" stands at[. . . .] The important factor is that it be in some way a launching out from all that we as women have been before into something new and uncharted . . . a voyage into the depths of your mind or a new connection you've discovered between something in your anthropology class and a book you were reading in herstory[. . . .] We are calling this an arts journal in the sense that art is communication. The standard we want to maintain is not arbitrary: we simply want the best of communication from lesbians who are consciously exploring new patterns in their lives. We hope you'll help us make it even more than we can imagine.[43]

You can see the recurring idea of the lesbian as the vanguard of the women's movement here—the epitome of the "free woman." Lesbians were creating "something new and uncharted," and the arts were the best way to explore these "new patterns." Aesthetic experimentation and lesbian identity are fused in this formulation.

Amazon Quarterly (*AQ*) published poems (including poems by Judy Grahn, Adrienne Rich, and Audre Lorde), essays on lesbian identity and the novel, and biographical sketches of little-known women artists, including Margaret Anderson. Both Rita Mae Brown[44] and June Arnold[45] published excerpts of their Daughters, Inc. novels in *AQ*. *AQ* also published a series of essays on "how to make a magazine," encouraging their readers to join the print revolution.[46] The journal regularly included lists of feminist publications, feminist presses, and feminist bookstores, creating a roadmap for an emerging lesbian nation.[47] It is a journal full of utopian possibility, creating a lesbian culture through the arts, without the prescriptivism and judgment of later lesbian feminism.

AQ was not framed explicitly as a southern periodical, but one of the editors, Laurel Galana, was from the South. In one issue, she noted this fact in a handwritten note: "As we go to press we are receiving more and more kind letters from around the country. The ones that touch me most are from my Southern sisters. I endured my first twenty-one years there. May you have the courage to change it."[48] Though southern writers like June Arnold and Rita Mae Brown were featured prominently in the journal, the South wasn't *Amazon Quarterly*'s primary focus. Southern lesbians were a small but vibrant part of the WIP movement and were overrepresented in the creation of a *literary* lesbianism. In the rest of this chapter, I outline some of the main trends of this literary lesbianism. One wing made the "esoteric" its ideal; another focused on lesbian feminist iterations of the "paperback original." The lesbian avant-garde was embraced by both Daughters, Inc. and *Sinister Wisdom*, inspiring the rise of a southern lesbian feminist literary culture.

Daughters, Inc., Avant-Garde Feminism, and the Lesbian Aristocrat

You might say that Daughters, Inc. began out of exigency. June Arnold couldn't find a publisher who would accept *The Cook and the Carpenter*, her experimental novel about the Fifth Street Women's Building takeover, so in the spirit of Virginia and Leonard Woolf, Arnold became her own publisher. Julie Enszer explains that "the vision of Daughters, Inc. was 'as kind of a Hogarth Press.' Daughters, Inc. would do what Virginia Woolf's press had done for her books for the Women's Liberation Movement. It would introduce to the world a different kind of novel that would change consciousness."[49] Arnold bought a farmhouse in Plainfield, Vermont, where her daughter Fairfax went to school (at Goddard) and where a number of New York radicals had moved. Blanche McCrary Boyd was living in a commune nearby, after a troubled sojourn at Duke University and a residency at the creative writing program at Stanford University with her husband, whom she left for a lesbian romance and a radical "intentional" community. Boyd would not only publish her first novel with Daughters, Inc. but also type up some of the other novels published in Daughters' first list. Despite her proximity to communes, however, and her own coalitions with political groups, Arnold did not embrace the communal model of publishing—an egalitarian division of labor, an opting-out of capitalist structures, and a rougher, do-it-yourself textual artifact, the product of inexperienced printers. Instead, Arnold started the press with a clear investment of capital, paid a commercial press to produce the manuscripts, and focused on selecting and shaping submitted manuscripts.

The first four novels she published plotted a new course in feminist writing: in addition to Arnold's *The Cook and the Carpenter*, Daughters, Inc. published Pat Burch's *Early Losses*, a coming-of-age novel that followed a young woman through 1960s protests to women's liberation, Blanche McCrary Boyd's novel of mother/daughter friction, *Nerves*, and Rita Mae Brown's *Rubyfruit Jungle*, which would become the most popular lesbian novel of the 1970s. Three of these four novels were by southern lesbians. Though Daughters did not maintain this ratio with its later lists, the press's publication of June Arnold and Bertha Harris, including reprints of their books, made it an important site of southern lesbian feminist writing.

Daughters, Inc. continued to publish interesting fiction that its founders believed created a "new" women's literature. It published what many consider to be the first feminist detective novel, M. F. Beale's *Angel Dance*, which featured the "macho" Latina detective, radical, and fugitive from justice Kat Alcazar, who helps the feminist celebrity Angel Stone (modeled on Kate Millet) extricate herself from a complicated conspiracy. Many of the press's novels deal with pressing feminist issues of the day, including alcoholism (Nancy Lee Hall's *Confessions of a Drunken Mother*), incest (*I Must Not Rock*, by Linda Marie), spousal abuse, violence, coming out, and coming of age.

But it was its embrace of the feminist avant-garde that made Daughters, Inc.'s reputation, thanks in great part to the public provocations of Arnold and Bertha Harris (who in 1975 became an editor for Daughters). Their rhetoric concerning the "right" way to do feminist and lesbian fiction was divisive, bracing, and sometimes hilarious. In Arnold's famous essay "Feminist Presses and Feminist Politics" she argues for the central importance of the WIP movement, which she describes as "a circle of media control with every link covered: a woman writes an article or book, a woman typesets it, a woman illustrates and lays it out, a woman prints it, a woman's journal reviews it, a woman's bookstore sells it, and women read it—from Canada to Mexico and coast to coast."[50] That autonomy was key, for Arnold, to prevent women's artistic vision from being coopted by the "Madison Avenue formulae" (20). Arnold argued that feminist writers should publish only with women's presses like "the Women's Press Collective, Diana Press, and Daughters, Inc.," because mainstream presses "will publish some of us— the least threatening, the most saleable, the most easily controlled or a few who cannot be ignored—until they cease publishing us because to be a woman is no longer in style" (19). Arnold ended her essay by denouncing as a traitor any feminist writer who published with a "finishing press": "Withdraw support from any woman who is still trying to make her name by selling out our movement" (26).

It is hard to argue with Arnold's assessment of the fickle nature of mainstream support of both feminist and lesbian writers; despite brief moments of interest (including the early 1970s and the early 1990s), mainstream publishing has rarely sustained an interest in diverse authors, including lesbians, feminists, and writers of color. But Arnold's absolutist stance did not take into account the struggles of writers without independent means of support who depended on advances from publishers. To dismiss every woman who published with a mainstream press as a sell-out was to impose a very narrow litmus test for authentic feminism. Very few writers (and independent publishers) could survive without dealings with commercial presses— including, as I discuss below, Rita Mae Brown and June Arnold herself.

The most important point in this essay was about the essential connection between independent publishing and avant-garde writing. Arnold argued that independent publishing *enabled* experimental aesthetics: "I think the novel—art, the presentation of women in purity (also I would include poetry, short stories)—will lead to, or *is* revolution. . . . Women's art is politics, the means to change women's minds."[51] By focusing on liberatory writing, not on big profits, feminist presses were more likely to take a chance on the daring and the difficult. Arnold believed that "the means to change people's minds" lay in language and in form. "One of the things we have noticed in reading women's press writings is a change in the language. . . . We've experimented with unpatriarchal spelling and neuter pronouns. I think we've changed our sentence structure, and paragraphs no longer contain one subject," Arnold argued, because women writers aimed for "the inclusiveness of many complex things."[52] Arnold described feminist literature as "experience weaving in on itself, *in*clusive, not ending in final victory/defeat but ending with the sense that the community continues. A spiral sliced to present a vision which reveals a whole and satisfies in some different way than the male resolution-of-conflict."[53] The autonomous women's press movement was essential to the feminist literary movement that Arnold embraced; for her, the feminist avant-garde required autonomy.

Bertha Harris was even more confrontational than Arnold in her advocacy of the feminist avant-garde, but she became less sure that an emerging lesbian feminist culture would produce the literary utopia she imagined. She feared the same literary desert that Allison would bemoan in 1990, where accessible popular novels would supplant the avant-garde. In a famous essay first presented at the Modern Language Association (MLA) meeting in 1974, Harris argued that lesbian art was by definition oppositional: "A lesbian form significantly differing from the patriarchal form I have described," she explained, "is not achieved through sexual substitution. . . . Individual turnabouts of heterosexual reality seem, to many, to constitute a literary expression of lesbian sensibility; and as such distract us from the apprehension of lesbian reality."[54] In pursuit of this goal, Harris rejected some of the most beloved characters of women's liberation, as well as the reading practices of the consciousness-raising novel—identification, emotion, and vicarious experience:

The great service of literature is to tell us who we are. . . . Lesbians, historically bereft of cultural, political, and moral context, have especially relied on imaginative literature to dream themselves into situations of cultural, political, and moral power. Twenty years ago, without Molly Bolt, we were Rhett Butler and Stephen Gordon and the Count of Monte Cristo. It is, of course, much more to the point to be Molly Bolt, or Patience or Sarah or Mrs. Stevens. The trouble with this process (vulgarly referred to as "identifying with") is that while the new lesbian hero is certainly safer for our mental health than Rhett or Stephen . . . and while we see her operating in what some might very loosely call a "cultural" context of tree-hugging, feminist folk-rock, vegetarianism and goddess-worship, her aggressive, strong, even magnificent image is by and large taken on by her beholder *still* inside the heterosexual/patriarchal definition of moral and political reality. Lesbian literature is *not* a matter of a woman plus a woman in bed.[55]

Harris rejects the egalitarianism of the WIP movement in favor of her ongoing commitment to an esoteric literary. June Arnold wanted literature to enable a truer, more radical vision of gender, but the list of Daughters, Inc. suggests that she still believed that a variety of forms could achieve this. Harris rejects the idea that simple representation—"a woman plus a woman in bed"—is enough. In trashing a number of groundbreaking lesbian texts— Rita Mae Brown's *Rubyfruit Jungle*, Isabel Miller's *Patience and Sarah*, May Sarton's *Mrs. Stevens Hears the Mermaid Singing*—she makes it clear that lesbian feminist literature needs to do more than change the characters; it must change narrative practice. French feminist writer Monique Wittig, who moved to the United States in 1976, articulated a comparable vision of lesbian identity and literature in *The Straight Mind and Other Essays*, *The Lesbian Body*, and *Les Guerilleres*. It seems clear that Wittig was an influence.

Harris's queer vision of both lesbians and literature concludes with a final plea for the lesbian literary: "Lesbians, instead, might have been great, as some literature is: unassimilable, awesome, dangerous, outrageous, different: *distinguished*. Lesbians, as some literature is, might have been monstrous—and thus have everything."[56] Harris's penchant for the monstrous is discussed in more detail in chapter 3, but note here that her embrace of the monstrous was specifically literary; she is suspicious of the lesbian culture ("tree-hugging, feminist folk-rock, vegetarianism and goddess-worship") that was already hardening into a dogma. Harris provoked several public skirmishes like this in the mid-1970s, both in print and in person. She had little patience for the democratic versions of literature bubbling in lesbian feminism; her protégée, Dorothy Allison, voiced similar frustrations in the 1990s.

But these absolutist manifestos aside, the feminist avant-garde was more invested in trash and assimilable narratives than Harris publicly admitted. This was partly because feminist presses published in paperback rather than hardback, and this connected them to the "paperback originals" that dominated early representations of lesbianism. In addition, although these books were larger in size than the standard pulp, they were often lumped in with the books of mass market paperback companies and pulp pornographers, and "respectable" review venues like the *New York Times* would not review paperback originals on principle. June Arnold saw Random House as her competition, but Random House saw Daughters, Inc. as a feminist version of Dell Books.

Privately, Bertha Harris expressed much more affection for those novels of "sexual substitution." She was, for example, a big fan of Gene Damon, and she wrote Barbara Grier a fan letter in 1975 that performed her love for lesbian pulp:

I MISS THE LADDER, I MISS THE LADDER, I MISS THE GOOD OLD LADDER!!! I MISS Ann Bannon and Beebo Brinker and Ann Aldrich and Love Among the Shadows and We Too Must Love and sentences that begin, "It was my first week in New York: and I was lonely, lonelier than I'd ever been at the farm where at least I had Sheba, my horse, for company—Sheba, who didn't care that I was different. . . . I had finally found a job, typing letters for a strangely fascinating older woman, who for some reason terrified me—although, for some reason, my heart lifted strangely, pumped insanely, everytime she entered the office, wearing her usual broad-shouldered pin-striped tailored suit and her crisp white shirts. But that was during the day; and, after five, I was left in my little rented room with only my own thoughts for company—unendurable thoughts, for they were of nothing but Marcie—Marcie of the long, glorious mane of golden hair who had, for some strange unutterable reason, broken my heart—Marcie, now Mrs. Tom Simpkins—and my sister-in-law! At last, I could bear it no longer. Instead of going home that night, I simply started walking. I don't know how long I walked, but some-how it helped to stretch my legs and fill my lungs with air. . . . Soon I was in a part of the city I had never visited—a place of little curving streets, doors leading down from the sidewalks, which, when they flashed open let out a beat of jazz and the sound of laughter—and that only made me lonelier, especially for that laughter, that gold laughter that matched the gold mane. Then my heart, for some reason, stopped—one of those doors opened, and out walked two women—hand-in-hand!!! They stood swaying in the shadows for a moment—then—oh my god!—they were kissing.

Kissing, passionately, mouth to mouth, melting into each other's arms as though they were one!!!!"[57]

This spot-on parody of the tropes of lesbian pulp (with its focus on Greenwich Village, butches, familial constructions of lesbian desire, and disingenuous femmes) opens new possibilities for reading the popular in Bertha Harris. Like many 1960s avant-garde writers, she incorporated pulp and popular culture references into her experimental fiction. And indeed, the follow-up to Harris's literary triumph of *Lover* was *The Joy of Lesbian Sex*, cowritten with Emily Sisley. Both *The Joy of Lesbian Sex* and *The Joy of Gay Sex* (by Charles Silverstein and gay literary icon Edmund White) built on the association of queer identity with explicit sexual acts, which was first established in the lucrative and titillating books of lesbian and gay pulp. Harris's participation in the project was an act of bravado, but it also says a lot about her radical ethos of lesbian feminism that she didn't believe that it hurt her cultural capital; if anything, it established her bona fides as a liberated radical unfettered by monogamy or respectability.

Daughters, Inc. was less prescriptive than the public proclamations of Arnold and Harris suggested. Julie Enszer notes that the "work of the women in the presses" was not "exclusively informed by any single feminist ideology,"[58] and instead incorporated an "oppositional consciousness" that was fluid, contingent, and pragmatic. Literature was a cultural category that early feminists believed had been defined in explicitly patriarchal ways and had excluded a host of women writers whom they found exemplary, including Virginia Woolf, Gertrude Stein, and Djuna Barnes. Coming up with new, fixed requirements for the literary didn't interest many in the early feminist reading community. Instead, the central purpose, Judy Grahn wrote, was to discover "women's real life stories" and "the truth we deserve."[59] Attempts to capture women's reality, beyond the screen of patriarchy, were made in a number of genres and formal styles; Grahn argued that "the more closely coordinated we allow the content and form of any art to be, the more accurate, useful and whole it is."[60] It wasn't until the middle of the decade that Arnold and Harris started evangelizing for a particular aesthetic style, but even then, Harris's avant-garde proclamations made the same assumption—that literature tells us who we really are. And despite Harris's sometimes strident tone, Daughters' book list always ranged far beyond Arnold's and Harris's particular literary preferences. In this, they had more in common with Barbara Grier than they would have admitted.

Daughters, Inc.'s inclusive tendencies became apparent in June Arnold's most important activist legacy: the formal creation of what we now call the women in print movement. In 1976 Arnold proposed a meeting of *all* women involved with bookselling and editing, distributing, reviewing, and writing feminist literature. The meeting was held in the center of the country, at a campsite in Nebraska, so that everyone could drive to it. The logistical challenges were immense, requiring multiple mailings, the planning of numerous workshops for every part of the book business, and the coordination of food, lodging, entertainment, and socializing for more than 100 women, many of whom were cantankerous and spoiling for a fight. Among the attendees were many who would later be important in the southern lesbian feminist network: "Dorothy Allison, Parke Bowman, . . . Harriett Desmoines, Barbara Grier, Bertha Harris, . . . Donna McBride, Catherine Nicholson,"[61] and representatives of the southern feminist journal *Feminary*.

The conference offered an exhaustive regimen of workshops dedicated to every aspect of the "media circle": publicity, reviewing, layout, distribution—nothing was left to chance. Barbara Grier was there, rubbing shoulders with Bertha Harris and other esoteric writers and publishers. They established a national network that was not beholden to outside influence, united against LICE (the literary industrial corporate establishment), their dismissive acronym for the mainstream publishing establishment.[62] According to Kristen Hogan, "This conversation among the bookwomen grew into a feminist literary advocacy network that would change both the vocabularies of feminism and reading and publishing in the United States."[63] One of the most important legacies of this network was the *Feminist Bookstore News*, started by Carol Seajay (of Old Wives Tales Press in San Francisco). Indeed, many of the successes of feminist publishers and bookstores over the next two decades grew out of this first WIP conference.

In the aftermath of the conference Daughters, Inc. became more successful than it had ever been; ironically, it was finally gaining mainstream recognition. Harris's *Lover* was widely reviewed in feminist publications as the prototype for a new kind of lesbian writing. Daughters, Inc. was the subject of an article in the *New York Times Magazine*,[64] featuring interviews with Arnold, Bowman, Harris, and Harris's lover Charlotte Bunch, that depicted the press as interesting, dogmatic, and unrealistic. Not long after the *New York Times* article came out, Arnold sold the rights to *Rubyfruit Jungle* to Bantam Books for $250,000 in an astonishing act of pragmatic flexibility. Arnold had denounced other writers for publishing their work with the "finishing press" and republishing small-press books with big publishers, and she had just told the *New York Times* that she would not sell the rights to any mainstream press.[65]

Brown wanted the sale; the money gave her financial security and independence for the first time in her life. And Arnold had invested enough of her own money—both in Daughters, Inc. and in the women's movement as a whole—that getting something back on her investment must have made sense to her. But the response of the women's community was vituperative as Daughters, Inc. was denounced in women's periodicals and in person. It was part of a larger pattern of critical and abusive behavior from fellow feminists that led Arnold to conclude that the community was no longer sustaining, and in 1978 she returned Texas, with her lover Parke Bowman, to write a novel about her mother (the posthumously published *Baby Houston*) and to embrace, in geographical terms, a long-term imaginative obsession. New York feminists felt that Arnold was abandoning both feminism and feminist publishing, but Arnold and Bowman incorporated Daughters, Inc. in Houston and planned to continue the business with the proceeds of the Bantam sale.

Arnold's diagnosis of cancer shortly after her return to Houston derailed these plans. In the time she had left—she died of brain cancer in 1982—she tried to finish her novel and beat her diagnosis. Her death was a tragedy for her children and for Bowman, who in her grief destroyed the bulk of the records of Daughters, Inc. It was also a loss for the literary movement as a whole, and without June to fiercely defend her own legacy, that task was left to others with scores to settle. In the early 1990s, Bertha Harris denounced June Arnold, brutally.[66] Yet, June Arnold deserves to be remembered for her work as a feminist publisher and a key contributor to the archive of southern lesbian feminism.

Periodicals and the Creation of a
Southern Lesbian Feminist (Literary) Culture

Though Arnold's active involvement in lesbian feminism ended in 1978, her influence, particularly in the creation of a lesbian literary aesthetic, lingered much longer. You could say that June Arnold had a hand in the launch of *Sinister Wisdom*. Catherine Nicholson had been living a closeted lesbian existence, like many of her generation and class. As a professor at the University of North Carolina at Charlotte, she lived on Country Club Drive, had discreet affairs, and worked unobtrusively within the university system. The women's movement changed everything for her. Bertha Harris arrived as a student in the late 1960s from Greenwich Village, full of radicalism and wild experimentation and sexual bravado, and her connections to the New York scene provided Nicholson with her first entrée to a different realm of possibility. When she began a relationship with the decades-younger Harriet Desmoines, Nicholson's journey from respectable middle-aged professor to radical feminist accelerated considerably. She and her collective, the Drastic Dykes, started making noise.

Harris provided introductions to New York feminist leaders, but they were first radicalized through print. Daughters, Inc.'s first list mesmerized them, as Desmoines explained: "In three nights and three days (in between making money, cooking, breaking up urchin battles, typing women's center stencils, vying for 'heterosexual acrobat of the year,' and various other Renaissance Girl activities), I read *Rubyfruit Jungle, Nerves, Early Losses, The Treasure*, and *The Cook and the Carpenter*. I read them again. I read them backwards, I read them middle to outside. I go through and pick out the juicy parts. I fall in love with the Carpenter, I fall in love with the Cook, I fall in love with Three. I end up falling in love with every single female character but one in June Arnold's novel."[67] Daughters, Inc. became one of their inspirations. So, too, did *Amazon Quarterly* and the C.L.I.T. papers in *Dyke Quarterly*, founded in 1975. In 1975 Nicholson and Desmoines traveled to New York for the Gay Academic Union conference and attended a party at June Arnold's house in Greenwich Village (which Barbara Grier also attended), and Arnold became a mentor to them.

When their favorite lesbian periodical, *Amazon Quarterly*, announced it was ending publication, they decided to start their own lesbian journal. It wasn't a very financially savvy plan, but it was an intellectually exciting idea. Nicholson resigned her job at the university and created, with Desmoines, *Sinister Wisdom*. They published their first issue on 4 July 1976—a declaration of independence. Desmoines's "Notes for a Magazine" in the first issue was both an introduction and a manifesto of sorts:

> We're lesbians living in the South. We're white; sometimes unemployed, sometimes working part-time. We're a generation apart. . . .
> A nightmare reveals our fears: Catherine dreams that she wakes next to me. I'm holding slides of mutilated bodies and soundlessly screaming. Catherine looks up at the blank TV. A single open eye stares at us from the screen.
>
> So why take chances? Because we needed **more** to read on, to feed on, more writing to satisfy our greedy maws. We'd become

lesbian separatists because no other political position satisfied. But that left us with scattered beginnings of a culture and no viable strategy. We believed with the CLIT papers that consciousness is women's greatest strength, and we both responded strongly to Mary Daly's call for "*ludic cerebration*, the free play of intuition in our own space, giving rise to thinking that is vigorous, informed, multidimensional, independent, creative, tough." But how to think that keenly and imaginatively, how to develop that consciousness?[68]

Their faith in the power of print—independent print—to create both a revolutionary consciousness and an independent lesbian culture harks back to both Arnold and Harris.

They had enough money for one year. It is unclear whether Arnold offered financial support, but she did bring the considerable weight of her influence to bear. Nicholson's extensive handwritten notes from the many practical sessions at the first WIP conference in 1976 (still preserved in the Sallie Bingham Center at Duke University) show that the sessions provided important mentorship. But even more important was the genesis of the journal's second issue, a special issue titled "Lesbian Writing." Arnold had participated in a special MLA session on lesbian writing in 1975 and Beth Hodges planned to edit a special issue on the session for *Margins*, but Arnold insisted that the material be given to *Sinister Wisdom*. It is likely that Arnold was trying to help Nicholson and Desmoines, but this was also part of the war that she and Harris were waging against the "finishing press": feminist writers should publish only with feminist presses; otherwise, they were sell-outs. *Sinister Wisdom* won the right to publish the proceedings, but the artifact of this battle—the second issue of *Sinister Wisdom*—suggests that the question was not entirely resolved. Indeed, Desmoines and Nicholson made the admirable decision to include in the special issue vigorous debate about the role of lesbian publishing, with dissents by several lesbian writers and a very personal letter from Beth Hodges, who defined the treatment she had received from fellow lesbians as "trashing" and "bullying."

Inside the cover, Hodges, Desmoines, and Nicholson included a photograph of Barbara Grier with the following homage:

This issue is for Barbara Grier (Gene Damon), who wrote sixteen years for *The Ladder*, editing it four of those years while averaging sixty letters a day to isolated lesbians across the country; who gathered the most complete bibliography of lesbian literature available; who knows with such clarity the importance of lesbian writing and publishing to our lives: "There are many women to find, many lesbians to write about and for. We are the women to do this . . . We have to go out on hills and listen for the wild sweet singing of our past and record it for our future." (Grier to Lesbians Writers Conference, Chicago, 1975.)

Beth writes: "I know you're a legend but I don't get choked up over legends. What moves me is the woman Barbara: not-very-humble, not-so-patient, but infinitely generous. For twenty years you've been encouraging lesbian writers and lesbian readers by sharing your time, your love, your energy, your knowledge. Thank you, dear Barbara. Your life blesses us all."[69]

Grier's status was unassailable in the early work of literary lesbians, where her catholic appreciation for all kinds of lesbian writing coexisted with the more avant-garde aesthetic of Arnold and Harris. But the debates that kept erupting suggest the difficulty of defining the lesbian aesthetic. Was it, as Grier maintained, anything with lesbian characters? Anything lesbian readers wanted to buy? Or was it, as the avant-garde wing of lesbian feminism maintained, something aesthetically distinctive, unassimilable, a means of revolution?

The "Lesbian Writing" issue didn't provide a consistent answer. Arnold's comments from the 1975 "Lesbians and Literature" MLA panel discussion (included in the special issue) made a clear case for the political efficacy of lesbian feminist writing and its role in creating a new form of literature. She suggested that the lesbian feminist genius is collective, based in groups of characters, which led to several key features: "a breaking down of distance between the writer and the reader," "a change in humor," and "a kind of unprecedented, complete honesty, however embarrassing."[70] "The feminist presses," she concludes, ". . . will be the ground in which this new art is brought to flower."[71]

In the published dialogue on lesbian literature between June Arnold and Bertha Harris, however, a more nuanced discussion about lesbian literature emerges. They discuss the freedom that women's presses gave them to tell the truth and take chances in their writing, but they also discuss the importance of not censoring themselves to satisfy an emerging lesbian consensus about appropriate characters:

> J: I wonder if there's another kind of censorship going on among lesbians now which hasn't been stated: that we're supposed to write about women being tender, sensitive, understanding, etc., about

women working in groups. But when you're in the middle of a novel and your character is doing something that's against that . . .

B: And you know it's true, what the character is doing.

J: You've got to stay with the character. Even if the character is a drunk and the critics say, Don't you know a lot of sisters are having trouble in the bars and they're becoming alcoholics and aren't you romanticizing alcohol? Do you think we have some responsibility to that, or do we have responsibility to the character?

B: No. We have only responsibility to the character. If you're writing from the absolutely raw place. Because responsibility to the character and what you're doing is ultimately responsibility to the women's movement and to all lesbians.

J: Even though it's not clear right now.

B: Even though it's not popular or clear, because, along with us writing fiction, we assume that women who read are also peeling off layers of consciousness. I think a big misunderstanding of what sex is, has been put about through the lesbian-feminist movement in particular. Sex among women sounds like early childcare sometimes.

J: Babies playing in the rain and all love and sweetness.

B: We all know that's not true. Sex can be violent, and devastating, and I think that to write a novel in which everything is sweetness and light, sexually among women, is lying. And lies always propagate not only bad literature but bad politics. And losing. People who believe lies lose.[72]

This exchange is remarkable: two women who were infamous for their strident attacks on sell-outs discuss the ways that prescriptive intolerance could hurt not only lesbian literature, but also the larger revolutionary claims that literature was intended to serve. A cynical interpretation would be that they didn't want anyone to question their own aesthetic choices, but they felt free to challenge everyone else's decisions. More broadly, they were grappling with the very real problem of prescribing a "right" way to do lesbian literature. No matter how responsible to the "community" one tries to be, it is always possible to violate another's deeply held beliefs about where one publishes, how and about whom one writes, and what situations and characters one creates. Arnold and Harris produced and published some of the most interesting lesbian fiction of the 1970s, but they also contributed to an atmosphere in which questions of authenticity led to self-destructive internal fights and the demise of Daughters, Inc. itself. Believing in literature without prescribing one definition of it is a difficult line to walk, and these literary lesbians often had difficulty maintaining their passion and their generosity simultaneously.

In her opening and closing remarks to the section "The Politics of Publishing and the Lesbian Community," Jan Clausen made clear her own discomfort with the push for "women's presses," mentioning the controversy about the special issue of *Sinister Wisdom*, the decision of former *Amazon Quarterly* editors Gina Covina and Laurel Galana to have Harper and Row publish their anthology of the magazine, and a panel discussion at the May 1976 New York City Lesbian Conference that became, in her words, "an acrimonious debate over the validity of publishing with 'the man.' While painting what seemed to me an overly rosy picture of feminist publishing alternatives, June Arnold, Parke Bowman, and Bertha Harris took such a strong stand against publishing with the male-controlled presses under any circumstances that some who disagreed with various points they made (myself included) felt reluctant to speak up."[73] Clausen's uneasiness with the stridency of this position is echoed in the responses of the lesbian writers who provided more nuanced perspectives about when and how lesbians should publish their work. Very few ruled out mainstream presses, and most reacted negatively to the proposition that "the lesbian writing community should act in any way to encourage or discourage certain publishing decisions on the part of its members."[74] Clausen's decision to publish the unedited responses of writers including Audre Lorde, Rita Mae Brown, and Jane Rule widened the range of voices of the "lesbian community," and collectively, these writers directly challenged Arnold and Harris. Nicholson and Desmoines were in many ways Arnold acolytes, but they did not shy away from criticizing her in these pages. Nor did they themselves avoid criticism: Beth Hodges's piece details her dismay at being bullied into choosing to publish in *Sinister Wisdom* and her anger at Nicholson and Desmoines.[75] Nicholson and Desmoines gave themselves the final word in the issue, reiterating arguments about revolution and the women's press that echoed Arnold's and Harris.[76] But they didn't claim final authority, and their final statement did not resolve the debate about the politics of lesbian publishing.

Perhaps because of the multiple voices involved in the debate, the special issue that Arnold had insisted be published by Nicholson put *Sinister Wisdom* on the map. The journal issue sold out, and women from across the country wrote looking for copies. The issue articulated a lesbian aesthetic that wasn't only about content but also about form—the culmination of Harris's and Arnold's vision for lesbian feminist literature.

Many supporters and contributors to *Sinister Wisdom* commented on the journal's location in the South, and Harriet Desmoines wrote about it in the third issue:

How to Go International on Grits and Turnip Greens:

Earlier this year it dawned on us that we were publishing a journal of Lesbian writing in the hometown of the "Praise the Lord" television network and that this was somewhat akin to raising pineapples on the North Pole. Our solution? Move to New York, move to Boston, move to L.A., move to San Francisco! Finally, we decided to just stay where we were. For one thing, it freaks people out in the Bay area. For another, most Lesbians live, love, work and politic outside the metropolitan centers. And the movement monster could surely stand a corrective dose of Southern Midwestern, "provincial" chauvinism. Then, too, we have our smug moments, like the evening one deeply closeted South Carolina Lesbian appeared, hopping from one foot to the other, sputtering, "I can't believe you all are *here*!"[77]

Desmoines's critique of the concentration of lesbian feminism on the coasts suggests that a bias existed long before official histories of the women's movement de-emphasized its "Southern Midwestern" factions. The sputtering South Carolina lesbian is a symbol of the southern inflection of the magazine, but ultimately, *Sinister Wisdom* aspired to be a national magazine of lesbian (literary) culture rather than a regional publication, as demonstrated by the heading "How to Go International on Grits and Turnip Greens." It published early poetry by Audre Lorde, reprinted influential essays by Adrienne Rich, and discussed lesbian identity in universal terms. So when Julia Penelope, formerly employed in the South but relocated to the University of Nebraska at Lincoln, invited them to move to Nebraska and gain the university's financial support for the journal, Nicholson and Desmoines moved.

Their departure inspired the creation of another feminist periodical more clearly rooted in a southern lesbian feminist consciousness. Mab Segrest, a former contributing editor to *Sinister Wisdom*, decided to transform a small feminist newsletter in the North Carolina Research Triangle into a southern lesbian feminist journal published by a collective that included herself, Minnie Bruce Pratt, and Cris South. The name of the collective, Feminary, was inspired by a term from Monique Wittig's *Les Guerilleres* for the books that "the women" carried around their necks, a sign of their liberation.[78]

In the inaugural issue of the magazine in 1979, when its name officially became *Feminary: A Feminist Journal for the South*, the Feminary collective explicitly thanked Harriet Desmoines and Catherine Nicholson "for their courage and example," and "their work for lesbians in the South." The issue also included an extended mission statement:

> *Feminary* is produced by a lesbian feminist collective in the Piedmont of North Carolina. As Southerners, as lesbians, and as women, we need to explore with others how our lives fit into a region about which we have great ambivalences—to share our anger and our love.
>
> We want to hear Southern lesbians tell the stories of women in the South—our mothers, grandmothers, aunts, cousins, and friends. We feel we are products of Southern values and traditions but that, as lesbians, we contradict the destructive parts of those values and traditions; and we feel it important to explore how this Southern experience fits into the American pattern.
>
> We are committed to working on issues of race, because they are vital to an understanding of our lives as they have been, as they are and could be—and to understanding and overcoming differences of class and age among lesbians as well.
>
> We want to encourage feminist and lesbian organizing in a region whose women suffer greatly in their lack of political power.
>
> We want to provide an audience for Southern lesbians who may not think of themselves as writers but who have important stories to tell—stories that will help to fill the silences that have obscured the truth about our lives and kept us isolated from each other.
>
> We want to know who we are.
>
> We want to change women's lives.[79]

The mission statement asserts essentialist notions of southern identity— "Southern values and traditions"—but then complicates them with race, class, and gender. It aligns itself with the transformative ethos of women's liberation, even as it embraces the "ambivalences" of the South and the founders' own identities. It celebrates the South and critiques it. *Feminary* quickly became a central imaginative meeting place for far-flung members of the southern lesbian feminist tribe, as an iconic cover suggested: over a map of the South, two lesbians kissed across Alabama and Georgia, and a woman reclined orgasmically in Virginia. It was explicitly and proudly southern, rejecting stereotypes of backward ignorance and southern belles. Despite its invocation of southern tradition, however, *Feminary* was not at all nostalgic. Class and race analyses were central to its work; southern patriarchy was the problem, and broad coalitions against that hegemony were seen as the only solution.

Feminary was also deeply interested in the literary. The second issue of the reimagined journal was devoted to poetry, and it is filled with poems, book reviews, and surveys of southern lesbian literature. References to Bertha Harris, June Arnold, and Rita Mae Brown abound in the review essays, but *Feminary* also had an egalitarian approach to writing; its mission statement encouraged contributions from women who didn't consider themselves writers. *Feminary* was an important space for a theorization of a distinctively southern lesbian feminist consciousness, and an heir to the projects of Arnold, Harris, Nicholson, and Desmoines.[80]

Members of the Durham collective burned up the roads between urban centers, giving talks, attending conferences, camping at writing retreats, and advocating for a distinctively southern lesbian feminism. Minnie Bruce Pratt, a Feminary member, recalls, "We used to joke about how we were the revolutionary answer to the Fugitives, a new literary tradition bent on turning the old values of the South topsy-turvy."[81] Trained in the "essential South" of the Fugitives, the Feminary collective claimed another South, grounded in multiculturalism, radicalism, and resistance. Their revolutionary and literary movement was linked by lesbian feminist centers in cities, college towns, and communes across the South, in Gainesville and Tallahassee, Atlanta and Durham, Charlotte and Knoxville.

Three other feminist publishing ventures not primarily grounded in southern lesbian feminism also provided places for lesbian feminist writers to publish. *Quest* magazine was edited by Charlotte Bunch, who had been a member of the Furies and was in a relationship with Bertha Harris (Harris became a guest editor for *Quest*, and Bunch was also involved in Daughters, Inc.). Bunch invited Dorothy Allison and her collective to move to Washington, D.C. to work on the journal, which they did in 1976. *Conditions* was overseen by another collective that would later include Allison and other famous lesbian feminists including Cheryl Clarke, Barbara Smith, Ely Bulkin (who coauthored a book with Minnie Bruce Pratt), and Jewelle Gomez. *Conditions* published African American writers who also published in *Feminary*, as well as Pratt and other southern lesbian feminist writers. The very talented editor and publisher Nancy Bereano published a number of southern lesbian feminist texts including, as editor at Crossing Press, Maureen Brady's *Folly* and Cris South's *Clenched Fists, Burning Crosses*, and as founder/editor of Firebrand Books, Allison's *Trash*, Segrest's *My Mama's Dead Squirrel*, and Pratt's *Crime against Nature*. At the same time, further south, Barbara Grier was reviving the paperback original tradition of lesbian writing.

Lesbian Feminist Trash: Naiad Press and Lesbian Genre Fiction

Naiad Press was one of a legion of feminist publishing ventures in the early 1970s. After the demise of *TL*, former contributor Anyda Marchant wrote to Barbara Grier asking for help in publishing her novel "about two women who come to love each other in what I consider a completely normal fashion. . . . It has a, for them, happy ending." She had trouble imagining that it would be published, "even by new women's presses, who all seem hung up on the idea of fiction as tracts with social significance. Of course fiction can be important in conveying ideas but to my mind the demands of fiction as art come first. However, I have decided to try printing the story myself and selling it as a paperback book moderately priced."[82] Grier wrote back with enthusiasm; she believed that *TL* readers, who liked "vicarious experience" and "tend to be readers for the sake of reading,"[83] would be the perfect audience. Grier used the pilfered *Ladder* mailing list to distribute it, Marchant and her partner provided start-up funds, and Naiad Press was born.

The press remained a modest operation in the 1970s, publishing a small but eclectic range of lesbian fiction. As Grier explained to a prospective author in 1976, "unlike Daughters we are a very poor press."[84] That year marked the high point of Daughters' cultural influence, but the dogmatism of Arnold and Harris was beginning to irritate people, including Grier, who had a much broader view of what constituted acceptable lesbian writing. However, Harris was a fan of Grier, remembering her from her days as Gene Damon at *TL*. In 1975 she invited Grier to a Daughters party in New York, where Grier met many southern lesbian feminist expatriates for the first time. Grier's description of that Greenwich Village party, in a letter to Marchant, reveals her ambivalence:

> The first night (not Thanksgiving) we went to the loft of
> Daughters[. . . .] It was a very impressive place in many ways . . .
> simple and dripping with the subtle things that sit in corners and
> scream quietly (money money money). The women are (meaning
> here Parke and June) fairly impressive . . . but too political for my
> tastes . . . though June is elegant looking much in the same way Jane
> Rule's Helen Szonthoff is . . . lean, well bred, good facial planes,
> quick bright eyes[. . . .] Parke and June are thinking of trying to get

a publishers conference going . . . with a Midwest location . . .
to get the women together who are active in publishing women's
material . . . It is an interesting idea[. . . .] I do love Bertha. . . . She
is funny and quick and well on her way to becoming an alcoholic.[85]

The gossip about Arnold and Harris is entertaining, but there is also the suggestion that Grier was alienated by both Arnold's strident politics and her affluence. Arnold's wealth and her sense of herself as part of an elite clearly rub Grier the wrong way, and her suspicion of the esoteric literary is likely linked to her sense of a class divide. If only the overeducated few could read it, how was such writing revolutionary? Daughters' avant-garde feminism sought to teach what a liberated lesbian future could look like. Grier was much more modest and practical; she sought lesbian fiction that lesbians wanted *right now*—especially lesbians like her in the flyover states, not the New York radical scene.

That tension continued to erupt between Naiad and a succession of feminist presses (including Persephone Press and Kitchen Table Press), but Grier's philosophy remained consistent: give lesbians what they want. She wrote in a letter to Marchant in 1977 about the decision by Diana Press to begin to publish fiction:

I am not so concerned about their announced intention to publish fiction. From what little contact I have had with them I should say that there is no likelihood of a real competition between us and them. One thing we must bear in mind is that Naiad has a definite publishing policy. . . . We are publishing for women who want real novels—you can call them romantic if you want to—and hopefully we will pick the kind that will go on being republished and reread. This is a slower kind of success, I am aware, and in that respect we are handicapped in dealing with both Diana and Daughters. . . . The writers who would please the critics that have called our books trash can, with my best wishes, go to Diana and Daughters for their way into print.[86]

Grier's clear sense of her own purpose, even in the modest beginnings of Naiad Press, is striking: she was the one publishing "real novels," and she didn't mind if those novels were characterized as romance. Diana and Daughters, by contrast, were publishing the esoteric fiction that didn't speak to her audience. Grier's embrace of what might be called a middlebrow aesthetic (though many termed it lowbrow or trash) and her rejection of a highbrow definition of the literary demonstrated an aesthetic commitment to accessible novels that remained consistent throughout her career.

Grier's discontent with the stridency of the women's press movement reached its breaking point over a controversy at Diana Press. Grier, a great supporter of feminist presses, had published her own *TL* anthologies with Diana Press and had also encouraged her mentor, Jeannette Foster, to reprint her groundbreaking anthology *Sex Variant Women* with them. Diana Press had promised 50 percent royalty payments for authors after printing expenses had been paid, but five years later, no royalties had been paid at all. Foster was suffering from dementia and could not afford nursing home care, and Grier felt guilty for leading her friend astray. Rita Mae Brown simply wanted what was owed her. They all sued the press.

Grier felt betrayed. As she wrote to the lesbian poet Elsa Gidlow, "It has managed to make it possible for me after about 25 years to turn my back on the movement and walk away . . . and this time I will not look back."[87] Grier remained involved in the movement, but something fundamental changed after this experience. From now on, she would run Naiad as a business, publishing what women wanted to read, not what political activists thought they should want. In 1979 she moved with her librarian partner, Donna McBride, to Tallahassee, Florida, to reinvent her press.

Grier wanted Naiad to be her full-time job, and for that, she needed commercial success. She published a wide range of books in the early 1980s, from reprints of lesbian classics (like Patricia Highsmith's *The Price of Salt* and Jane Rule's *Desert of the Heart*) to lesbian sex manuals (Pat Califia's *Sapphistries*). Shortly after moving to Tallahassee, Barbara Grier met Florida State University professor Sheila Ortiz Taylor, who had written a novel called *Faultline*. Grier was convinced she had found the new *Rubyfruit Jungle*—a clever, funny, and formally interesting novel with a heroine to rival Molly Bolt: Arden Benbow, a motorcycle-riding, poetry-writing, Latina lesbian mother of six, ex-wife of Malthus, lover of Alice. Grier was ready. She arranged for a first printing of 10,000, a large run for a small feminist press without much capital. She had promotional material made, including buttons, t-shirts, and bookmarks, all depicting a rabbit—a play on the name Malthus and a reference to the novel's rapidly reproducing rabbits (and Arden's own fecundity). She solicited jacket blurbs from famous writers, including two iconic southern lesbian feminists. Rita Mae Brown enthused, "*Faultline* is faultless. Sheila Ortiz Taylor has written an earthquake of a book."[88] Bertha Harris praised the book as a literary triumph and an example of authentic lesbian literature: "*Faultline* is a family narrative done to a brilliant surreal turn. An American standup comic masterpiece sired by Buster Keaton out of Gertrude Stein, born on the San Andreas fault and danced on the ceiling by a Black Fred Astaire. How otherwise can you talk about the adventures of a Lesbian mother with six children, three hundred rabbits and a very relaxed attitude? A laugh out of life at last."[89] Harris's preferences for avant-garde literature, popular culture, surrealism, and humor seemed to be satisfied by this book, which featured multiple narrators, flashbacks, and subversive queers but which also, unlike Harris's novel *Lover*, was remarkably accessible. Grier was convinced that *Faultline* would make Naiad solvent and successful.

Faultline marked a significant shift in tactics for Grier. Published the same year that Alice Walker's *The Color Purple* became a literary sensation, *Faultline* was promoted using strategies invented by LICE. As Joanne Passet explains, "Determined to get Taylor's *Faultline* 'into the hands of every woman in America (and all over the world too),'" Grier promoted the book at the American Booksellers Association meeting, arranged for publication in "England, Germany, Spain and France," and contacted Bantam Books about a mass-market edition (which didn't happen).[90] *Faultline* was a success for Naiad, but not on the scale of *Rubyfruit Jungle*. As it turned out, Grier's financial stability came not from a funny literary novel but from a romance novel.

Published in 1983, Katherine Forrest's *Curious Wine* detailed the deliciously slow seduction of Diana Holland by Lane Christianson at a women-only weekend in Reno, Nevada. Forrest deftly writes a lesbian fantasy—the perfect blonde woman, the isolated bird's-eye room (with a ladder that pulls up for perfect privacy), the easy, intense physical connection, and most importantly, the happy ending: love at first sight becomes the one true love unlike any actual relationship, gay or straight. Readers know exactly how this story will end up—with Diana and Lane in bed together—but Forrest's tantalizing manipulation of the conventions of romance makes the journey thoroughly satisfying for the reader.

Curious Wine became Naiad Press's bestselling novel and remained a constant on its "top ten bestseller" lists. Grier was a savvy enough businesswoman to recognize that she had found her meal ticket. Forrest became "the press's supervising editor,"[91] encouraging first-time authors to tap into the lucrative market that *Curious Wine* had uncovered. Naiad published lesbian detective novels, lesbian mysteries, lesbian science fiction, coming-out novels, and, of course, lesbian romances. A wide range of authors, including many first-time novelists, fed the insatiable demand of its lesbian readership.

Its forays into nonfiction, particularly the notorious *Lesbian Nuns,* led to mainstream recognition.[92]

Naiad Press quickly became a symbol of everything the lesbian feminist avant-garde abhorred, what Harris disparagingly referred to as "woman plus woman in bed." For many, Naiad represented the degradation of the dreams of June Arnold, Bertha Harris, and Catherine Nicholson to create a distinctive aesthetic of lesbian writing. And yet Harris, the queen of the literary lesbians, remained on friendly terms with Grier. She blurbed *Faultline* in 1982, and in the late 1980s negotiated with Grier to bring out a new edition of *Lover.* Though Harris ended up reprinting with New York University Press, she had high praise for Naiad Press. As she wrote in a letter to Grier: *"I am very proud of you.* Because of you, lesbians have something to read—virtually anything we want. Immediately after food, sex, shelter, work, friendship, comes the next vital necessity: something to read. I call Naiad an International Treasure. I (and you) recall the horrible days well when there was nothing to read."[93]

Grier saw her work at Naiad as providing lesbians with what they wanted, not what the urban activist vanguard thought they should have. For this lesbian book collector and bibliographer, reading remained a good in and of itself. What women readers did with that reading was less important to Grier than getting them to read at all. If feminist reading led to consciousness raising and political transformation, great, but Grier was content with other outcomes—the construction of identity, a virtual sense of community, even pure pleasure. "I suppose if I could," she explained to Houston bookstore owner Pokey Anderson, "I would make better readers, but you can't do that. . . . There is a place in the world for all of it, there's a place for all this reading."[94] Grier insisted that we open up our understanding of feminist reading practices. Her populist ethos fueled Naiad's success in the 1980s and 1990s.

Literary Lesbians and Mainstream Success in the 1990s

The rise of Naiad Press transformed lesbian fiction into a recognizable and lucrative literary category available in bookstores and accessible to a wide array of readers, lesbian and otherwise. By the end of the 1980s, Naiad's visibility and accessibility exceeded anything Grier might have imagined when she was writing her *Lesbiana* column back in the 1960s. But not everyone was happy about the rise of lesbian genre fiction. Dorothy Allison's 1988 letter is representative of the discontent that existed:

I want so to write mean stories—work that pushes the envelope of what people allow themselves to think, work that stretches the lesbian imagination. Most "lesbian" fiction doesn't even make me mad; it just sits on the shelf like stale white bread so bland I don't even want to call it Lesbian. . . . There is so much more that can be done with fiction than most lesbians seem to realize, so many more lesbian realities to explore, so much more I want to try to do. So much stuff, I need to see for myself, the edge of fear mostly, the place where fear skirts lust and the way it breaks. . . . I want the ambiguity. . . . I want the uncertainty and the surprise.[95]

Allison had been a lesbian feminist true believer, living in a commune, running a women's center and women's bookstore, attending the Sagaris Institute, and working for iconic feminist journals including *Quest* and *Conditions*. Bertha Harris was her mentor, but the transgressive, monstrous lesbian Harris championed did not become the ideal in 1980s lesbian feminism. The "lesbian sex wars" led to Allison's almost total disillusionment with feminism. It also prompted her to starting publishing. Her 1983 book of poetry, *The Women Who Hate Me*, was a direct response to her detractors; her 1988 collection of stories, *Trash*, was similarly transgressive and courageous. Although Allison was fed up with the women's press culture that Naiad represented—"stale white bread"—she still needed women's presses to get published.

But this was about to change. The first hint of what was to come was an unexpected prize. In 1989 Minnie Bruce Pratt won the Lamont Poetry Prize for her book *Crime against Nature*, which detailed Pratt's loss of parental rights after coming out and divorcing her husband. It is hard to overstate what a milestone this was. The Lamont was one of the most prestigious poetry prizes in the nation; an award of the Academy of American Poets, it was designated specifically for a poet's second book and was meant to honor up-and-coming poets. It was comparable to being named a Yale Younger Poet or winning a Pulitzer Prize for poetry; some of the most famous American poets have been honored with a Lamont Prize. James Merrill was the host at the ceremony at which Pratt received the award.

This recognition by the Academy of American Poets was widely seen as lesbian literature's coming of age; with the exception of Adrienne Rich (who had been a Yale Younger Poet but lost much of her academic reputation when she embraced lesbian feminism), Pratt was the first lesbian feminist poet to receive mainstream recognition, particularly for content that was explicitly queer. She emphasized this in her acceptance speech, and placed the genesis of these poems in the South:

> The gay bar that I went to, in 1975, when I was first coming out as a lesbian, was called The Other Side; it was an old warehouse on Russell Street, in Fayetteville, North Carolina, and was, in fact, located on the other side of the tracks. When I went with my friends, we'd stand in a clump in the narrow doorway, then squeeze an awkward entrance between a cigarette machine and the counter where we paid our money and someone stamped our hands with blacklight ink. . . . The entrance was deliberately narrow so it could be easily blocked by one person while we all ran out the big double doors in the next room. . . .
>
> I was never arrested in a raid on that bar or any other. Judgment on me as a lesbian came down in another place in my life, when I was told that I was not fit under the General Statutes of the State, not fit under the sodomy law, to be both a lover of women and the mother of my two sons. The poems in the book *Crime against Nature*, for which I am receiving this award tonight, are a reconciliation of these ways of loving, as a mother, as a lesbian; are a reconciliation of a contradiction that I do not accept, that I have defied in my life and in my writing.[96]

Pratt constructs a poet's metaphor for the treacherous narrow space for queer life in the South, structured for secrecy, protection, and escape. Her reconciliation was not just as a lesbian and a mother but also as a southerner who refused the narrow confines to which she had been relegated.

Pratt gave explicit credit for her achievement to women's liberation, gay liberation, and (implicitly) the WIP movement. "I would not have begun to live as a lesbian nor have survived to write these poems without the women's liberation and the gay and lesbian liberation movements. Many of the people who made the political and cultural realities that helped me survive are here tonight: Women who've excavated and saved the facts of lesbian history, women who've written the poems, edited the magazines, newspapers, and journals, taken the photographs, taped the radio shows, run the bookstores, and begun the women's studies and gay studies programs, women who have created the places where lesbians can live and think and flourish."[97] Pratt's acknowledgment of the WIP movement, with its network of journals, bookstores, writers, and academics, gives it credit for her development as a writer. She called her winning the award "the trajectory of the eighties around us breaking through into the mainstream.

It was one of those moments. . . . I mean, nobody could believe it. Like, what happened? And of course, all of our conversations were around, how did this happen? How is this possible? Very interesting, because we were trying to calculate the impact of the movement on the cultural arena."[98] The big names of the "lesbian feminist cultural establishment"[99] were there, staging an uncomfortable encounter between lesbian feminists and the mainstream cultural establishment.

It was a warm-up for the literary phenomenon to come: Dorothy Allison's 1991 *Bastard out of Carolina*. Allison had been working on the novel for many years. After the publication of *Trash* in 1988, she received a big advance from Dutton, a subsidiary of Penguin established in 1986. The contract with Dutton gave her the benefit of wide distribution of her novel, including in the increasingly significant big box bookstores Barnes and Noble and Borders. Allison had reservations about publishing with a mainstream press; they had first suggested a book cover that she described to Firebrand publisher Nancy Bereano as "a Steven Spielberg cleaned-up version of *Tobacco Road*."[100] But the advance allowed her the time to finish the novel, and the money the publisher budgeted for a book tour, promotion, and distribution gave her a remarkable opportunity to reach a far larger audience than she had ever enjoyed.

One would not think that a coming-of-age novel about poverty, abuse, and incest would become a runaway bestseller, but like Alice Walker's 1982 *The Color Purple*, *Bastard out of Carolina* exceeded all expectations. The novel prompted national conversations about incest, became a finalist for the National Book Award, was turned into a movie directed by Angelica Huston, and made Dorothy Allison a literary star. It continues to appear on college syllabi for a variety of courses including southern literature, "grit lit" surveys, queer studies, and gender studies overviews.

Other southern lesbian feminists took advantage of the interest in queer topics and received renewed attention. Blanche McCrary Boyd had a reset, of sorts; in 1991 she published a collection of linked short stories, *The Revolution of Little Girls*, which, because she would not allow her first two novels (*Nerves* and *Mourning the Death of Magic*) to be reprinted, was treated much like a first book. She also reprinted her collection of essays, *The Redneck Way of Knowledge*. Bertha Harris came back in 1992 with a reprint of *Lover*; her new introduction detailed her experience with radical feminism and settled scores with June Arnold. Minnie Bruce Pratt published *Rebellion*, a collection of essays, in 1991, and Mab Segrest's *Memoir of a Race Traitor* came out in 1994; both were published by independent presses. Even in a moment of mainstream acceptance, feminist presses remained an essential part of the publishing ecosystem.

One could call this a return of the literary lesbian, except that the literary lesbian had never really gone away, even if mainstream presses had lost interest. Allison and Boyd were invested in traditional notions of the literary and did not appreciate the rise of lesbian genre fiction that Naiad Press represented. But Allison's own literary tastes were not limited by the experimental ethos that her mentor Harris advocated. She wrote in a letter about lesbian writer Sarah Schulman's novel *Empathy*, "Everything I say should be taken in the context of my own biases and interests in fiction, [and] the fact that while I understand and enjoy traditional narratives, I have little to say about experimental writing. I read very little of it."[101] Allison's preference for "traditional narratives" complicates her own embrace of the literary. For avant-garde lesbians like Harris, "traditional narratives" were not literary enough.

Allison's own relationship to the literary was complicated, and in some ways, she was closer to pulp queen Barbara Grier than her public persona suggested. Privately, she wrote S/M science fiction erotica. One story, "Predators," was published; the rest were sent by mail to private subscribers for a fee.[102] It could be said that Allison started the niche market for lesbian S/M erotica, just as her friend Jewelle Gomez began the lesbian vampire trend with *The Gilda Chronicles*. Allison has been careful not to publish the erotica under her own name, but she was writing it at the same time she was finishing *Bastard out of Carolina*. As it was for Harris, for Allison the line between literary and trash was permeable.

Even as Allison became the most widely known southern lesbian feminist writer, she understood the continued perils of depending on mainstream publishers. As she wrote to her agent,

> I worry a great deal how any lesbian writer who takes herself and her writing seriously can survive in mainstream publishing where the bottom line is sales. I believe that there will always be a barrier between the lesbian writer and the straight audience that has to be overcome if a trade publisher is to make a profit. The lesbian audience is just not big enough to get the kind of sales that warrant hardcover profits, though the combined, lesbian, feminist and gay audience may be. Nor do I believe in the universal audience—the idea that if the work is good enough it will draw in the readers. I know far too many good writers whose work is obscure and marginal.[103]

So the problem of the literary and the literary lesbian continued, even as many lesbians went mainstream in the 1990s. By and large, Allison was treated as if she had come out of nowhere to write a first novel, though she had been publishing throughout the 1980s and had been nurtured by the feminist movement for her entire career. In a conversation with Boyd not long after the publication of *Bastard*, Allison critiqued the mainstream press's fascination with her:

> *BB*: So, how are you feeling about being a crossover artist?
> *DA*: Hi, darlin'. It's bullshit. What about all those straight writers who are read in queer communities? If you're talking about crossover only in terms of small-press lesbian and gay writers who suddenly sell some books to straight people, it's insulting and trivializing.[104]

Allison notes the continued myopia of the mainstream about the "small-press" system set up by the WIP movement. The fact that *New York Times* reviewers didn't notice, she insists, doesn't negate the importance of that sustaining network of small presses, alternative bookstores, queer and feminist writers, and readers. The media wanted to treat Allison as a singular oddity, rather than as part of a southern lesbian feminist tradition, but she knew better.

Ultimately, the WIP movement created a distinctive literary network whose members believed literature could liberate women from the ravages of the patriarchy. Its interrogation of the literary led to a remarkable production of literary artifacts that critics have yet to appreciate. Those productions ranged across levels of sophistication and tastes, united in a fearless examination of women's experiences and a commitment to writing previously unspeakable truths.

This small press revolution enabled, both in the books it published and the mainstream interest it commanded, the creation of the archive of southern lesbian feminism. The main interests and contours of that tradition are the focus of the next three chapters, which explore the radical South, queer sexuality, and the reconstruction of southern space. In the spirit of the WIP movement, these cultural and literary investigations proceed topically, with a diverse range of southern lesbian feminist voices chiming in. Whatever their differences, these southern lesbian feminist writers were engaged in a radical critique of the South—its racism, its hypocrisy, its control of physical and intellectual space—and their common critiques and inventions deserve to be understood together.

Politics and the Lesbian Feminist Imaginary

· ·

Coming Out in the South

It was big news when the Human Rights Campaign, the biggest gay rights organization in the country, announced that it was starting a multimillion-dollar initiative in three southern states: Arkansas, Alabama, and Mississippi. The investment of money and time in a region long considered, in the words of a *Daily Kos* article about the initiative, the "very heart of our homophobic Mordor"[1] marked a new moment in national gay political organizing.

The executive director of the Human Rights Campaign (HRC), Arkansas native Chad Griffin, and Academy Award–winning screenwriter (and Texas native) Dustin Lance Black visited the University of Mississippi in the fall of 2014 as part of the "One America" initiative. Their message was essentially the same one the gay rights movement has been emphasizing since the time of Harvey Milk: come out. Telling their own coming-out stories, Griffin and Black suggested the same happy ending: if we all come out, we will transform our home states and the homophobia that continues to reign in our legislatures.

I knew a number of people in the audience who had already come out, bravely and at potentially great personal cost in a state where there is no protection from employment and housing discrimination. My friend Stacey Harkins had become a marriage equality activist after travelling to New York to marry Anna, registering their license in the Lafayette County courthouse, giving interviews in print and on camera, and otherwise embodying the ethos of coming out. A feature on the anything-but-liberal hottytoddy .com website foregrounded their insistence on claiming both southern and gay identities.

> They are aware that Mississippi does not recognize them as a couple, but they do not let that define their relationship.
>
> "People have told us, 'If you don't like our laws, just leave.' But Anna and I were both born and raised in Mississippi. We are both

second generation Ole Miss graduates," Stacey said. "When we planned our wedding in New York, we still planned it around the Ole Miss football game. I don't understand how people can discriminate against us, but I really don't understand who has a wedding on a football game day! Ha!" . . .

"We work and pay our bills and go to dinner with our friends and spoil our schnauzer, Andy, rotten," Stacey said. "We eat at Ajax, support our Rebels, and love Oxford just like anyone else. This is our state, too. We love Oxford. We love the people and the land that generations of our family members have chosen as their home."[2]

Gay marriage had been pushed to the forefront of the national conversation by ordinary citizens like Stacey and Anna, residents of flyover states who wanted the practical protections marriage could afford them and were willing to hire lawyers to claim their rights as citizens. It is easy to forget now that national groups like the HRC wanted nothing to do with gay marriage in the 1990s and were annoyed that these lawsuits kept forcing them to take a stand. Through marriage equality, Americans discovered that their neighbors were gay and lesbian when they lined up for licenses across the nation. Many queer southerners were already out—and some resented hearing a simplistic, celebratory narrative that suggested coming out would automatically transform the region.

By the end of 2017 the HRC could not point to any legislative victories in Jackson, Mississippi; the governor had not altered his homophobic rhetoric, despite widespread rumors that his own son is gay.[3] The passage in the spring of 2016 of HB 1523—by far the most far-reaching antigay legislation in the country, framed by "religious freedom"—suggests that the Obergefell backlash trumped the sunny coming-out narrative of Griffin and Black. Indeed, the HRC's most inspiring work in Mississippi has been done by Denise Donnell, Rob Hill, and Daniel Ball, who have built partnerships with Mississippi's church communities. Convincing some of the churches in the state to tone down their rhetoric and reach out to needy communities, including homeless LGBTQ (lesbian, gay, bisexual, transgender, queer) youth, could make an enormous difference in a state where tirades against gay marriage and gay equality often make life unbearable for LGBTQ citizens and the friends and family who love them. Grassroots gay rights organizations have similarly emphasized religious communities as a site to wage the battle for gay equality.

Perhaps the most troubling thing about the HRC investment in the South was the suggestion that this sort of intervention was brand new; it is not.

Queer feminist radical activism thrived in the South since the 1970s, emphasizing intersectional and coalition politics. Framing the South as "the heart of our homophobic Mordor" has a long history; the South is usually figured in contemporary discourse as a reactionary no-man's-land, a space so mired in tradition and averse to change that it is dragging down the nation. And obviously, evidence for this view abounds—an abundance of Republican governors, the rejection of the Affordable Care Act, the public denunciation of Syrian refugees, and the steady stream of legislation restricting abortion rights and discriminating against queer citizens.

But the lived reality has always been more complicated. Southern studies scholars have been arguing for decades that the South is more an ideology than a real place, a hegemony of heritage that has made a certain version of history, obsessed with the Confederacy and the nostalgia of the Lost Cause, a litmus test for "authentic" southernness. This test has always excluded a majority of actual residents of the South, then and now; its power depends on willful un-remembering. Specifically, it depends on commemorating the South as conservative while ignoring its ongoing relationship with radical political movements.

Perhaps the best known example of radical politics was the drive to end racial segregation in the South. Martin Luther King Jr.'s nonviolent movement was clearly southern, rooted in Christianity and the tradition of black southern Baptists. But so too was the Student Nonviolent Coordinating Committee (SNCC), started by southern African American students at a historically black college in Greensboro, North Carolina. The SNCC organized some of the most dramatic events of the early 1960s, including the Freedom Rides. Its strategy of using white northerners to increase the visibility of the movement and prompt the federal government to take action (as it did during Freedom Summer) was constructed and debated by a core of southern radical students.[4]

Less remembered are other political movements that grew out of the civil rights movement: African American activism focused on the sexual assault of black women by white men;[5] the beginnings of the black power movement in Lowndes County, Alabama;[6] and early feminist organizing.[7] The SNCC also had far-reaching effects: their systematic campaign to register to vote black Mississippians across the state, in communities large and small, and to introduce new ideas through Freedom Schools and the Free Southern Theater was an almost military-style operation to retake the territory occupied by Jim Crow, in both physical space and the southern imaginary. This focus on culture and liberated consciousness for black southerners continued through the 1960s and 1970s through the black arts movement.[8]

Go back to the early nineteenth century and you find radical southerners everywhere. They lived in maroon societies formed by groups of escaped slaves in the Carolinas and Florida;[9] they plotted slave uprisings;[10] they escaped to the North and spoke on the abolitionist lecture circuit;[11] they turned against their own planter families and adopted the mixed-race children of their relatives;[12] they rioted against the Confederate government.[13] Whatever percentage of the population they comprised (and if one includes enslaved Africans along with abolitionists, Unionists, and deserters, that percentage is considerable), they succeeded in dramatically redefining the economy, American citizenship, and the Constitution during Reconstruction. The period following the Civil War saw the most radical reinvention of citizenship and governance ever attempted in the United States, greater than even the New Deal. The southern denunciation of that era, epitomized by *Birth of a Nation*, has hidden its successful radicalism, which was first recuperated by W. E. B. Du Bois in his 1930 *Black Reconstruction* and more recently in scholarship by Eric Foner, Douglas Egerton, and Allen Guelzo.[14] More than 1,500 African Americans held legislative office during the period; Reconstruction's insistence on creating an equitable interracial democracy inspired both the counterreaction of Jim Crow and the subsequent civil rights movement.

Still other examples of radicalism simmer under the surface in southern history. Robyn D. G. Kelley's *Hammer and Hoe* details the almost forgotten history of black Communists in the South, who continued to exert influence from the Scottsboro trial to the broadcasts (from Cuba) of Radio Free Dixie to anti-Klan organizing in the 1980s.[15] At the same time, the New Deal created conditions that allowed the rise of organized labor in the South, which destabilized efforts by southern politicians to take money from federal programs while enforcing segregation. In textile mills, loading docks, coalfields, and tobacco factories, thousands of southerners went on strike for fair wages; their organizing would later feed the civil rights movement.[16]

We keep forgetting these eruptions of the radical South in our literature and our history, but they inform the southern lesbian feminist writers of *The Lesbian South*. History was crucial to their understanding of themselves as feminists and southerners, and that buried history provided the key to their own radicalizations.

(Lesbian) Feminist Activism and the South

Women's liberation activism in the South has also been largely overlooked. The 2014 special issue of *Sinister Wisdom*, "Southern Lesbian-Feminist Herstory 1968–1994," documents the wide range of feminist activism in the South during the first twenty-five years of the women's liberation movement in the United States. Rose Norman points out that in 1968, one of the twenty women invited to attend the "first national women's liberation organizing meeting," Judith Brown, was from Gainesville, Florida. Brown had co-authored one of the most influential early women's liberation documents, "Toward a Female Liberation Movement," known as the "Florida Paper."[17] Brown returned home from the meeting and formed Gainesville Women's Liberation, the first women's liberation group in the South (16). Two members of the New York Redstockings, Carol Hanisch and Kathie Sarachild, moved to Gainesville in 1969 ("at least part-time," says Norman). Sarachild wrote "the first pamphlet.on principles of feminist consciousness-raising (CR) groups" in Gainesville, and Hanisch "wrote the famous essay 'The Personal Is Political' while living in Gainesville" (16). Gainesville, in other words, generated some of the most important concepts and publications of early women's liberation, and southerners were central to women's liberation from its earliest iteration.

This is not how women's liberation has been commemorated, as a number of southern scholars have pointed out. Even Rose Norman, "a lifelong Southerner . . . involved in feminism since the 1970s," didn't know about "the significance of Gainesville, Florida, in the women's movement" (16). Southerners tend to be left out of these national narratives, or their locations or origins are elided. Many feminists moved to New York and Washington, D.C., Connecticut and California, Oregon and Illinois, but they never ceased to identify as southerners, to engage with the South imaginatively and emotionally, and to live as expatriates who might at any moment go "home." But not all southern feminists were expatriates, as the "Herstory" issue makes clear. The oral histories in *Sinister Wisdom* map a wide feminist campaign in the South involving university towns and urban centers, women's communes, and underground communities. Oral histories from Gainesville, Miami, Atlanta, Nashville, and Kentucky, Mississippi, and North Carolina suggest the geographic scope of southern feminist activism. From the creation of women's resource centers and women's studies programs on university campuses to the establishment of battered women's shelters and rape crisis centers to legal battles over reproductive rights, domestic violence, rape laws, custody of children, child care, and the Equal Rights Amendment, southern feminists were involved the full range of what have commonly been understood as "women's issues."[18] They were also involved, simultaneously, in issues of economic inequality, mass incarceration, animal welfare, and what we now call "critical race studies."

Scholarship on southern feminist movements has increased in the last ten years.[19] *The Lesbian South* contributes to this growing body of knowledge by investigating the intersectional focus of the archive of southern lesbian feminism. Southern lesbian feminists were not the only voices advocating radical critiques and solutions, of course, but they were prominent in women's liberation. Blanche McCrary Boyd suggested in her 1998 retrospective novel about women's liberation, *Terminal Velocity*, that southerners made particularly good radicals: "'There's nobody better than a Southern white girl who gets liberated,' a well-known black militant had told me, leaning his face down close to mine, repeating almost word for word the line a white SDS leader from Wisconsin had used a few months before. Southern white girls, their theory seemed to go, grew up with such crazy, restrictive notions of feminine behavior that when we broke out, we broke out completely. 'Outlaws with charm,' the SDS man said, then asked me if my house was one of those big white mansions with columns."[20] This stereotype of southern "bad girls" is problematic, to say the least, as it assumes a certain version of white planter-class femininity, defined by Scarlett O'Hara; nonwhite and working-class southerners are excluded. Southern feminine norms come up again and again in the archive of southern lesbian feminism as something toxic to be deconstructed and moved past.

As lesbians, these southern writers placed themselves beyond the boundaries of "acceptable" southern ladyhood. Minnie Bruce Pratt is a case in point.[21] She describes herself as a femme former sorority girl who enjoyed all the benefits of traditional southern femininity. When she was older she recognized that chivalric protection was also a cage, when she lost custody of her children after coming out as a lesbian. The fragility of her racial and class privilege led to greater insights:

> If I have begun to understand that I am entrapped *as* a woman, not
> just by the sexual fears of the men of my group, but also by their
> racial and religious terrors; if I have begun to understand that when
> they condemn me as a lesbian and a free woman for being "dirty,"
> "unholy," "perverted," "immoral," it is a judgment they have called
> down on people of color and Jews throughout history, as the men of

my culture have shifted their justification for hatred according to their desires of the moment; if I have begun to understand something of the deep connection between my oppression and that of other folks, what is it that keeps me from acting, sometimes even from speaking out?[22]

That "deep connection" of oppression—of racial and religious intolerance, and the ways that accusations of "perversion" serve to keep those others in their place—helped Pratt to critique the injustices of her southern upbringing. This intersectional critique marks the archive of southern lesbian feminism. Those excluded from the myth of the southern belle, notable southerners of color and working-class southerners, felt less investment in ladyhood but approached their politics in a similarly intersectional way. Deconstructing the status quo led to complex radical coalitions.

Minnie Bruce Pratt also challenged the legacy of the Fugitives, whose values were "love of the land and denial of those who had done the work on the land, despair and a belief in death, a fascination with the past of the old heroes, a failure to understand the new heroes and heroines who were liberating the present."[23] But the Fugitives also taught Pratt about the power of words to create new realities, new political configurations, new mythologies. This belief in the creative power of literature had immediate practical and political aims as well. Southern lesbian feminist writers, like the Fugitives, already considered themselves to be outside the American mainstream, and they understood the power and resistance of a community of outsiders. Why couldn't their own literary visions, supported by independent presses, create a new South, a better South? The archive of southern lesbian feminism imagined a *radical* South full of deviants and race traitors and carpetbaggers and racial, cultural, and sexual others, empowered in a system that supports them. Some wrote these creations from afar; others worked for change *in* the South, in protests and activism. This radical South took many forms and engaged multiple political issues, but it made cultural rebellion and intersectionality central to a southern lesbian feminist imaginary.

Radical Politics and the (Southern) Lesbian Feminist Imaginary in Early Women's Liberation

A number of southern lesbian feminists were involved in early feminist activism. June Arnold was a member of the Fifth Street Women's Building takeover; Pat Parker was involved in a number of actions in the Bay Area, supporting victims of domestic violence and parental rights for lesbian mothers; Blanche McCrary Boyd lived in a Vermont radical commune and helped organize the Sagaris Feminist Institute; Rita Mae Brown organized a number of notorious political actions including the Lavender Menace action at NOW and the presentation of the "Woman-Identified Woman" at another feminist gathering; Mab Segrest worked in anti-Klan activism; Minnie Bruce Pratt protested the Supreme Court after the Hardwick decision in 1986; Alice Walker participated in civil rights activism in Mississippi in the 1960s; Dorothy Allison ran a women's center in Tallahassee in the 1970s; even Fannie Flagg, not a particularly political person, signed a petition in favor of the Equal Rights Amendment in the 1970s. Politics was the air they breathed, and 1960s radicalism—particularly antiwar protests and nationalist groups like the Black Panthers—informed their provocations. The southern lesbian feminist writers of this study manifested their radical politics in a host of political issues, and their embrace of cultural forms to explore them and change "consciousness" in their readers was of a piece with the consciousness-raising groups that motivated direct political action.

This flexible focus on radical politics and consciousness raising through art is apparent in some of the earliest women's poetry of the period. Poetry readings united nascent feminist communities at feminist bookstores and coffeehouses, and many southern lesbian feminist writers got their starts writing poetry. There were two national stars in the earliest days of this egalitarian feminist poetry movement—Rita Mae Brown and Pat Parker.

Brown's early collection *The Hand that Cradles the Rock* contains numerous references to the pressing "women's issues" of her day, and it was a touchstone for early women's liberationists. The book depicts the contemporary world of the patriarchy, a male culture that is sick and dying. The title of the opening poem makes this clear: "On the Rooftop Where All the Pigeons Go to Die: A Litany for Male Culture." She embeds images of decay and the sea in a repetition of the word *before*: "before great hulks of decomposed intelligence / bobbled on the Hudson flowing endlessly," "Before universities and warmakers fed off each other like incestuous crabs."[24] The longing for a lost, prepatriarchal culture takes an unexpected turn when she notes the "sunken temple of Jupiter's ancient encrusted marble maze" (13). Those familiar with Adrienne Rich's "Diving into the Wreck" will note similar themes here; "male culture" is already doomed in Brown's poem. She dismisses "Radical Man" as nothing more than "A marvelous me of malevolence" (16).

Brown's "triptych" "The New Lost Feminist" garnered considerable attention in the feminist journal the *Furies* when it was first published in 1971, and Coletta Reid's long appreciation of the poem was reprinted in her introduction to the Diana Press reprint of *The Hand that Cradles the Rock*: "The left panel is the expression of the deep personal frustration, powerlessness and suffering of a woman. . . . The center panel gives the societal picture . . . America is dying. . . . But before the end comes, the cause of death is made clear: the demise of the system was part of the nature of the system itself. . . . The right panel is a recognition of what has been done to us by the society and what we have to do about it."[25] From the poem's dramatic start—"A woman is dying for want of a single unrealized word, / Freedom" (23)—through images of "blacks, / Women and the young / Fleeing a Troy that has built its own horse / America becomes a bloated corpse" (24) to its final call to action—"It's time to break and run" (25)— Brown allows for no compromise with "America's rotting rib cage [that] frames the gallows / Of her putrid goals" (24).

The apocalyptic images of what we now call "heteropatriarchy" are relentless. In a play on Yeats's poem "The Second Coming," Brown describes "leav[ing] in wider and wider circles / Turning to where the center should be, Amerika," and ends: "You find him, syphilitic whore / An international festering sore" (35). And she is at no loss for specific examples: the dry irrelevance of universities, the brutality of repression. In another poem from *The Hand that Cradles the Rock*, "Hymn to the 10,000 Who Die Each Year on the Abortionist's Table in Amerika," Brown insists on remembering the dead through making "death masks" and touching "the crevices of the slain faces/ For slivers of truth" (40). The spelling *Amerika* suggests an America wounded by racism (the KKK) as well as a German allusion that may imply a fascist state; in using this language, Brown is similar to a number of New Left writers. She concludes, "Though painful in its pushing / We must hunt as wounded women / The balm to heal one another" (40). Another poem, "For Lydia French, Shot and Killed, August 13, 1970," condemns domestic violence: "Women know / Women have always known / As marrow to the bone / Death is at the heart of men. / I touch your solitary, senseless death / and run for my life. / Men shall yet know / The fruits earned / Of death. / Goodbye, Lydia" (58). She touches on the issue of mass incarceration with images of the women's prison located in Greenwich Village, the Women's House of Detention: "Here amid the nightsticks, handcuffs and interrogation / Inside the cells, beatings, the degradation / We grew a strong and bitter root / That promises justice" (67). As in her political essays (collected in *A Plain Brown Rapper*), Brown connected women's issues to a variety of radical political causes.

In San Francisco, Houston native Pat Parker was also building up an impressive following.[26] Her early poetry published by the Women's Press Collective includes saucy rebukes to various lovers, activists, and strangers, and criticizes America and the South as fascist, movement brothers for their sexism, feminist sisters for their racism and homophobia, and fellow lesbians for their racism. Unlike Rita Mae Brown's poetry, Parker's work is often very funny. (Brown saved her humor for her fiction.) Parker's humor often softens the sting of her pointed poetic critiques. The poems from her 1973 collection *Pit Stop* show her wry wit. "For Willyce," a poem about having sex with her girlfriend, finishes with a commentary on patriarchy: "When I make love to you . . . / & your sounds drift down /oh god! / oh jesus! / and i think— / here it is, some dude's / getting credit for what / a woman / has done, / again."[27] Themes of invisible women's work abound in earlier women's liberation, but there are no poems as naughty and witty as Pat Parker's. In "The *What* Liberation Front?," she includes a humorous satire on "liberation" political rhetoric by including her dog's critique of her own oppression.

> Today I had a talk with my dog
> he called me a racist—chauvinist person
> told me he didn't like the way
> i keep trying to change him. . . .
> And property—he wanted to know why
> people expected dogs to protect their capitalist interest
> he never watches television or plays
> records. & how come I put tags on him.
> My dog—he laughed. He is his own dog.
> And what's this bullshit about his sex
> life. If he wants to fuck in the streets it's
> his business.[28]

The poem is printed with a facing-page photograph of Parker kneeling and her dog, standing on his hind legs, towering over her with his paws on her shoulders, and it ends with the dog going to a "consciousness-raising meeting." This poem shows a sense of humor about the conventions of identity politics in 1973 that we don't usually give lesbian feminists credit for. But how should we read this poem? She clearly isn't dismissing the principles of "liberation"; indeed, she doesn't mind Marxist critiques of dogs (and wives) as "property." Recent scholarship on the queer nonhuman that argues that distinctions between humans and other animals mirror hierarchies of gender, race, and sexuality would embrace much of the sentiment behind this funny poem.[29] Indeed, the disturbing colonial rhetorical tradition of framing Africans as animals to justify slavery comes under critique in this dismissal of animals as property. And Parker's implicit support of "fucking in the streets" might also be embraced by queer studies' investigations of public sex.[30] Parker's seemingly simple poetry is actually extraordinarily nuanced and layered and performs often dangerous critiques of normative American society.

Other poems by Parker continue this theme of seemingly simple structure and complicated intersectional critiques. The opening poem of *Pit Stop*, "My Lover Is a Woman,"[31] is a good example:

1

My lover is a woman
   & when i hold her—
      feel her warmth—
      i feel good—feel safe

then i never think of
my families' voices—
never hear my sisters say—
bulldaggers, queers, funny—
come see us, but don't
bring your friends—
it's okay with us,
but don't tell mama
it'd break her heart
never feel my father
turn in his grave
never hear my mother cry
Lord, what kind of child is this?

2

My lover's hair is blonde
& when it rubs across my face
it feels soft—
feels like a thousand fingers

touch my skin & hold me
and i feel good.

Then i never think of the little boy
who spat & called me nigger
never think of the policemen
who kicked my body and said crawl
never think of black bodies
hanging in trees or filled
with bullet holes
never hear my sisters say
white folks hair stinks
don't trust any of them
never feel my father
turn in his grave
never hear my mother talk
of her back ache after scrubbing floors
never hear her cry—
Lord, what kind of child is this?

3

My lover's eyes are blue
& when she looks at me
i float in a warm lake
    feel my muscles go weak with want
        feel good—feel safe

Then—i never think of the blue
eyes that have glared at me—
moved three stools away from me
in a bar
never hear my sisters rage
of syphilitic black men as
guinea pigs—
    rage of sterilized children—
        watch them just stop in an
        intersection to scare *the old*
        white bitch

never feel my father turn

in his grave
never remember my mother
teaching me the yes sirs & mams
to keep me alive—
never hear my mother cry
Lord, what kind of child is this?

4
And when we go to a gay bar
& my people shun me because I crossed
the line
& her people look to see what's
wrong with her—what defect
    drove her to me—

and when we walk the streets
of this city—forget and touch
    or hold hands and the people
        stare, glare, frown, & taunt
          at those queers—

I remember
    Every word taught me
    Every word said to me
    Every deed done to me
        & then i hate
i look at my lover
& for an instant—doubt—

Then—i hold her hand tighter
    And i can hear my mother cry.
    Lord, what kind of child is this.

The structure is deceptively simple—from observations about her white lover to the hauntings of her own traumatic experiences, culminating in the refrain about her parents, "Lord, what kind of child is this?"—but Parker weaves a complicated vision of cultural interpellation here. She switches focus from one form of prejudice to another within a stanza, even within a line. Her sisters go from being victims of "syphilitic black men" to terrorizing a white woman, without any transition. There is no simple identity as either victim or oppressor, no stance that makes one immune to this hate. The repetitions of "my lover is a woman" and "what kind of child is this?" reveal racism within queer communities; homophobia within black communities; white supremacy and its devastating consequences in the black community; and the painful rejection by her family. A personal love story cannot transcend the complicated structural limitations that thwart an interracial lesbian couple.

Ultimately, Parker is concerned with how this hostile cultural environment affects her own psyche and identity. One way she explores the infection of cultural hate is through form. Like many of her other poems, "My Lover Is a Woman" capitalizes the first word of each sentence and the "Lord" of the last line, and leaves the rest lower case. In the the second-to-last stanza, when the narrator allows her cultural marginality to drive her to doubt her lover and her own experience, she capitalizes every line, perhaps to symbolize the hateful cultural mode that has infected her. She retreats away from this standard position in the final stanza, and rewrites her mother's lament. Instead of "my mother cries, Lord, what kind of child is this," she writes "i can hear my mother cry," ending the thought with a period. Her final line, "Lord, what kind of child is this" also ends with a period, not a question mark, and becomes, rather than her mother's homophobic lament, her own somber mediation on how to resist a hateful, destructive culture.

In this poem, Parker is haunted by her southern childhood—images of lynching, of police violence, of her mother's servitude in white homes, and of her own subservience as she is taught "the yes sirs & mams / to keep me alive" as a second-class citizen. Other poems by Parker juxtapose a Jim Crow South against the idealistic claims of a free America, foregrounding her own distinctive positionality as a black southerner. She often focuses on a racist, militarized presence, as in her poem "Tour America." Parker considers safety on a potential road trip, but every remedy requires another protection from the previous one: "there are things I need: / travelers checks in new york / gas mask in berkeley, / face mask in los angeles, / National guardsmen to protect me/ - in the south, / Marines to protect me / from guardsmen / - in the mid-west, / Police to protect me / from hustlers/ - in the ghettos, / Bullet-proof vest and helmet / to protect me from police / -everywhere."[32] Parker packs a number of cultural references into this short poem—political protests in Berkeley, the Kent State massacre, civil rights protests in the South, and the ongoing specter of police brutality across the United States. The complexity of oppression in the United States means that no one solution is right; protectors in one context become oppressors in another. Following a reference to the venality of the police everywhere, Parker concludes the poem with her most revolutionary sentiment yet: "perhaps,/ it would be better/ to blow it up."

Parker has a complicated relationship to the South in her poetry. As an expatriate, she had already voted with her feet; she rejects the subordinate legacy of African American manners and a legal system that defined her as a second-class citizen. In her poem "Her children arise up, and call her blessed . . . .", from the 1978 collection *Womanslaughter*, Parker considers another southern legacy she rejected as a young girl—saying "sir" and "mam," a practice intimately tied to an apartheid system.

> when i was a child
> i was punished—
> i refused to say
> yes sir & yes mam. . . .
> now, my mother
> is dying
> & i wish to say
> so much,
> to thank her
> to say—i love you
> to hold her in my arms.
> these things
> i cannot do
> we have too
> many years
> of not touching—
> of not saying. . . .
> i am afraid of death
> fear to touch a cold body
> yet, i know
> in the final viewing,
> i will lean over my mother
> & whisper in her ear—
> yes mam, mama, yes mam.[33]

Parker's careful evocation of her mother's physical and emotional distancing finds an unexpected resolution when she bestows a southern mark of respect on her mother (which neither of them would have received in their native Houston). Revolutionary egalitarianism meets her southern background in a particularly moving way in this poem.

Parker reclaims the South in "To My Vegetarian Friend," too, when she rebukes a vegetarian with a paean to southern African American foodways:

> It's not called soul food
> because it goes with music.
> it is a survival food. . . .
>
> And when I sit—
> faced by
> chitterlins & greens
> neckbones & tails
> it is a ritual—
> it is a joining—
> me to my ancestors
> & your words ring untrue
> this food is good for me
> it replenishes my soul.[34]

Parker's insistence on "soul food" as "survival food" connects southern cooking to a mystical communion with a slave past and an African one (something that has become an emphasis in Southern Foodways Scholarship[35]). Soul food becomes a kind of sacrament that is superior to the vegetarian dogmatism popular among Bay Area lesbians.

Parker's focus on complex intersectional issues, however, doesn't prevent her from pointedly criticizing the patriarchy. The title poem in *Womanslaughter*, a heartrending account of her own sister's murder by her husband and the court's reduction of the charge to manslaughter, is an extended critique of how the killing of women is accepted, even celebrated, in a misogynist culture. Forty years after its publication, the poem is still a devastating indictment of a system in which "womenslaughter" is endemic. Parker's sister was failed by the police and the justice system. The police said, "Lady, there's nothing we can do / until he tried to hurt you."[36] In court, lawyers suggested she was a slut and a lesbian, his white boss vouched for him, and he was given one year for manslaughter. Parker exposes how, in a patriarchal America, womanslaughter is the prerogative of every man, even those subordinated by race and class: "What was his crime? / He only killed his wife / But a divorce i say. / Not final, they say; / Her things were his / including her life. / Men cannot rape their wives. / Men cannot kill their wives. / They passion them to death."[37] The realization that woman-slaughter is foundational to patriarchal culture is the chilling and unavoidable conclusion drawn from this particular familial grief.

The poem's final paragraph merges into a cross-racial appeal to "sisterhood":

> The three sisters
> of Shirley Jones
> came & cremated her.
> & they were not strong.
> Hear me now—
> It is almost three years
> & I am again strong.
> I have gained many sisters
> And if one is beaten,
> or raped, or killed,
> I will not come in mourning black
> I will not pick the right flowers.
> I will not celebrate her death
> & it will matter not
> if she's Black or white—
> if she loves women or men.
> I will come with my many sisters
> and decorate the streets
> with the innards of those
> brothers in womenslaughter
> No more, can I dull my rage
> in alcohol & deference
> to *men's* courts.
> I will come to my sisters,
> not dutiful
> I will come strong.[38]

Parker universalizes the theme of her poem in the end, shifting from her literal sisters—the "sisters of Shirley Jones"—to her feminist sisters, of all races and sexual orientations. Parker's unflinching indictment of fellow feminists for sexism and racism does not mitigate their unity against a common foe—in this case, the structural violence of a patriarchal system. Her proposed response to that system is vigilante vengeance: to "decorate the streets with the innards of those brothers in womenslaughter." That violent radical solution recurs in a number of Parker's poems.

This simultaneous embrace of radical critique, coalition politics, and disreputable femininity also appears in writings by other southern lesbian feminists. Rita Mae Brown's essays, for example, critique figures of the mainstream feminist movement—the Betty Friedans, the Kate Millets—and praise the sort of women who weren't supposed to be involved in women's liberation: "the women who won't make a mockery of the word Liberation . . . women who trust deeds not the promise of then . . . poor women, Black women, Puerto Rican women, Asian-American women, working women and women who love their sisters . . . women who will bypass rhetoric and make a revolution."[39] Early women's liberationists like Brown were "question[ing] the basic structure of our nation,"[40] and many were deeply suspicious of the priorities of white, middle-class reformers. Indeed, Brown states in the introduction to her collected essays: "By now, thanks to those early anti-lesbian campaigns, we've all learned to mistrust a mystique of unity which comes at the expense and silence of minority women. Women who are safely white aren't going to be quiet about it, nor are poor women, nor are lesbians. Lesbianism was the first issue to break ideological ground on the real meaning of multiplicity rather than conformity. Because of that initial, bitter struggle I hope the issues of class and white bias can be handled with more maturity than any of us handled the lesbian issue."[41] Particularly important in critiques of sexuality and heteronormativity was the trope of the revolutionary lesbian, a queer figure who allowed for a broad appraisal of the role of sexuality in contemporary American culture. But lesbian identity, for many southern-identified lesbian feminists, also served as an impetus for coming to terms with multiple differences among women. That was especially true in the intimate connection of feminism and antiracism in the archive of southern lesbian feminism.

Intersectional Analysis, Antiracism, and Cross-Racial Organizing in the Lesbian Feminist South

For southern lesbian feminists, race was not something that was later "added" to feminism; it was always an essential part of their understanding of their region and their identities. Many southern lesbian feminist writers came to feminism through civil rights activism and continued antiracist work as a key part of their feminism. The best known of these activists is Alice Walker, and though she didn't publicly claim lesbian feminism (or even identify as a lesbian, despite writing one of the most famous depictions of a lesbian relationship in *The Color Purple*), her voice is essential in reckoning with the alignment of civil rights and feminism. Walker lived in Jackson, Mississippi in the 1960s with a Jewish husband who worked as a lawyer for the NAACP. Her involvement with *Ms.* magazine and with feminism (or womanism, as she called it in her germinal essay collection *In Search of Our Mothers' Gardens*) connected civil rights activism and feminism in palpable ways. In *Gardens*, she laid claim to the South as an African American and a radical, in terms that defined a whole generation of Southern lesbian feminists: "Those red hills of Georgia were mine, and nobody was going to force me away from them until I myself was good and ready to go. . . . No black person I knew had ever encouraged anybody to 'Go back to Mississippi . . . ,' and I knew if this challenge were taken up by the millions of blacks who normally left the South for better fortunes in the North, a change couldn't help but come. . . . We would fight to stay where we were born and raised and destroy the forces that sought to disinherit us. We would proceed with the revolution from our own homes."[42] Walker's decision to "proceed with the revolution from our own homes" resonated with many southern lesbian feminists. *In Search of Our Mothers' Gardens* was one of many southern lesbian feminist texts in the 1980s that linked antiracism and feminism.

The next year, Cris South's novel *Clenched Fists, Burning Crosses* considered the connection between anti-Klan activism and feminism. The epigraph to the novel comes from Pat Parker's essay "Revolution: It's Not Neat or Pretty or Quick," which places the Klan in a systemic feminist critique of a patriarchal society: "The Klan and the Nazis are our enemies and must be stopped, but to simply mobilize around stopping them is not enough. They are functionaries, tools of this governmental system. They serve in the same way as our armed forces and police. To end Klan or Nazi activity doesn't end imperialism. It doesn't end institutional racism; it doesn't end sexism; it does not bring this monster down, and we must not forget what our goals are and who our enemies are. To simply label these people as lunatic fringes and not accurately assess their roles as part of this system is a dangerous error."[43] South frames her novel within a systemic critique of contemporary culture and refuses to consider the Klan an aberration; for South, the Klan is emblematic of a racist patriarchy.

The main character of *Clenched Fists, Burning Crosses*, Jessie, gets a brutal education about the function of white male power. Her sexual coming out—she has sex with a woman for the first time only twelve pages into the novel—is connected to her political coming out. When she dismisses reports about Klan activity as "silly," her business partner, Laura, teaches her southern history:

> Let me give you a little piece of reality to think about. In the early
> 1900s, my grandfather and grandmother bought fifteen acres of
> land in northern Georgia. They were farmers. The Klan paid them a
> visit. They burned my grandfather's house to the ground and rode
> through all the crops. Two years later, because my grandparents
> wouldn't leave, they came back. They burned the place again. They
> tore up the crops. But this time, they beat my grandfather and left
> him a cripple for life. He was a young man with a wife and five kids.
> They had to move into town and my grandmother had to do maid's
> work to support the family. Some local white men visited my
> grandfather and told him that they had heard there was some
> mischief brewing, but they hadn't taken it seriously. *Mischief!* Then
> those good-intentioned white men offered to buy granddaddy's land
> from him. They bought it for twenty-five cents on the dollar.[44]

Laura suggests a seamless system of economic disparity constructed through violence—the shock troops do the terrorizing and the rich planter class scoops up the rewards. And though Laura's story focuses on African Americans, Jessie soon learns that white people who break with white supremacy also face racial terror.

Jessie finds herself under surveillance. When she appears at a gas station wearing a "Stop the KKK" button, the owner "read the button out loud, and you could've heard a pin drop in there. All the men stared at me, and one guy came over and sort of leaned against the counter beside me, looking at me hard. . . . Just as I was leaving, David asked didn't I rent that old farmhouse down at Ben Carpenter's place."[45] They continue to watch her, and when Jessie is a witness to a murder at an anti-Klan demonstration, she becomes a direct target of harassment that includes the trashing of her home, the hanging of her dog, and hate speech written in letters and painted on her wall: queer, niggerlover. It culminates in Jessie's grisly gang rape—an act of political terrorism intimately connected to the murder that prompted it.

That rape happens in the first third of the novel. The rest of the novel considers the aftermath of sexual and racial terror and how she not only survives but also resists it. Jessie discovers that no one in her circle is unaffected by sexual violence. Her own lover, Kate, was beaten by her father and raped by her brother; her best friend's lover was gang raped; her business partner Laura was beaten; and Laura's white lover, Moon, was shot and left for dead by the Klan in Mississippi in the 1960s. And the violence is not limited to her lesbian feminist circle; one of the rapists, Hank, a police officer, a Klan member, abuses his own wife, Beth, beating and raping her viciously.

The friends' successful resistance is achieved through their support for one another and through the institutions they build. They nurse Jessie back to health, and it is Laura and Moon, the former civil rights activist, who discover the Klan members in the printing shop and prevent their escape from the police. Kate starts a battered women's shelter, and when Hank's wife escapes there, having finally found the courage to leave her husband, she corroborates Jessie's rape charge and allows Jessie to regain control. A fellow police officer tells Hank where the shelter is (despite knowing that Hank has been arrested for arson and that his wife has left him), and when he appears, Jessie protects Beth, sinking a maul into the wall as she aims for his head, and leaving him whimpering in the corner as she swipes an ax inches from his face. "Lizzie Borden,"[46] she says later, laughing, and this archetypal image of that murderous woman releases something in Jessie that cannot be taken away. The final scene of her celebration with her lesbian feminist community underlines their resolve: southern lesbian feminists will not be intimidated, and they will not be driven out of their communities.

Cris South was one of the key members of the Feminary collective, whose mission from 1978 to 1982 was to queer the South. The journal it produced, also called *Feminary,* made an excavation of the radical South central to its embrace of a multicultural lesbian feminist South. It framed itself as a distinctively southern, antiracist publishing forum that deconstructed a toxic, nostalgic South and created a just and inclusive one. That new South explicitly included women of color. The journal emphasized the voices of African Americans, all of whom had roots in the South, whether they themselves had lived there or not (thus Pratt included the writing of Kitchen Table Press founder Barbara Smith). These voices of black migration were central to *Feminary*'s southern vision, in memoirs, interviews, short stories, and poetry. *Feminary* also sought out Native American and Hispanic voices. It aimed to create new ways of remembering and defining, new maps, and new conceptions of the South. *Feminary* was an experiment in a truly intersectional analysis of a lesbian South, overseen primarily by white southern lesbian feminists but created by a diverse collective of lesbian feminist writers.

Nowhere was this emphasis clearer than in the collective's final publication, a *Feminary* issue titled "The South as Home: Leaving or Staying," which includes Raymina Mays's short story "Delta," detailing the narrator's exile from her African American home because of her lesbianism,[47] and a memoir about return to the South by Anita Cornwall, an African American lesbian feminist from Greenwood, South Carolina who wrote for *TL*.[48] Almost all the writings by African Americans are stories of migration and displacement, a theme that runs through the issue. The issue also includes multiple maps, as if lesbian feminists must, literally, remap the territory to make it their own. On the back cover, one woman stands with arms akimbo (taking her stand, if you will) over the map of the South; another woman strides purposefully away from the map of the South, with only her ankle touching the tip of Florida as she moves out of the frame. The maps of the South on the cover have been modified from an earlier version to include half of Oklahoma and Texas—accommodating, perhaps, both Native American displacement and June Arnold's inescapable shadow. Maps recur throughout the issue, overlaid with lists and bullet points detailing different radical histories. One emphasizes Native American displacement; others depict Jewish migration, African American traditions of resistance, and labor and the industries of the South. Each one transforms a seemingly known quantity.

Minnie Bruce Pratt comments on this remapping of the South in her poem "Reading Maps: Two," which concludes the issue. She starts, "I have no map for the past,"[49] because her mother has given her none: "About her life, mostly silence, a blank piece of paper. / I want to rip that up, useless guide to this land / we were both born and raised in, / the place I drive through now . . . on dirt paths once marked by Choctaws with painted trees, / past fields where, within her lifetime, good christian men / made bonfires, burned black folk like pine, while the women / lifted up the children to see."[50] A sense of violent haunting by the past, and its continued resonance in her present, continues throughout the poem. The "hidden road" marks a radical past and her own more recent queer rebellion:

I did not see
the hidden road, the one made in the dark blue sands,
the grey, brown, yellow red sands, the river sands

on the shore of an ancient sea,
the one made
by the feel of the Choctaw people wailing from
the Tombigbee . . .
made by the feet of the Ibo people stolen
from the land where they hoed their sweet yams, beans,
walking to chop cotton in strange fields at dawn[51]

Walking off the map and finding a new genealogy of knowledge grounded in native and African ways of knowing is central to Pratt's, and *Feminary*'s, radical lesbian feminist vision.

Feminary lasted only four years as the vanguard of a multicultural lesbian feminist South, but it produced aftershocks that went on for over a decade. Cris South's 1984 novel *Clenched Fists, Burning Crosses*, for example, was one result of the collective. In many ways, the careers of both Mab Segrest and Minnie Bruce Pratt demonstrate the importance of *Feminary*. Segrest's 1985 collection of essays, *My Mama's Dead Squirrel*, was dominated by pieces that had first appeared in *Feminary*. The book was published by the newly formed Firebrand Books, founded by Nancy Bereano, which would publish a number of intersectional analyses about the South by lesbians including Mab Segrest and Maureen Brady (discussed below), as well as Dorothy Allison's *Trash* and Pat Parker's *Movement in Black*.

After *Feminary* folded, Segrest worked as an anti-Klan activist, partnering with civil rights organizations across North Carolina. Her 1995 book *Memoir of a Race Traitor* details this work. Coalitions, and her complicated decisions about how her own sexuality factored into her activism, drive the narrative. She explained the dynamic:

> I had begun to feel pretty irregularly white. Klan folks had a word
> for it: *race traitor*. Driving in and out of counties with heavy Klan
> activity, I kept my eye on the rear-view mirror, and any time a truck
> with a Confederate flag license plate passed me, the hair on the back
> of my neck would rise. My reaction was more like the reactions of
> the Black people I was working with than of a white woman with
> three great-grandfathers in the Confederate Army. . . . I was in daily,
> intimate exposure to the cruel, killing effects of racism, which my
> Black friends spoke of in the same way that they commented on the
> weather, an equally constant factor in their lives. I often found
> myself hating all white people, including myself. As I took on racism,
> I also found its effects could be turned on me. The possibility of

overt violence or the reality of subtle ostracism gave me a sense of shared risk, not the same as dangers faced by my friends of color, but close enough.[52]

Segrest describes how white antiracist activism weakened the privileges of white supremacy. The sense that white allies are not just traitors but inauthentically white circulates throughout the text. Segrest notes the links between racism and homophobia at the point in her narrative when white supremacists murdered men in an adult bookstore known to be a gay hangout and then set the bookstore on fire; the victims' own families are hesitant to identify their loved ones as gay. Her careful interactions with those families shows her own complex understanding of the intersectionality of oppression:

> As a lesbian, I had a lot personally invested in this case. . . . This time, the issue was not the Klan and racism; it was neo-Nazis and homophobia. My heart went out the Godfreys and the Meltons as they sorted through the information. Were the victims, their loved ones, gay? After hearing Dorlene's vehemence and Fay's questions, I knew this was not the issue. They were killed because their attackers perceived them to be gay. The perpetrators' motive, rather than the victims' identity, was the place to focus. But I couldn't help wondering. Did the young men gathered that night at the Shelby III offer some window onto small-town life for homosexuals?[53]

Segrest's queerness makes her more aware of the connection of racism and homophobia; queer bashing was a way to smear opponents of segregation, as Bayard Rustin and James Baldwin well knew. "Queers" and "nigger lovers," as Cris South notes, often go together.

But Segrest is also careful (much more so than Rita Mae Brown, for example) to distinguish between these two kinds of oppression, noting that being queer doesn't erase her white privilege but does make that privilege more tenuous. She also recognizes the challenge in persuading black communities to recognize homophobia as a linked issue; she often felt that she needed to hide her queerness. *Memoir of a Race Traitor* is a nuanced analysis that exemplifies Segrest's careful work of intersectionality.

Minnie Bruce Pratt has an equally important cultural resonance, both for her work and for her long partnership with the transgender activist Leslie Feinberg. The amnesia of southern history was a constant theme in Pratt's writing; she was raised in a South that insisted that nothing has changed, or can change. As she wrote in her collection of essays *Rebellion*: "To talk, to gossip, to complain, to raise your voice, to shout about what was happening to you or around you was useless; it was not reasonable; it was *foolish*, if not crazy, since the social order, the nature of people was set, doomed, and no amount of shouting would alter creation. It was not a possibility that talking about something would release a passion for change and thus bring about change."[54] Yet her insistence that history provided multiple models of radical transformation fuels her essays.

In one, Pratt writes about the erasure of the South's radical past in Fayetteville, North Carolina, where she was teaching:

> I had no knowledge of any woman like me who had resisted and attempted to transform our home in preceding generations. I had no knowledge of other instances of struggle, whose example might have strengthened and inspired me in mine. For instance, I knew nothing of the nearby Lumbee Indians . . . who succeeded in the 1950s in breaking up Klan rallies and cross-burnings that had warned them to "keep their place."
>
> Even though I was teaching at an historically Black college, I had no understanding of the long tradition of Black culture and resistance in the town, a tradition which reached back before the Civil War, and which had produced Charles W. Chesnutt . . . author of novels that described the market house town, political organizing by Blacks, their massacre by whites during the 1898 Wilmington elections. . . . I knew nothing of the nourishing of Jewish culture in that hostile Bible Belt town, nor of Jewish traditions of resistance. . . . Nor that Carson McCullers, a woman very like me, living there in the 1930s, had written of the maddening, rigid effects of military life and thinking, and of the resistances of an Army wife. . . . Later I discovered Bertha Harris' novel of being a lesbian lover, with extravagant stories that might have been told in that bar, being a passing woman in the Wilmington shipyard, being lovers with a movie star who had "hair like gold electricity," hair like my lover's hair, a book that was published the year I moved to the town that outrageous Bertha had long since grown up in and left.
>
> I knew nothing of these or other histories of struggle for equality and justice and one's own identity in the town I was living in. . . . It was a place with so many resistances, so much creative challenge to the powers of the world: which is true of every county, town, or city

in this country, each with its own buried history of struggle, of how people try to maintain their dignity within the restrictions placed around them, and how they struggle to break those restrictions.[55]

Pratt's extraordinarily detailed rewriting of the history of Fayetteville notes the layered history of Native American, African American, queer, and working-class southerners. Throwing Carson McCullers and Bertha Harris into this queer genealogy was an added bonus. Each southern community is a palimpsest, its radicalism willfully forgotten yet essential to the activist work Pratt embodies in the present. Other essays in *Rebellion* build on this legacy, demanding a complete rewriting of the history of South. Pratt's encounters with family secrets and hidden queer enclaves create a South dramatically different from the conservative vision of the South that circulates in contemporary media.

Pratt addresses race (including African American and Native American history), sexuality, and class in her excavations of the South. Her discussions of class are particularly notable because these economic critiques are rare in the archive of southern lesbian feminism. (Rita Mae Brown included some Marxist references in her early poetry, but they seem pro forma and disappeared when she began to write fiction.) In one essay in *Rebellion*, Pratt argues that she

needed an economic history of my region, my country, that would have disclosed the irony and injustice of a state government doling out, through my mother, pitifully inadequate sums of money to women, and men, and their children, the sale of whose *selves* and whose slave labor, prison labor, hired-out convict labor, unpaid and underpaid domestic work, factory work, all kinds of work, had erected the white state, universities, houses, hospitals, factories, office buildings, fortunes. I would have had to understand that I had no knowledge of this economic analysis because there had been systematic and often violent state suppression of information and organization about class issues, from the beginning of our country until the most recent example—at that time the McCarthy purges. I would have had to see the red-baiting and Communist-hunting of McCarthy was based not on patriotism or love of democratic freedom, but on the assumption that capitalism *is* freedom.[56]

Maureen Brady's novel *Folly*, discussed below, takes up this interlocking economic, racial, and sexual analysis of the South in a more sustained way, but Pratt's awareness of the economic means of gender and racial oppression makes her writing a significant contribution.

Pratt's interest in intersectional analysis also runs through her most lauded work, the Lamont Prize–winning poetry collection *Crime against Nature*. She links her own branding as a sexual other with the terrorizing of African American communities in a number of its poems, including one in which she describes discussing with her black nanny, as an adult, the details of her divorce:

> She nods at how I answer her questions:
> I left the man; he got the children.
> She inclines her head to signify us two
> in the long story of women and children
> severed. With a nod she declares us
> not guilty, and begins to give advice.
>
> Her sibilant words I scarcely understand,
> delta language, her a child on a plantation
> talking to her own people, Mr. John Ed's land.
> (Did she talk to the child before memory?
> Did the child understand?) What I hear is
> the slash of machete on cane, a heavy sack
> dragging through the sand, the thud of a gun,
> dead bone at the spine, and a voice crying,
> Her children cry out to her, but which ones?
>
> The words I salvage are few, fierce, clear:
> *Bind them to you, bind them while you can.*[57]

Pratt draws a parallel between her own experience of losing her children and the systemic theft of children from mothers under slavery ("signify us two / in the long story of women and children / severed), but she does so in a way that recognizes the crucial differences between their experiences. The middle section, in which Pratt recognizes a "delta language" she cannot fully comprehend, suggests the incommensurability of their experiences while still recognizing a common source of oppression under white heteropatriarchy. She communicates the difference through images of experiences she doesn't share ("the slash of the machete on cane," "the thud of a gun"), allowing her to make connections without erasing the specificity of difference. She respects her distance from African American dispossession but doesn't render it inscrutable (as June Arnold would do, famously, at the end of *Sister Gin* when she makes several attempts to speak in the voice of an African American servant and then concludes that she cannot do so as a white writer[58]). The African American character in Pratt's poem issues a clear imperative, "Bind them to you while you can," which gives her both agency and authority.

This is the only poem in which Pratt explicitly links her own experience with African American dispossession, but it serves to anchor this collection that explores Pratt's betrayal by both those closest to her and the law that declares that her existence as a lesbian mother is "against nature." Her understanding of the dominant narrative that brands her a deviant erupts in several poems but gets its most explicit telling in the final poem, "Crime against Nature," which pushes back against Alabama's antisodomy law by suggesting that it is the state's disciplining of "sexual deviants," not the "deviants" themselves, that is "against nature":

The ones who fear me think they know who I am.
A devil's in me, or my brain's decayed by sickness.
In their hands, the hard shimmer of my life is dimmed.
I become a character to fit into their fictions,
someone predictable, tragic, disgusting, or pitiful.
If I'm not to burn, or crouch in some sort of cell,
at the very least I should not be let near children. . . .

But what about my mother? Or
the man I lived with, years? How could they be so
certain I was bad and they were not. . . .
I left
certainty for body, place of mystery. They acted
as if I'd gone to stand naked in a dirty room, to spin
my skin completely off, turn and spin, come off skin,
until, under, loomed a thing, scaly sin, needle teeth
like poison knives, a monster in their lives who'd run
with the children in her mouth, like a snake steals
eggs.
I've never gotten used to being their evil,
the woman, the man, who held me naked, little and big.
No explanation except: the one who tells the tale
gets to name the monster. In my version, I walk

to where I want to live. They are there winding
time around them like graveclothes, rotten shrouds.
The living dead, winding me into a graveyard future.

Exaggeration, of course. In my anger I turn them
into a late-night horror show. I've left out how
I had no job for pay, he worked for rent and groceries,
my mother gave me her old car. But they abhorred me:

my inhuman shimmer, the crime of moving back and forth
between more than one self, more than one end to the story.[59]

Pratt's indictment of the intimate violence of her interpellation as a "crime against nature" draws on a number of discourses, including popular horror films (zombies), Christianity (demonic possession), and medical diagnoses (sickness). She also recognizes her own complicity in demonizing the oppressor. But ultimately, her crime is insisting on "uncertainty," on a multiplicity of selves without clear boundaries and set endings. It is this embrace of uncertainty at the heart of Pratt's intersectionality that makes it distinctive. If this is a version of identity politics, then that identity is flexible, changeable, coalitional, and dynamic, bringing out unexpected alliances and, perhaps, transformational politics.

The same belief in the transformative potential of intersectional alliance fuels Maureen Brady's novel *Folly*. Brady, a Tennessee native, was involved with Spinsters Ink, wrote for *Sinister Wisdom* and *Feminary*, and corresponded with the Feminary collective. While working on *Folly*, Brady wrote to Minnie Bruce Pratt, explaining why she wanted to set the book in the South: "It is, I guess about my adolescence and that was spent in the South, and I want to write about black/white relations, beginning awareness in the way it comes to you in the South as that's the way I knew it. Also about the strength of chains of women in the South."[60] Brady asked for extensive details about working in a factory and asked if she could "talk to someone on a sewing line" and "get inside and spend some time observing."[61] Pratt volunteered to introduce her to Mab Segrest's "landlady in Hurdle Mills [who] worked in a hosiery mill for years and tells wonderful stories."[62] The resultant research grounded *Folly* in the experiences of southern working-class women.

Though many lesbian feminist southerners consider the role of class in their narratives, few focus explicitly on labor issues, which makes Brady's *Folly* a rarity in the archive of southern lesbian feminism. The women of

Victory Mills support parents and children, enduring speed-ups and constant surveillance as they labor under the interpellating eye of a foreman known colloquially as Fartblossom, until the fateful day they have had enough. One of their coworkers, Cora, has left her sick baby to go to work (because the mill has no sick days or family leave policy), and the baby dies. When a daughter calls frantically to tell the mother, the foreman calls the police and then sends Cora home to be arrested for negligence. Folly, a single mother of two, is outraged, and she and several others confront him:

> "What right you got stealing our break?" Folly asked. "What right you got callin' the cops on Cora? What right you got makin' her come to work when her kid was sick? Answer me that?" . . .
>
> "Every one of us has to come to work every single night whether our children are sick or not, or you wouldn't keep us on," Martha said, "And you know it." . . .
>
> "We ought to have time off even if there's no pay for it so nobody's got to run off and leave a real sick baby so's they don't lose their job. I know'd Cora since the first grade 'til now. Went all the way through school with her, sitting next to her most of the time because of our last names falling together. She didn' do nothin' the rest of us wouldn't have done. Ain't no fairness in you calling the law out on her. Law ought to be called out on you." It was Shirley White who made this speech and made it clear from the back of the room where her machine was located right next to Cora's empty one. . . . Every eye was on Fartblossom. Every woman could feel the others' feelings and Shirley had spoken their mind.[63]

Folly's bravery prompts many other women in the room to ask questions, and a collective outrage gathers force to a dramatic conclusion:

> Shirley's voice came clear from the back again. "You ain't answered our questions, Mr. Blossom." She made the Mr. Blossom sound real polite.
>
> "I've no intention to," he said.
>
> "I've no intention to go back to my machine then," Folly said. They looked over at Martha. So many times they had talked this out on the way home and said all the things they would say just before walking out on Fartblossom. Now Folly didn't feel she had anything more to say and Martha didn't look like she did either. Martha just nodded and made the first step toward the door. Folly followed.

Emily had been standing behind them all along. She followed Folly, but Folly still wasn't sure Emily wasn't going back to her machine until she went right past it. A couple more women stepped out from the first row and made a single file line behind Emily. Folly couldn't believe it. She thought maybe she hadn't heard Fartblossom declare second break or something. The way people exit from a church they were getting up, one right after the other and falling into line. She didn't dare turn around to see what she knew was happening. There was silence except for the sounds of feet walking until they got past the door, and then there was everyone talking at once.[64]

After this dramatic Norma Rae moment, the real work of the novel begins. The workers must contend with the shenanigans of management in collusion with the legal system, and even with the patriarchal cluelessness of the union organizer, who drops family leave policies at the last moment without their knowledge. The entire system is against the empowerment of working-class women, and this narrative is aware of that fact without making it the central focus of the novel.

The central drama of *Folly* turns on the problem of individual agency within collective action and empowerment. Sexuality is one key fulcrum—Folly's relationship with her friend and neighbor Martha, which becomes sexual over the course of the strike, is paired with Folly's daughter Mary Lou's burgeoning friendship with the lesbian butcher Lenore, demonstrating the complicated negotiation of love, desire, and identity. But it is overcoming the barrier of racism in this small southern town that becomes most crucial for the success of the women of Victory Mills. The white characters are forced to confront the ways they have allowed themselves to be willfully ignorant of their own privilege, meager though it is in their working-class existence, and both mother and daughter must face it and unlearn it. The ultimate betrayal of the union by the male union organizer leads the women to a radical solution: they decide to run their own factory, without management—an anarchist/socialist fantasy in which workers own the means of production and govern themselves. Given the real history of nonunion labor in the South, the novel is utopian, but the careful consideration Brady gives to economic and racial issues makes it a model of intersectional feminism in a region not known for utopian solutions.

The works of Segrest, Pratt, and Brady are important both for the archive of southern lesbian feminism and for the way they complicate larger narratives of the evolution of feminism and lesbian feminism during the late 1970s and early 1980s. This was the era that saw the publication of some of the most famous critiques of the whiteness of lesbian feminism, including *Home Girls*, *This Bridge Called My Back*, and *All the Women Are White, All the Men Are Black, but Some of Us Are Brave*. These works are still cited in evidence of the racism of lesbian feminism. Even Barbara Grier's attempts to broaden her own publishing vision of lesbian feminism into a multicultural space with the publication of Ann Allen Shockley, Anita Cornwall, and Sheila Ortiz Taylor did not gain wide currency; Julie Enszer suggests that Naiad's publications represented an older, civil rights version of activism (rather than the emerging coalition of women of color), and women of color increasingly wanted control over their own publications and venues.[65] So one might assume that the Feminary collective—dominated by southern white lesbian feminists—was similarly criticized, but it was not. Indeed, the archived letters and published writings of Mab Segrest and Minnie Bruce Pratt indicate that they had close relationships with Barbara Smith, Cheryl Clarke, and others now remembered primarily in the "women of color critique." Segrest wrote about the importance of her network of lesbian feminists: "The larger, vibrant lesbian writers' movement (the *clitterati*, one friend joked) gave me a diverse, expanded circle of friends, people like Barbara Smith at Kitchen Table: Women of Color Press; Cherrie Moraga, Dorothy Allison and Elly Bulkin at *Conditions*, a New York lesbian magazine; Lou Blackdykewoman from South Carolina. Black, working-class white, Jewish, Chicana—they were my new queer cousins, with whom I was determined to keep faith."[66] The correspondence from the archives bears out this notion of "queer cousins." Segrest and Pratt had extensive correspondence with Moraga and Lou, initially through their work for *Feminary* and later in independent friendships on their own. Barbara Smith, whose impatience with Barbara Grier was well known, felt close enough to Pratt that she shared details of some of the interracial rivalries with other lesbian feminists of color.

This understanding of the interconnections of sexism, racism, and homophobia was broadly embraced in a 1980s lesbian feminist culture that continued to include southern lesbian feminists. The feminist journal *Conditions*, started by four white lesbian feminists, focused its fifth issue on African American writers including southerners Ann Allen Shockley and Pat Parker. That issue, Julie Enszer maintains, had enormous influence, selling out two print runs (10,000 copies) and inspiring the publication of a number of germinal essay collections listed above. It also led to the transformation of the Conditions collective into a multicultural collective that featured Cheryl Clarke, Jewelle Gomez, and Dorothy Allison.[67]

Enszer's study of *Conditions* led her to conclude that "feminist investments in racial-ethnic formations were successful as a means of interrogating power and creating organizations to transform power relations between white women and women of color, institutionally and interpersonally. The story of *Conditions* highlights the possibilities that feminists imagined and created for multicultural, transformative, and visionary activism in the production of print culture."[68] Equally notable was the inclusion of Dorothy Allison, who more a decade later would become a startling "new" voice in literary fiction. Allison's development as a writer was tied up more broadly in the feminist movement, but her experience at *Conditions* was decisive. Working with other serious writers like Jewelle Gomez and Cheryl Clarke gave her role models, and *Conditions* provided early readers of her work. The collective's racial and regional diversity was sometimes uncomfortable for Allison; as she said in an interview, "I mean I was suddenly working with Yankee black women, and they looked at me like, Who is this cracker? And I'm like, Ooh, they're going to eat me alive."[69] But the political coalitions and close friendships created new means of activism and identification.

What is notable is how important the contribution of southern lesbian feminists was to the wider investigation of gender and race in 1980s feminist movements. Pat Parker continued to be an inspiration, Ann Allen Shockley continued to publish in available venues, Mab Segrest, Minnie Bruce Pratt, and Cris South (of the Feminary collective) added their voices, and Dorothy Allison evolved and grew through these multiple encounters. That race was inseparable from gender was not news to any of these southern women, black or white, and their versions of radical politics were always informed by this fact. But it also suggests a more complicated coalitional feminism than we often acknowledge. Personal relationships and explicitly antiracist activism made such coalitions possible and suggested that whatever critique of feminism these pioneers were articulating, it was from *within* a lesbian feminist community in which they were still invested.

Popular Translations of the Radical South

In addition to the discussions about intersectional politics that happened in independent lesbian feminist presses and periodicals in the 1970s and

1980s, there were also conversations about the radical South erupting for readers more interested in entertainment than in political instruction. In 1982 Ann Allen Shockley published *Say Jesus and Come to Me* as a paperback original with Avon, a paperback press.[70] The novel features a (closeted) black lesbian preacher, Myrtle Black, who proposes an interracial women's march to protest the ongoing problem of prostitution in the city; almost immediately, white feminists attempt to coopt her vision for their own benefit—and to use her as a token black woman in their campaign. Shockley is unsparing in her depictions of white women's cluelessness, but she also allows for the possibility of cross-racial partnerships, as long as white women confront their own misconceptions in the process. Shockley believes that the black church, especially its queer membership, both male and female, needs to be the driving force behind such movements in the South.

In one of the novel's telling debates, a San Francisco organizer, Rita, insists on making the march explicitly feminist. "We need to put it in the political logistics of the overall Women's Movement," she argues. "Focus attention on the *oppression* of women by male patriarchs. Bring to the forefront woman *power*—the power to control our lives, our bodies, our identities, as well as the destruction of sexism in our institutions!"[71] Myrtle considers Rita a zealot whose speech is reminiscent of the "Black Movement's once fiery oratory, a movement whose eloquence was now reduced to ashes without even the heat of the flames" (129). She replies, "I am against sexism. . . . But my plan was simply to march against crime, corruption, and vice in the city. A moralistic concept" (129). The contrast of "moralistic" and "feminist" frames the tensions of the exchange. Elsewhere in the novel, many black women refuse to align themselves with the feminist movement because it is perceived to be a white woman's trivial pastime. When Myrtle asks an organizer about "black feminists," she replies, "What black feminists? . . . This is the South. . . . The word feminist was anathema. It antagonized the black men, and men *are* important to black Southern women, you can believe it! To top that, they equate the word feminist with man-haters, white women, and lesbians. And like wow! Lesbians are something that can't be dealt with in the black community—queers and funny people" (133). This attitude leads Myrtle both to insist on a "moralistic" focus for the march and to hide her own lesbianism—at least, until the final scene of the novel.

Myrtle encourages feminist organizers to recognize how different their experiences are: "As a *black* woman," Myrtle said icily, "I *know* about oppression, being victimized by racists *and* sexists alike. I catch it from black women who are prime endorsers of black male chauvinism, white sexists and racist women. I know *all* about oppression!" (130). And she will not allow white feminists to coopt her leadership: "As the one who conceived this idea and as a minister, I am going to *insist* that there be moralistic and humanitarian objectives. We must not lose sight of intrinsic human values" (130). This model of faith-based feminist activism can be used to build a coalition that could, the novel suggests, transform politics in urban spaces in the South.

Say Jesus and Come to Me couches its radical politics in a romantic love story between Myrtle Black and an R & B singer, Travis Lee. The melding of radical politics with the emerging genre of lesbian romance meant that happy endings muted some of the intensity of the political critique, making it, perhaps, less radical. Naiad was stepping up production of lesbian romance and other genre fiction in the 1980s when it reprinted *Say Jesus and Come to Me* in 1987; another of its releases that set romance in the radical South was Catherine Ennis's *South of the Line*. Ennis, whose real name was Hobby Van der Weyden, was a member of a women's artist collective in rural Louisiana who wrote several novels for Naiad Press in the 1980s in a variety of genres (speculative, romance, mystery).

Plantation stories are ripe with homoerotic subtext, as Michael Bibler's *Cotton's Queer Relations* discusses at length.[72] *South of the Line* may be the most explicitly queer plantation romance ever written. Dashing plantation mistress Dominique first appears as she is winning a horse race, in "men's clothing, filthy breeches, a rough white shirt open at the throat, rolled up at the sleeves, and mud-caked, scuffed boots. A long black pigtail escaped from under her faded, floppy hat."[73] Dominique makes quick work seducing Faith, her poor cousin from Illinois: "She lay on me, her tongue at first tentative as she tried to match its movement to the surging of my hips. Then the fire caught her and we were joined, as one, our mouths wet, warm, moving together."[74] Unlike most lesbian romances, which invent obstacles to the lovers' union, Ennis puts the lovers in bed together within the first thirty pages. The sex/romance is a hook to get the reader interested in Ennis's revisionist version of the radical South: Faith discovers that her beautiful, seductive plantation mistress lover is working for the Underground Railroad; she is, in fact, a "race traitor" who passes as a member of the white supremacist elite to undermine the system. Ennis upends the tropes of abolitionist literature that treats southern whites as the villains and northern abolitionists and slaves as the heroes/heroines, and plantation romances in which northern brides come south and are converted to the superiority and wisdom of southern ways. Here, the Yankee "bride" comes south and is seduced by the glamorous plantation mistress, which leads not to an embrace of the peculiar institution but to Faith's conversion to abolition and activism. In Illinois she had been pro-Union but not engaged with questions of slavery or equality; in Tennessee she becomes an active agent of abolition.

Dominique takes escaped slaves north with Henry, the husband of her half sister Malissa, a freed slave; the couple pass as slaves in Dominique's household as they subvert the plantation hegemony. But Faith doesn't discover this until long after her seduction by Dominique, when they are attempting to reach New Orleans by riverboat and are put ashore to make their own way by land. After they are menaced by pirates and saved by their alliance with a poor, illiterate woman named Blest, who gives Faith a gun, they meet a group of ordinary white farmers who feel no loyalty to the Confederacy: "'I don't aim to get into any fighting,' the man said adamantly. . . . 'I ain't got time to shoot at no Federals 'less they get bothersome. Live and let live.' He often saw blue uniforms on the road but they had not disturbed him or his crop. He and his family were isolated, close to, but out of the political turmoil. They were Southerners, yes, but uninterested in the Confederacy's claim to sovereignty, probably not even sure what the word meant."[75] Victoria Bynum's research about Jones County's resistance to the Confederacy resonates in this passage that suggests that the Confederacy was a creation of the planter class that had little relevance to other southerners.[76]

Ennis also shows us the complexity of African American experiences in the South. Henry and Malissa establish a haven for free blacks in New Orleans; as Dominique explains to Faith: "'There were thousands of free blacks in New Orleans then,' she began again. 'Many of them owned homes and businesses and some were land-owning farmers. And Malissa had cousins there. So she and Hank and Henry moved to New Orleans, too, and they were more my family than my grandparents. You see, even if they weren't proud of it, Malissa was their grandchild, too. . . . I love Malissa. She's my sister and my dearest friend and we've been together all my life.'"[77] This portrait of New Orleans as a refuge from the racist hegemony becomes a backdrop to their own escape to freedom—south, instead of north.

It is significant that it is a lesbian seduction, by a woman who wears men's pants and a shirt without a bra, that leads to Faith's political radicalization. In these tales of the radical South, lesbian desire is the gateway drug, so to speak, for other transgressions. That fundamental difference leads to sympathy with other differences and to coalitions among the many southerners who are opposed to the nostalgic white supremacist version of the South that still dominates political discourse and popular culture.

It is interesting that Catherine Ennis—a Louisiana native and resident who wouldn't use her own name on her books and wouldn't do readings too close to home, so as not to be recognized—should construct this version of southern history that dramatically rewrites the meaning of southern identity and southern heroism. It speaks to the need for southern lesbian feminist writers to create a usable past, a genealogy of their South, in which even those timid about radicalism can feel at home.

Consider one of the most popular writers discussed in this study, one most southern readers still don't know is a lesbian. Fannie Flagg was never an activist and certainly never a radical. Her career was built on her likeability and her unchallenging southernness and femininity, and in spite of her relationship with the famous lesbian and feminist activist Rita Mae Brown, she has maintained that reputation. When *Fried Green Tomatoes* was released as a movie, Flagg resolutely refused to identify her *characters*, much less herself, as gay. So she may seem a strange choice to conclude this chapter about the radical South, but Flagg's writing is marked by an often radical deconstruction of identity categories thought to be fixed and unchangeable in the South, and her undogmatic, entertaining stories make these radical transgressions seem like the most natural thing in the world.

The ongoing legacy of southern lesbian feminists' radical South can be seen in Flagg's 2010 novel *I Still Dream about You*, a love letter to Birmingham, Alabama. Flagg's story follows Maggie Fortenberry, a blond former Miss Alabama who decides to kill herself but can't seem to free herself from her myriad social obligations in order to do the deed. This dramatic situation provides the opportunity to introduce, through Maggie, a host of southerners who don't fit traditional definitions of conservative southerners. As the book jacket puts it, "Maggie discovers, quite by accident, that everybody, it seems, has at least one little secret."[78]

Indeed, one of the charms of this novel is the way that Flagg holds back specific details that are usually considered defining; structuring categories of identity are folded in casually, after the reader has formed an attachment to a particular character. We learn that Hazel, the boss at Red Mountain Realty, is a brilliant businesswoman—and a little person; that Brenda is a treasured friend, an African American, and a lesbian (or at least had a lesbian affair in college); and that blonde, perfect Maggie had a years-long relationship with a married man, a fact she is ashamed of, and which, along with the rejection of her childhood sweetheart, makes her want to end it all.

Contending with difference is a struggle for every member of the team. When Brenda meets Hazel, she asks Ethel, "Does she know she's a midget?"[79] This prompts an awkward exchange: "'Why, no,' said Ethel, never looking up. 'But I'm sure if you want to go back in and tell her, she'll be delighted to know why she's so short.' 'Oh no . . . I didn't mean it that way[. . . .] What I meant was that she acts just like a real person. . . . Oh [. . .] I'm not saying she's not a real person. It's just [. . .] well [. . .] she didn't sound like a midget on the phone[. . . .] I thought they all had funny little voices like the Munchkins in *The Wizard of Oz* or something" (59; author's ellipses in brackets). Flagg's tone here is humorous but not satiric; Brenda's discomfort doesn't mark her as bigoted, but simply uninformed. This attitude runs through most of the novel; difference is both important and inconsequential, and the characters have a sense of humor about their own identities. At one point, Brenda and Hazel joke about their shared minority status:

> Brenda had such a good sense of humor about herself—a trait you more or less had to have if you worked for Hazel. Brenda and Hazel had a lot in common on that score. In Brenda's lifetime, she had gone from being Colored to Negro to Black, and now African American, and it was a running joke between them. Hazel would come in the door and ask Brenda how she was feeling today, and Brenda would say, "Well, I felt very black yesterday, but today I'm feeling a little colored. How about you?" Hazel would think and say, "I think I'm feeling a little more short-statured than height-challenged today."
>
> Brenda always said to the new people, when they were surprised at some of Hazel's humor, "She may not be politically correct, but she's hired more minorities than any other company in town." (70)

Flagg's creation of a multicultural haven at Red Mountain Realty balances the importance and the irrelevance of differences. Hazel is everyone's best friend, the most fun and charming person in the office. Ethel is a diehard white conservative who watches Fox News and can't stand Obama, but she loves Brenda and congratulates her after the 2008 election. Although her sister was traumatized in a Birmingham civil rights demonstration, Brenda loves her coworkers; she and the former Miss Alabama are best friends. Political differences have no deleterious effect on the "beloved community" that Red Mountain Realty represents.

Maggie is allowed to be both sympathetic and clueless in relation to southern racism. She is shocked by the Birmingham protests: "This was not the Birmingham she lived in. She had never heard her parents or anyone she knew say an unkind word against black people. . . . She had been told that they preferred to be with their own" (83). Her cluelessness about the roots of southern racism would not have survived even one issue of *Feminary*, yet Flagg softens her critique of Maggie and, by extension, of well-meaning, shocked white southerners who might be reading the novel. Maggie can love her friend Brenda, and recognize that racism was worse than she knew, and still long for the good old days; both southern nostalgia and a multicultural present are valued in *I Still Dream about You*. Flagg celebrates the progress that would allow Brenda to run for mayor: "The way things were changing so fast, anything could happen. A black woman from Birmingham had already been America's secretary of state, and Regina Benjamin, a black woman from southern Alabama, had just been named surgeon general of the United States" (227). And yet, Flagg notes that "progress had not come without a price" (227), and immediately shifts to the harassment of Maggie at the Miss America pageant for being a white southerner. This equation of two kinds of prejudice unifies southern identity, black and white, against "outside agitators" in a way that is unthinkable to white supremacists and antiracist activists.

That radical South of the present extends back into a southern past. When Brenda and Maggie discover a corpse in the attic of a grand estate they are selling, they uncover a secret: Edward Crocker, a scion of Birmingham industry, one generation removed from Scottish indentured servitude, was a woman who passed as a man. With this plot turn, Flagg is able to explore feminist themes directly. "As Edward, the son, she'd had total control of her own life. . . . When he had championed women's causes, he had not been dismissed as just another emotional female. When Edward had ordered men about, they had not balked at receiving orders form a woman. And her life had not been without fun. She and Lettie had laughed over the years, picturing the faces of men: if they had only known a female was running one of the largest companies in the world and had bested most of them at golf" (297). Edward Crocker becomes, in Flagg's telling, a kind of feminist activist, disproving all misogynist assumptions. That Edward/Edwina was able to pass as a man without surgery or hormones suggests a willing suspension of disbelief that is essential in Flagg's oeuvre. In Flagg's fictional universe, race, gender, and sexuality are unfixed, malleable, and ultimately unimportant.

Such cavalier erasures of racial and gender differences and easy resolutions of the divisive politics of the contemporary South are possible only, perhaps, in the happy, quirky South of Flagg's imagination. And even in that world, Flagg is not convinced that everything needs to be discussed publicly. When Brenda and Maggie reveal their secrets to each other—that Maggie had been involved with a married man, and Brenda had an affair with a married woman—they agree to keep these secrets to themselves:

> She looked over at Maggie and said, "Well, then . . . now that both our cats are out of the bag, like the song says, 'Tain't nobody's business but our own,' right?"
> "Right."
> "Life is hard enough. I say everybody deserves at least one little secret, don't you think?"
> "I do." . . .
> They both smiled all the way home. I was so good to have a best friend. (304)

This implicit repudiation of the "come out" mantra of gay liberation extends far into the past, as Maggie considers the talk that revealing Edward's secret would bring: "Anything involving someone's sexual life (dead or alive) was fodder for the worst kind of titillation and gossip, and his life would wind up being just another amusement for people to speculate about" (313). So she decides to keep his secret as well.

Flagg's insistence on the dignity of the closet is maddening, considering the chances taken by her fellow southern lesbians decades before. But Flagg is doing more than she lets on here; while her characters don't know the full complexity of the radical South, the readers do. No secrets are ever actually kept in the novel. And when she creates an impossibly happy ending for all her characters (including a surprise million-dollar legacy), she makes the black lesbian Brenda the new mayor of Birmingham—as radical a premise as any that southern lesbian feminists have imagined. Flagg depicts a world that contemporary political discourse would have us believe is impossible in the South, in a wildly popular novel that has reached many, many more readers than the brilliant analyses in *Feminary.* That this vision is both romantically idealistic and often accurate is Fannie Flagg's peculiar genius. In the end, as a fictional creation of the archive of southern lesbian feminism, the radical South is both transformative and entirely unremarkable.

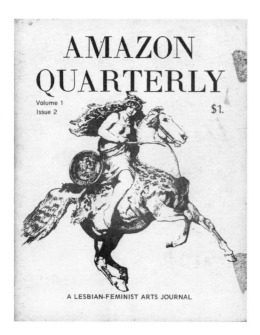

The second issue of
Amazon Quarterly.

Rita Mae Brown (right) at the Lavender Menace action, New York City (photo by
Diana Davies, Manuscript and Archives Division, The New York Public Library).

June Arnold, novelist and publisher, Daughters, Inc.
(Tee A. Corinne Papers, Coll 263, Special Collections and
University Archives, University of Oregon Libraries,
Eugene, Oregon).

Rita Mae Brown, *Rubyfruit
Jungle* (Daughters, Inc., 1973),
front cover.

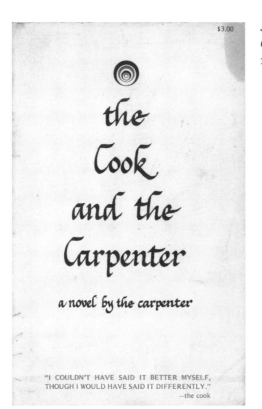

June Arnold, *The Cook and the Carpenter* (Daughters, Inc., 1973), front cover.

Pat Parker, *Pit Stop* (Women's Press, 1973), front cover.

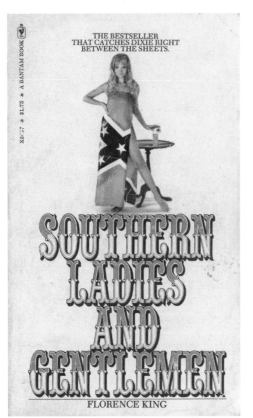

Florence King, *Southern Ladies and Gentlemen* (Stein and Day, 1975), front cover.

America's
sexiest southern
exposure!

THE SOUTHERN WOMAN:
She is required to be frigid, passionate,
sweet, bitchy and scatterbrained—all at the same time.
Her problems spring from the fact that she succeeds.

THE BAD GOOD OLE BOY:
He makes his grand exit
seven seconds after the grand entrance and murmurs:
"I sure pleasured you, Velma Lee, dint I?"

THE SELF-REJUVENATING VIRGIN:
She claims it never really happened because:
a) she was drunk and b) "We didn't do it in a bed."

THE GOOD GOOD OLE BOY:
He holds out a dozen pink carnations and says:
"I'm mighty sorry 'bout last night,
I wasn't gonna rape you. I just wanted to hold you a li'l."

Florence King, *Southern Ladies and Gentlemen* (Stein and Day, 1975), back cover.

Feminary collective.

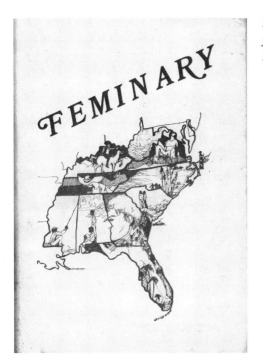

Feminary: A Feminist Periodical for the South, Emphasizing the Lesbian Vision, front cover.

Sheila Ortiz Taylor, *Faultline* (Naiad Press, 1982), front cover.

Maureen Brady, *Folly* (Crossing Press, 1982), front cover.

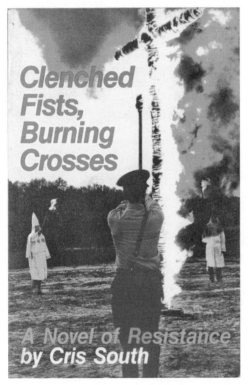

Cris South, *Clenched Fists, Burning Crosses* (Crossing Press, 1984), front cover.

Catherine Ennis, *South of the Line* (Naiad Press, 1989), front cover.

Fannie Flagg, novelist (Birmingham Public Library Archives).

Dorothy Allison, novelist (photograph by Jill Posener).

Queer Sexuality and the Lesbian Feminist South

. . . .

Floating on the Yalobusha River in kayaks with my partner and "Big Sexy"—a fifty-eight-year-old, bisexual, cross-dressing construction worker—I begin to believe that the entire state of Mississippi is queer. It's mainly because of Big Sexy's patter as we slowly drift:

> "Do you know John? He is gay as hell. Of course, he just got himself a girlfriend. I texted him and wrote, 'What the fuck is up with that?'"
>
> "My first marriage ended when my wife told me she prefers women to men. Of course she got married again. I ran into her at a bar with her new husband and she came and kissed me on the mouth. I said, 'That tastes good but I had it first.' Ooh, she was MAD at that."
>
> "Bruce? That town is gay gay. Eupora, too."
>
> "Have you been to Drew's Place in Memphis? Nice little neighborhood lesbian bar. I like to go there fully dressed."

And so on. As the hours pass, I wonder if there is a man in this state who hasn't had a guy back behind his barn, if all the women have "special friends" in their bridge clubs or sororities or church socials.

There was a reason these stories seemed familiar to me. This is the world of the southern gothic, made flesh: sexual perversion behind every decaying mansion, gender nonconformity bristling behind the magnolias, the landscape pulsing with deviance. Southern gothic literature—with its focus on claustrophobic, dysfunctional family relationships, the supernatural, and sexual deviance that produced an impression of the South, and humanity more generally, as "grotesque"—was made famous by a group of writers from the 1930s through the 1950s. Even before then, abolitionists made accusations of sexual deviance on plantations, of adultery, miscegenation, and even (Harriett Jacobs whispers in *Incidents in the Life of a Slave Girl*) homosexuality, a precursor to the construction of the South as the nation's "other."[1] During the Cold War, William Faulkner, Erskine Caldwell, Carson McCullers, Flannery O'Connor, Tennessee Williams, and Truman Capote depicted a South bursting with taboo sex, including incest, rape, necrophilia, and bestiality. From Charles Bon's kimono to cousin Randolph's kimono, from McCullers's dwarves to Capote's dwarves, from Quentin's Canadian "husband" to Brick's lost "friend"—all circulated sexual tropes that continue to inform impressions of the South. Sexual deviance is one of the South's most successful exports; indeed, from the 1930s through the 1950s, the southern grotesque made queer transgressive decadence a key part of the southern literary brand. To be southern was to be, by definition, a sexual freak.

The southern gothic—its sins, its stereotypes, its sexualization of southern identity—has been so extensively studied (by scholars as varied as Louis Rubin, Susan Donaldson, Patricia Yaeger, and Ann Goodwyn Jones) that the editors of the *Undead Souths* (2015) declared that "old tropes of *the* Southern Gothic are themselves now decayed, long-standing images and ideas mummified and cracking into dust."[2] The southern gothic has been invoked in criticism in a cornucopia of ways (indeed, in Patricia Yaeger's *Dirt and Desire*, that variety exists in one chapter), including as resistance, as critique of southern segregation, and as feminist appropriation. Yaeger argues that the grotesque operates differently when women appropriate it, that it becomes a protest and an exposé of the ways that patriarchy makes women's bodies vulnerable and frames insubordinate women as deviant.

The broader implications and meanings of the southern gothic are beyond the purview of *The Lesbian South*; what is significant for this study (and for the southern lesbian feminist writers discussed herein) is that the southern gothic provided a mechanism to explore queer sexuality. Sarah Gleeson-White's 2003 *Strange Bodies* shows how Carson McCullers's "grotesque" narratives allowed for multiple explorations of female adolescence, male homosexuality, carnivalesque gender performance, and androgyny. She argues, "McCullers's grotesque is similarly productive of new worlds, new subjects, albeit strange in the context of the dominant motifs of southern gendered and sexual behavior. . . . By engaging with contemporary accounts of gender and sexuality, I emphasize and celebrate McCullers's menacing and ultimately transgressive vision, and its emancipatory and empowering potential."[3] But McCullers did not depict lesbianism directly; it would take southern lesbian feminist writers to cross that final taboo—a challenge they accepted with gusto.

The southern gothic had its queerest iteration in the work of Carson McCullers and Truman Capote, whose haunting fictions made queerness central to the South. They didn't necessarily believe that sexual deviance would transform society, but simply that queerness, unvarnished, was true, and sometimes beautiful. McCullers and Capote championed characters who make others uncomfortable: the drug addict and seeming pedophile Randolph and the sissy boy Joel in *Other Voices, Other Rooms*; the masculine Amelia, in love with a vindictive dwarf in *The Ballad of the Sad Café*; the closeted homosexual and animal abuser Major Penderton in *Reflections in a Golden Eye*. These characters' outsider status is clear, their suffering is immense, and their ends are tragic. Compassion and identification fuel their depictions. McCullers stated that perspective most clearly in her essay "Notes on Writing: The Flowering Dream": "Nature is not abnormal, only lifelessness is abnormal. Anything that pulses and moves and walks around the room, no matter what thing it is doing, is natural and human to a writer. . . . I become the characters I write about. I am so immersed in them that their motives are my own. When I write about a thief, I become one; when I write about Captain Penderton, I become a homosexual man; when I write about a deaf mute, I become dumb during the time of the story. I become the characters I write about and I bless the Latin poet Terence who said, 'Nothing human is alien to me.'"[4] For McCullers, the human transcended all categories of normality.

McCullers's and Capote's commitment to the queer and the grotesque wasn't simply a perverse pleasure or campy ironic homage. Their identification with cultural others led them to critique the brutal regime of the normal and expose the violent disciplining of the abnormal. The "unspeakability" of sexuality made its role in violent repression invisible. In Capote's *Other Voices, Other Rooms*, the gang rape of Zoo, which prevents her migration and freedom, demonstrates the cruel power of "transgressive" sexuality. In addition, both Joel and Idabel are punished for their violations of gender norms: the truck driver in the novel's opening sequence wants to pull down Joel's britches and "muss him up" to make him a "real boy"; Idabel is kicked out of public restaurants for her violations of gender norms, and in the end, her beloved dog is killed and she is sent to a gay conversion camp of sorts, where she is forced to wear dresses and endure Baptist sermons. McCullers's queers are even more embattled. Allison Langdon cuts off her nipples during a depressive episode—an attempt to liberate herself from femininity, apparently—and is committed to an asylum against her will; Major Penderton, longing for the company of men but forced, through convention, into marriage with a woman, kills the voyeur who chooses his wife over him. Miss Amelia's queer passion for Lymon, her hunchback cousin, leads to her own destruction as a triangle of unrequited love—Amelia's for Lymon, Lymon's for Marvin Macy, a former Klansman and Amelia's husband, and Marvin's for Amelia—leaves her bereft and isolated in a small-minded southern town. The brutality with which queer grotesques are punished exposes the deeper codes of violence that sustain the normal and guides the reader into sympathy with these outsiders, not in spite of but *because* of their radical difference. It has taken queer theory decades to articulate and unravel what writers like Capote and McCullers portrayed in their fiction: queerness as a resistance to and exposure of regimes of the normal.[5]

An exchange between Mab Segrest and Dorothy Allison suggests the importance of the southern gothic for southern lesbian feminist writers. In *My Mama's Dead Squirrel*, Segrest had critiqued the southern literary tradition for framing women's sexuality and agency as monstrous: "Both McCullers and O'Connor were casualties of the war of the female mind with the female body."[6] Feminist southern writers, Segrest believed, would create a new form of southern writing, "seeking new forms and language" (19). This new tradition did not include Bertha Harris and her famous essay on lesbian monsters; "I don't care to be a monster," wrote Segrest, who instead advocated "imagining and visioning ourselves out of patriarchally prescribed roles that depend on their power on oppression of the Other" (40). Southern feminist writing, Segrest maintained, would leave the grotesque behind.

Dorothy Allison would have none of it. Segrest's rejection of the grotesque and her attempt to separate feminist writing from the gothic tradition provoked a sharp rebuke from Allison, who framed the debate in both literary and personal terms: "Grotesque is a buzz word to me and it has taken me years to sort it out. *I am grotesque.* Do you realize that? Not just me, but my family, all blacks, all poor people, all lesbians. We don't have to do anything 'grotesque'—we simply are by definition. Of course if you throw in incest, child abuse, rape, s/m, violence, poverty, self-hatred and homosexuality, we've got no argument, right? All those grotesque realities, right?"[7] Allison ties the grotesque to the marginal in the South—African Americans, lesbians, and the poor; if the grotesque interpellates all these groups as deviant, then Allison embraces that label, in solidarity with all the South's cultural others. Allison continues with concrete examples from her own life, suggesting that Segrest's rejection of the "grotesque" stems from her disgust at the working-class realities of southern women like her. Indeed, she advocates claiming the label "grotesque," much as queer theorists reclaimed "queer" in the 1990s. "What is grotesque Mab? What is it you think is happening in those novels by Williams, O'Connor and McCullers? Do you know that what I see is compassion and love, a *championing* of what the world calls grotesque? Do you see how I might believe that a radical act, the only christian act I believe in—loving what the world tells you is sick and hateful and contemptible? For me it is about loving my own life."[8] For Allison, rejecting the grotesque meant rejecting the reality of her own queer life in the South. Her insistence that to write about the deviant is to champion "what the world calls grotesque" frames the southern gothic as an act of queer defiance.

One could argue that southern literary critics developed their version of the southern literary tradition *against* this notion of southern sexual deviance, embracing tradition, family, and a grounded "sense of place"—in a word, normality. Even otherwise progressive southerners chafed at the image of the southern grotesque as a blot on the honor of the South. But for most of the southern lesbian feminists discussed in this book, the southern grotesque was the only cultural narrative that made visible southern queerness—not just homosexuality or even nonnormative sexuality, but unassimilable queerness, the disturbing, the repulsive, and the true. Indeed, it made queerness *central* to southern culture.

That radically queer embrace—to "champion what the world calls grotesque"—dominates the archive of southern lesbian feminism. Detailed descriptions of transgressive sexuality are found in the works of nearly every writer discussed in *The Lesbian South*. These writers were exposing the hidden queer dynamics of literature and culture long before Eve Sedgwick's complex readings exposed the central role of queerness in the Western literary tradition. They did so, variously, to challenge patriarchy and suggest more empowering sexual roles for women; to shock and invert the negativity surrounding the "decadent southerner"; and to expose the ways that "deviant sexuality" is actually a tool of the status quo. In every case, these southern lesbian feminist writers were committed to explicit descriptions of a wide range of sexual practices, refusing euphemisms and encoding for discomfiting and often distressing depictions of sex. This is perhaps the most notable achievement of the archive of southern lesbian feminism; it is simultaneously traditional (in its linkage of southernness and deviance) and radical (in its insistence on explicit description).

This chapter frames southern lesbian feminist depictions of transgressive sexuality within contemporary queer studies and the gay and women's liberation commitment to liberatory sexuality, but traces their distinctive contribution back to the southern grotesque. I argue that their embrace of transgressive sexuality emerges from a specifically southern conversation, one which queer theory helps us articulate and appreciate. Southern lesbian feminists' combination of the southern gothic and sexual liberation informed their insistence on frank depictions of specific sexual acts and gender identities purposely transgresses community norms. In the sections that follow, I explore Harris's, Allison's, and Florence King's explicit invocation of the Southern Gothic; women's liberation's interest in sexuality as a means of empowerment and revolution; and queer theory's investment in the disruptive power of nonnormative sexuality. Weaving these strands together, I then analyze the archive of Southern lesbian feminism's varied interrogation of sexuality, through a variety of specific examples: sex scenes, polyamory, intergenerational sex, female incest, prostitution, and rape.

There is little consensus among Southern lesbian feminist writers about these sexual pratices; some are celebratory, some outraged, some embrace certain practices as liberatory, while others condemn those same practices as a tool of patriarchal oppression. But what these writers share is a commitment to discarding euphemism for explicit, frank description. Not for them the shadowy insinuations of the Cold War southern gothic. Whether it exposes the hidden workings of a homophobic and misogynist culture or champions the grotesque, the archive of southern lesbian feminism makes transgressive sexuality, described in explicit detail, a central focus. Taken collectively, the archive of southern lesbian feminism is still astonishing in its capacity to shock, to challenge, to outrage, and to inspire.

Grotesque Camp: Bertha Harris, Dorothy Allison, and Florence King

No southern lesbian feminist writer was more committed to the southern grotesque than Bertha Harris, whose devotion was inflected as camp. Her 1972 novel *Confessions of Cherubino* made that embrace clear. The description on the cover of a 1978 reprint explains:

Under one Southern gothic roof, Bertha Harris packs the most comic and outrageous family ever assembled in fiction . . . then sends its members into the world to drive the rest of us crazy with desire.

The temperamental little genius of love, Cherubino, is as gifted with disguise as with sexual delight: Cherubino is
    —A baby-faced soldier gone AWOL
    —Sanctissima with her passion for pianos, airline stewardesses
        and prima donnas

—Robert, the postman, who specializes in Special Delivery
—Miss Nina, with her ambition for the perfect perversion
—and clairvoyant Venusberg, musical May-Ellen, deaf Beloved,
  heroic America: Margaret, the born-again sweetheart[. . . .]
  But especially *Cherubino* is Ellen, who is all the dreams made
  flesh.[9]

Confessions of Cherubino contains virtually every stereotype of the southern gothic—rambling southern manor, queer elder sons, adulterous husbands, incestuous mother/daughter and sister/sister relations, cross-dressing, decadence—but it goes much further than other novels of the genre. It is the southern gothic on crack: the characters are crazier, the sexual liaisons are more outrageous, and the queerness is not shadowy but explicit. Harris's open embrace of the queerness of the southern gothic becomes a particularly effective literary weapon that merges sexual otherness and humor.

References to famous southern gothic novels abound in *Confessions of Cherubino*. Ellen's sexual liaison in the garden with Venusburg, the black daughter of the "servant" and probable half sister, is reminiscent of the Judith/Clytie liaison in *Absalom, Absalom!*; Miss Nina's too-close relationship with her gay son—even living together with him and his lover—suggests the refrain "Violet and Sebastian, Sebastian and Violet" from Tennessee Williams's *Suddenly, Last Summer*; Ellen's drag performance of her father evokes Frankie's cross-dressing in McCullers's *Member of the Wedding*; America's rape by Ellen's father, Roger, depicted as a visitation by an angel, alludes to Zoo's narration of her gang rape in *Other Voices, Other Rooms*.

The South's "sense of place" takes on new meaning when Ellen, after a night of walking the streets in her father's clothes, writhes against the earth in the garden of her southern home. That garden is later the site of her sexual liaison with America's daughter, the clairvoyant Venusburg:

She took off the cape with a flourish that Roger had never accomplished and spread it over the girl. Venusberg huddled; then she relaxed and waited. The cape's heavy braided collar covered nearly all her face; one of her pigtails, bristling into a rotten tomato, was becoming soaked in yellowish juice[. . . .]

With two slow movements, with one harsh clumsy movement, Ellen went beneath the cape.

Venusberg whispered, through her sighs, into Ellen's shoulder: ". . . Sincerely yours, Venusberg. Book, Castle, Music, Piano, Drum Marjorette, Valedictorian, Up North, Good Eye, Dresses, Beauty,

Home . . . home . . . home . . . Ellen, Ellen, Ellen," finally she
gasped.

Ellen's feet jutted from beneath the cape; her toes dug into the
gray vegetable earth. Before long, their pink wetness became thick
with dust. The cape rocked.[10]

Hiding the actual sex under a cape, Harris toys with explicit images including the "yellowish juice" oozing under the cape and the "long, pink wetness" of her toes in the dirt, Erskine Caldwell–esque. Sexual deviance ties
all these outrageous flights of fancy together, and the southern setting gives
Harris cover to depict queer sexuality.

Harris's campy embrace of the gothic as decadent lark influenced her
most famous student, Dorothy Allison. Allison's collection of stories *Trash*
(1988) uses the southern gothic to celebrate lesbian lust. The narrator of
"Monkeybites" describes having sex with her butch lover in the lab where
she worked, with monkeys in cages as voyeurs:

> She grabbed my wrists and pulled my hands behind my back,
> holding them there with one hand while she used the other to rip
> the snaps of my blouse open and unzip my jeans slowly. . . . I heard
> my sobs like they were echoes in a wind tunnel. She inched my jeans
> down over my butt until I was whining like a monkey strapped to a
> metal table. "Oh, fuck me. Goddamn it! Fuck me!" I begged. Toni slid
> me on to the edge of the table and my hair swept the floor. When her
> fingers opened my cunt and her teeth found my breast, I started to
> scream and the monkeys in the wall cages screamed with me. . . .
> When I finally started to come, I swung my head until the cages
> blurred and the monkeys became red and brown shimmering
> cartoons.[11]

Allison toys with dangerous grotesque imagery here, depicting animals and
queer desire in tandem. Like Harris, Allison makes queer desire explicit;
though significantly less playful, she is equally invested in tropes of the
southern gothic.

Indeed, in "Monkeybites" Allison comments on the continuing relevance
of the southern gothic as Toni critiques the narrator in a speech that serves
as a metafictional commentary on *Trash* as a whole: "Shit girl, it's just too
much, too Southern Gothic—catfish and monkeys and chewed-off fingers.
Throw in a little red dirt and chicken feathers, a little incest and shotgun
shells, and you could join the literary tradition. . . . If you were to work on

your stories well enough, someone would be sure to conclude they had something to do with your inverted proclivities, your les-bi-an-ism. Something like you constantly re-enacting the rescue of your little sister. Hell, you could make some psychiatrist just piss his britches with excitement."[12] Allison's reference to the southern gothic suggests that the gothic authorizes her to discuss sexuality explicitly, using the trope as license for unsettling frankness in sexual depictions. It emphasizes the gothic as a vehicle for critique that inspires voyeurism but also exposes deeper cultural trends.

Another aspect of the southern grotesque suggests that sexual deviance may become a means of social control, and this also has a strong legacy in the archive of lesbian feminism. Florence King has made transgressive sexuality central to southern experience in her devastating satires of denials and double standards in the South.[13] King's 1975 essay collection *Southern Ladies and Gentlemen*, full of trenchant critiques of the schizophrenia of "normative" gender roles, is a much more accessible version of Judith Butler's later analysis in *Gender Trouble*. In one of her most famous essays, King argues that "The cult of Southern womanhood endowed her with at least five totally different images and asked her to be good enough to adopt all of them. She is required to be frigid, passionate, sweet, bitchy, and scatterbrained— all at the same time. Her problems spring from the fact that she succeeds."[14] Her explanation of the "self-rejuvenating virgin"—the southern belle who is both frigid and passionate—is one of the funniest descriptions of schizophrenia ever penned:

"IT DIDN'T REALLY HAPPEN BECAUSE . . ."

1. I was drunk.
2. We didn't take all our clothes off.
3. We didn't do it in a bed.
4. He didn't put it all the way inside me.
5. He didn't come inside me.
6. I didn't come.
7. . . . Well, not really. (34)

In King's depiction of southern womanhood, extramarital sex is both rampant and condemned. She is equally incisive in her discussion of the "Town Fairy" who exists in every town, usually without problem, even as "straight men in smaller towns are always bragging, "We don't have no queers 'round cheer'" (156). How is possible that "Nobody minds him, and he is no threat to even the worst queer-hater" (157)? King explains, "The reason he isn't is that Southerners believe in heredity, not environment, and Town Fairy is universally considered to be nobody's fault: the Lord did it. Town Fairy's problems are blamed on the fact that he was—are you ready for this? A change-of-life baby. This is perhaps the South's neatest sleight of mind, one that cheers both men and women" (157). Thus, the South can be both homophobic and accepting at the same time—as long as the "town queer" is single and connected to a prominent family. Tolerance for the eccentric Town Fairy can obscure the rampant intolerance of African Americans and of queers who do not come from well-to-do families. King, a staunch conservative, did not see this penchant for the kinky or the transgressive as progressive or revolutionary. Instead, her essays show how southern transgressive sexuality is essential to "normal" southern life. That awareness of both the transgressive power of sexuality *and* its potential for cooptation by the ruling power was central to the southern gothic, and it would be central to women's liberation and queer theory as well. The latter iteration, however, would insist on queer community, a prospect more threatening to the status quo.

Women's Liberation and Liberatory Sexuality

In the early days of women's liberation, some lesbians combined their critique of patriarchy with explicit queerness, resulting in a confrontational, cheerful sexual rebellion. Lesbianism was seen as the vanguard of the movement, a site of transgressive and liberatory sexuality. As Bertha Harris explained: "Women's liberation in New York was, at its onset, about sexual liberation; too many men were not interested in finding out what makes a woman come. Too many women had sedulously anaesthetized libidos. The women's liberation movement was about the American woman's American orgasm. It was that simple. Every other thing that the women's liberation movement was about during the sixties and seventies in New York followed from that, including the fact that I looked out my window one morning and saw lesbians everywhere. It's easy to recognize lesbians; they look like you, only better."[15] Harris's explanation of feminism as primarily about sex is incomprehensible in our current narrative of women's liberation (which tends to characterize feminism as sexless and cheerless), but it reminds us that for one influential group of women's liberationists, sexuality itself was a prime site of women's liberation. By remaking the most intimate patterns of sexual life, women would use sexual pleasure to remake the culture as a whole.

Harris's claim that women's liberation was about "the American woman's American orgasm" was not unusual in the early days of women's liberation. Sexual pleasure for women was revolutionary. Jane Gerhard argues that "Within second-wave feminism, the female orgasm came to represent women's self-determination, making 'the great orgasm debate' central, not incidental, to the project of women's liberation."[16] Women's autonomous desire was unthinkable under patriarchy; any suggestion of it would result in the dreaded interpellation *slut*. The radicals of women's liberation embraced *slut*, but the word they used more often was the worst thing a man could say about a woman: *lesbian*. This led to a split between the mainstream and the radical. As Harris explained:

> The more intimate the women, the higher their consciousness, . . . the greater their pleasure in one another. That's how liberation initially worked. But pleasure frightened many women; so did the displeasure of men. Betty Friedan, a social reformer from Peoria and the author of *The Feminine Mystique* . . . put the fear of pleasure into words; she accused lesbians of trying to subvert the women's liberation movement with orgasms. A sexual panic broke out.
>
> When the dust cleared, the movement was roughly divided between the sexual subversives and the rest of the women's movement—women who feared both the displeasure of men and the pleasure they felt with one another.[17]

Commemoration of "sexual subversives" and their central role in early women's liberation is common in memoirs from the era, which are replete with salacious and sometimes hilarious details. Jeanne Cordova, for example, recalled living with a partner but having set "free days" when they could pursue and sleep with other women.[18] Karla Jay describes going to a sex party in California that included men and women, featuring gay, straight, and lesbian sex, and having a threesome with a lesbian couple in a sleeping bag; all three got crabs from the sleeping bag, putting a damper on their sexual liberation.[19] The San Francisco lesbian community on Valencia Street included not only several lesbian bars but a women's bathhouse, Osento. Though it functioned differently than men's bathhouses—the rule for Osento was "no sex, even with yourself"—it still was an essential part of a radical and sexually liberated women's community. Feminist periodicals from the 1970s detail a full range of transgressive sexual practices.

Sex, then, was serious business in early women's liberation, a means of liberation and revolution. Blanche McCrary Boyd's retrospective novel about the early women's movement, *Terminal Velocity*, summarizes the perspective succinctly:

> "Only radical lesbians, by introducing pleasure and fun into the revolutionary equation, can liberate sex from power, thus liberating women from men. . . ."
>
> "You see Red Moon Rising as a place where pleasure and fun are goals? Isn't that, um, decadence?"
>
> "Revolutionary pleasure and revolutionary fun are not decadent," Ross said primly. "Not in the context of the sexual oppression of women."[20]

Such theorizing was common in early consciousness-raising groups, manifestos, and feminist treatises. The notion of a distinctive women's sexuality liberated from patriarchy and the male gaze became an obsession.

Southern lesbian feminists were often poster girls of liberated feminist sexuality. Rita Mae Brown's sexual conquests, for example, were as legendary as her activism and her writing. She slept with the actress Alexis Smith in New York; seduced Charlotte Bunch in Washington, D.C., breaking up her marriage; had a relationship with Elaine Noble, one of the first women elected to the statehouse in Boston; and went to Hollywood and stole Fannie Flagg away from her long-term partner, only to leave Flagg for Martina Navratilova. Brown enjoyed her status as lesbian sex symbol; she published photos of herself on her books and encouraged her fans to circulate them and post them.

Brown may have been the most visible womanizer among lesbian feminists, but she was hardly unique. Bertha Harris's conquests were also notorious; they included Charlotte Bunch, who had terrible luck with partners in the 1970s, and possibly a liaison with June Arnold. Blanche McCrary Boyd's archive contains letters from distraught former lovers, and Boyd reported an acid-fueled one-night stand with country music star Marshall Chapman. Pat Parker's commitment to nonmonogamy made her a rakish figure on the West Coast. Minnie Bruce Pratt explored polyamory when she had relationships with both Cris South and JEB (Joan E. Biren, a lesbian photographer who had been part of the Furies collective).

Dorothy Allison became a symbol of this sexual liberation in the 1980s, when lesbian feminism turned from sexual transgression to what many called sexual puritanism. As a member of New York's Lesbian Sex Mafia and a public advocate for sadomasochism, Allison became a pariah in lesbian feminist circles after the Barnard Sex Conference in 1982, which marked the beginning of the "lesbian sex wars."[21] Those skirmishes over "right" and "wrong" ways to have sex were a dramatic departure from the earlier optimism about the liberatory power of transgressive sexuality, and they made clear an important distinction between southern lesbian feminists and the wider lesbian feminist movement. Southern lesbian feminist writers made the most of the enthusiastic attitude toward sexuality in early women's liberation, but they were more committed to the strange, the disturbing, and the transgressive than to simple celebrations of liberatory sexuality. Their hybrid of the southern grotesque and the sexual subversiveness of women's liberation produced a commitment to direct, explicit depictions of transgressive sexuality.

Queer Theory and the Critique of the Normative

Southern lesbian feminist writers understood transgressive sexuality within a larger matrix of power, and their focus on sexuality is an important genealogical link to queer theory, which emerged in the early 1990s. Queer theory made the very notion of "normal" sexuality its primary critique; for queer theorists, the nonnormative and transgressive are exemplary. Grounded in Michel Foucault's analysis of society's disciplinary regimes, queer theory surfaced in the fierce political backlash surrounding AIDS, which fueled its suspicion of assimilation and its critique of the status quo. Many queer theorists are wary of the "pride" narrative, exploring shame;[22] more broadly, they mistrust the mainstreaming of queer sexuality that has led to the legalization of gay marriage and the "normalizing" of queer relationships.[23] Queer theorists are also, Annamarie Jagose argues, skeptical of orgasm as a "register of normativity,"[24] and therefore dismissive of feminists' equation of liberation with the "American woman's American orgasm." To mainstream queer relationships for the approval of society at large is to mute their potentially transformative power.

One of the most trenchant critiques of assimilation is Leo Bersani's influential 1987 essay "Is the Rectum a Grave?" Written at the height of AIDS panic, the essay refutes the "redemptive reinvention of sex" as "lies" we have been telling for political reasons: "The immense body of contemporary discourse that argues for a radically revised imagination of the body's capacity for pleasure . . . has as its very condition of possibility a certain refusal of sex as we know it, and a frequently hidden agreement about sexuality as being, in its essence, less disturbing, less socially abrasive, less violent, more respectful of 'personhood' than it has been in a male-dominated, phallocentric culture."[25] Rejecting this "refusal of sex as we know it," Bersani argues that we should understand sex as "anticommunal, antiegalitarian, antinurturing, antiloving" (215), thus becoming spokespersons for the "anti-communitarian thesis"—a queer intellectual movement that separates queer sexual acts from redemption, group action, political progress, and even identity itself. Bersani believes that sex is so powerful that it destroys society and the very notion of self: "The self which the sexual shatters," he explains, "provides the basis on which sexuality is associated with power. It is possible to think of the sexual as, precisely, moving between a hyperbolic sense of self and a loss of all consciousness of self" (218). Sex, particularly queer sex, is a disruptive force that undermines the very basis of society itself.

Other queer theorists are so utopian in their understanding of the transformative nature of nonnormative sexuality that "queerness" itself becomes an ideality. In the hands of José Muñoz, one of the most lyric of the queer utopians, the queer becomes almost a koan. In the opening chapter of *Cruising Utopia*, he writes:

> Queerness is not yet here. Queerness is an ideality. Put another way,
> we are not yet queer. We may never touch queerness, but we can feel
> it as the warm illumination of a horizon imbued with potentiality.
> We have never been queer, yet queerness exists for us as an ideality
> that can be distilled from the past and used to imagine a future. The
> future is queerness's domain. Queerness is a structuring and edu-
> cated mode of desiring that allows us to see and feel beyond
> the quagmire of the present. . . . Some will say that all we have are
> the pleasures of this moment, but we must never settle for that
> minimal transport; we must dream and enact new and better
> pleasures, other ways of being in the world, and ultimately new
> worlds. Queerness is a longing that propels us onward, beyond
> romances of the negative and toiling in the present. Queerness is
> that thing that lets us feel that this world is not enough, that indeed
> something is missing. Often we can glimpse the worlds proposed and
> promised by queerness in the realm of the aesthetic.[26]

Whether dystopian or utopian, queer theory insists on the transformative, disruptive value of the queer. A commitment to unassimilability and rejection of the normal still unites the diverse field of queer theory. Though the roots of its radical suspicion are clearly grounded in the AIDS crisis, it also draws on an earlier faith in the transformative power of sexuality that was evident in early women's liberation and gay liberation.

Recent work in queer theory has looked at how the mainstreaming of LGBT people can make homosexuality complicit with normative systems of state power. Jasbir K. Puar calls this "the powerful emergence of the disciplinary queer (liberal, homonormative, diasporic) subject into the bountiful market and the interstices of state benevolence"; this move involves "full-fledged regulatory queer subjects and the regularization of deviancy."[27] Puar contrasts homonationalism "against queer*ness*, as a process intertwined with racialization."[28] Gains in LGBT rights, including marriage equality, have raised concerns among queer theorists that the revolutionary potential of transgressive sexuality—its queer*ness*—is being lost. The controversy over "pinkwashing,"[29] for example—the charge that Israel touts gay rights to obscure its colonial oppression of Palestinians—suggests that nonnormative sexuality can sometimes be a tool of oppressive dominant power structures.

Queer theory, then, mistrusts the lure of the normative as much as it celebrates the transgressive. The normalization of LGBT sexuality risks losing the transformative power of the queer. Like McCullers and Capote, contemporary queer theorists insist on the transgressive in its disturbing, unassimilable iterations. Southern lesbian feminist writers, a bridge between these two queer forms of protest, similarly rejected normalized depictions of lesbian sexuality for challenging, risky, grotesque textual explorations.

Queer Sexualities and the Archive of Southern Lesbian Feminism

Southern lesbian feminists contributed to a broader critique of heteronormativity in their explicit descriptions of deviant sexual identities. Influenced by the southern gothic, gay pulp, women's liberation, and gay liberation, these writers were committed to open, explicit descriptions of the specific sexual behaviors and practices of transgressive sexuality. They rejected the transgressive as simply a metaphor, or a shadowy allusion, in favor of describing a broad range of sexual behaviors in language that blurred the line between the literary and the pornographic. The archive of southern lesbian feminism sometimes condemns or critiques these sexual depictions, but it always embraces a politics of visibility.

This tradition described sex between women in exhaustive detail. Not for these writers was the encoded tomboy, adolescent or carefully linked romantically to men, that marked the Cold War southern grotesque. They eschewed Carson McCullers's heterosexual marriage, which made her baby dyke style safe in the late 1940s and early 1950s. Romantic, lustful, sentimental, funny—the styles range, but sexual content remains central.

Bertha Harris's *Lover* was so explicit that Harcourt Brace rejected the manuscript. "In a three page letter," Harris wrote Barbara Grier, "they told me in mincing terms that *Lover* is perverse (Perverse!). . . . In simpler language, it is a dirty book."[30] One wonders whether the editors were reacting to passages like this : "Flynn fucks women. All she must do to maintain paradise is to fuck women; and she does; she fucks them behind the arras, the tuppenny stand-ups; and in the rowboats on her river; and in the swimming pool and in the grass and in great four-posters and on fur rugs before fires huge enough to roast a cow. Face-to-face with them, she fucks them. . . . A vagina is a long, deep swoon."[31] Harris's often difficult literary style opens up here for a direct embrace of women's lust. *Lover* answers the question "What do two women do in bed?" in inventive, glorious detail:

> Her fingers bump across the other's knuckles until her fingers are caught in the other's palm. It is an irresistible takeover; and then she has three loose fingers and a thumb with which to cup the other's fist. That is the way she frequently begins—and it could end with only that. But not this time—because, almost immediately, her free hand starts. It takes the other's waist, it slides around to the other's back, the small of her back; then enters the clothing, insinuating beneath the waistband and shirt. At this point, the tips of her fingers are resting against the initial curve of the buttock. In this manner, she draws her toward her; until the shoulders, the breasts, bellies, *pubi*, the knees indent, one against the other.
>
> Then she moves, but only from the hips, and a little to the left. The lover's right thigh is then between the legs of the beloved. It is a tight fit, and the entire length of the thigh. The lover's first kiss is on that curve where the neck becomes shoulder. She kisses; then she licks there, then she sucks there. Sometimes she tastes perfume; sometimes she tastes sweat, or soap.
>
> The beloved, too, becomes necessary. Some point is eventually reached at which one cannot tell lover from beloved. A conglomerate of picture, sound, smell, noise charges past her on the red-carpet pavement. There are cloudbursts, dingdong bells, shoo-fly pie, yumyum and the lover's indrawn breath (taken, now, from within

the beloved's ear). But if she is smart she will neither grab, gesticulate, nor roar. She will take deep breaths. She will close her eyes, and hold on; but not too tightly.

The wizard tongue collects the eyelid, then the mouth's first corner, then its second, then all its insides—teeth, tongue, gums, palate; while the hands go up and hold tight underneath the arms, and the two thumbs press, once, against the nipples. Once more, then, they touch the hips then leave the body entirely. The lover and beloved are separate now, so the lover says, "I love you." (61–62)

In an homage to Carson McCullers's *Ballad of the Sad Cafe*, Harris refers to the two as "lover" and "beloved," eschewing gender-specific descriptions of their sexual roles. To claim lesbian sex as a universal act of love is as audacious as McCullers's framing of a love affair between a mannish woman and a dwarf. Harris's language pays attention to women's bodies in exhaustive detail: the unnoticed curve of shoulder to neck, the detailed list of thumbs, hips, nipples, teeth, tongue. Harris replaces specific descriptions of sex for a stream-of-consciousness collection of "picture, sound, smell, noise," and then lists hilariously ironic metaphors for the act: "cloudbursts, dingding bells, shoo-fly pie, yum yum."

Other passages give more detail about what two women actually do together: "She has two fingers inside the movie star's vagina, stroking the round of the cervix; and the stranger is crooning, 'O, my dear little vagina!' . . . I dreamed I was making love to you. . . . I want you to know that it was me making love to you but not like a husband does, it was with my tongue. And suddenly, in this dream, that little thing that grows at the top of a woman down there, that little bud, turned into two separate little pieces of electrical wire—two little gold electric things" (145). The precision of this description of lesbian sexual acts—stroking the round of the cervix, the "little thing that grows at the top of a woman down there"—puts most pornographic writing about lesbianism to shame, mainly because it does not presume the primacy of the phallus or the necessity of a man. Two women, Harris maintains, are more than adequate for the fulfilment of desire.

Joyful depictions of lesbian sexuality are common in the archive of southern lesbian feminism. Indeed, the freedom to write about lesbian sexuality openly often made writers downright giddy. Consider the first sex scene in June Arnold's *The Cook and the Carpenter*, which uses the gender-neutral pronouns *na* and *nan*:

The carpenter's hand reached into the cook's hair, long curved
fingers cupping nan skull as if it were most fragile wood, carving so
coveted nan hand trembled[. . . .] Crickets and leaves and the
brook's game with its pebbles and their own breath and motion
surrounded them, but that was outside; inside was silent. "I've never
kissed anyone before except in the presence of thoughts in words. A
thousand comments. Do this. Think this. What if . . . . ? What are
you doing? My mind is six hours old." A frog croaked and na smiled
and grew serious. "I've never done this before."

On the damp dark earth smelling of summer and insects, the
carpenter felt nan nose fill with the smell of the cook's face and nan
mouth with the tang of saliva; nan hand on the cook's chest tin-
gled[. . . .]

A sudden rain made the leaves over their heads flap and the
sound of the rain reached them before its wetness. They licked the
water from each other's faces, "God thinks sex is dirty," the cook said.

"Na doesn't. That was applause. Didn't you hear it?"

"Your face has changed, " the cook said. Na stopped at the edge of
the trees and stared at the face of a friend two years, now lover.[32]

The scene foregrounds women's experience; both women are active agents,
not passive recipients. The recurrent natural imagery—crickets, a creek,
"damp dark earth," rain—marks this sexual encounter as a liberated one, free
from coercion and hierarchy, and having sex in the garden rewrites Garden
of Eden mythology; they are two Eves before the Fall, and the gender-
neutral pronoun *na* makes the "masculine" and "feminine" partner impossible to determine. Arnold confronts the "Adam and Eve, not Adam and
Steve" invocation of the garden when at the end of their encounter the rain
(uncontrollable wetness) is interpreted by the cook as criticism and by the
carpenter as "applause." Arnold tries to write a new language for sex in
this scene, outside of heteropatriarchy—even as her language draws on religious imagery and themes.

On the other side of the cultural hierarchy, Naiad Press sex scenes were
distinctive—evocative, euphemistic, and sometimes unintentionally funny.
Witness a sex scene between the two lovers in Ann Allen Shockley's *Say
Jesus and Come to Me*:

Travis emitted a low moan, closing her eyes and tightening her arms
around Myrtle's neck. The kiss was long, deep and exploring,
wonderfully new and fresh to them as first lovers' kisses can be.

Myrtle contoured her face between the groove of Travis's breasts, inhaling the woman-smell of sweetness and salty dampness. . . . Tenderly Myrtle began to disrobe her, pausing to kiss, nibble, and lick unexpected places on bare flesh. Travis had a mole on her right shoulder blade which Myrtle now sucked gently. Hands deftly unfastened the flimsy tissue of brassiere to make the pendulous breasts fall freely in view. Myrtle bent, kissed and tongued the eye of each brown nipple. Easing down the sheer lattice of panties, she uncovered the coarse black curly bush of hair securing the Venus of her loving.[33]

It's easy to make fun of the language here—"woman-smell," and "Venus of her loving" are particularly unfortunate—but it is similar to the euphemisms of women's romances (like "throbbing manhood"). Happy, romantic endings for lesbians were rare, even in the 1970s, and many lesbians wanted their own versions of romance novels. Sex scenes like this one—romantic, euphemistic, and earnest—were the backbone of Naiad's success in the 1980s and 1990s.

Nevertheless, direct, sometimes disturbing, and transgressive depictions of sex dominate the archive of southern lesbian feminism. Writers risked confirming negative stereotypes about decadent southerners and degenerate queers to depict a wide range of sexual deviance—including polyamory, intergenerational sex, female incest, prostitution, and rape—with a fearlessness that distinguishes the archive of southern lesbian feminism.

Polyamory

Polyamory was common in early lesbian feminist texts in the 1970s, and southern lesbian feminist writers continued to explore it in the 1980s. Rita Mae Brown's irrepressible narrator from the 1973 *Rubyfruit Jungle*, Molly Bolt, has numerous lovers from the age of thirteen; her rejection of monogamy is part of a devil-may-care lesbian identity. When talking with her lover Holly's older lover, Kim, she casually answers Kim's question about her sexual relationship with Holly. Kim doesn't mind: "Once I got beyond thirty-five I stopped being torn up about those things and I definitely gave up on monogamy. Maybe I can do it but no one else seems to be able to." Molly answers flirtatiously, "Well, don't test yourself. Non-monogamy makes life much more interesting"[34] That attitude rules over the rest of the novel. Near the end, Molly's first lover, now "reformed" and married unhappily to a man, asks her if she wants to settle down and what she'll do when she gets old, and Molly answers, "I'm going to be arrested for throwing an orgy at ninety-nine and I'm not growing old with anybody. What a gruesome thought" (219). Polyandry runs through Brown's 1978 novel *Six of One* as well.[35] Ramelle has an affair with the Curtis, the brother of her lover Celeste, and insists that she loves them both: "I don't feel guilty. I don't feel I've betrayed her. I feel it's the most natural thing in the world to love you. Loving you makes me love her more and loving her makes me love you. Do you think it's possible that love multiplies? We're taught to think it divides. There's only so much to go around, like diamonds. It multiplies."[36] Celeste doesn't confront Ramelle because "it was none of my business. You belong to yourself."[37] When Ramelle becomes pregnant, all three of them raise the daughter collectively.

Alice Walker's 1982 *The Color Purple*, one of the best-known novels in the archive of southern lesbian feminism, grew out of a rumination on a love triangle. Walker explained: "I don't always know where the germ of a story comes from, but with *The Color Purple* I knew right away. I was hiking through the woods with my sister, Ruth, talking about a lovers' triangle of which we both knew. She said: 'And you know, one day The Wife asked The Other Woman for a pair of her drawers.' Instantly the missing piece of the story I was mentally writing—about two women who felt married to the same man—fell into place."[38] Love triangles structure most of the relationships in the novel, and they are often overlapping: Albert, Shug, and Celie; Albert, Shug, and Grady; Celie, Shug, and Germaine; Harpo, Sophia, and Mary Agnes (Squeak); Harpo, Sophia, and Buster; Corrine, Samuel, and Nettie. As Linda Abbandonato puts it, "Triadic combinations proliferate; characters are constantly realigned in an intricate network of combinations, apparently in a continual state of metamorphosis until the final utopian vision."[39] The novel frames these multiple relationships as, simply, "family." When Sophia introduces Buster to her husband (who is there with Mary Agnes), she says, "This Henry Broadnax. . . . Everybody call him Buster. Good friend of the family."[40] All these relationships transcend jealousy; the interlocking triangles unite for the common good. Mary Agnes goes to the sheriff to save Sophia from prison, risking her own safety for her lover's wife; Sophia cares for Mary Agnes's daughter when Mary Agnes leaves for Memphis; Grady and Shug, who are married, take Shug's lover Celie back with them to Memphis; Albert consoles Celie when Shug leaves her; Nettie marries Samuel when his wife dies.

Walker suggests that these complex familial relationships are based on African models. When Nettie arrives in Africa with Samuel and Corrine, the members of the village assume that both women are Samuel's wives. Walker frames monogamy and jealousy as patriarchal corruptions of human nature. Albert has to unlearn his misogyny, and by the end of the novel he is transformed from an abusive husband to a nurturing member of the larger family; as Celie explains, "When you talk to him now he really listen, and one time, out of nowhere in the conversation us was having, he said Celie, I'm satisfied this the first time I ever lived on Earth as a natural man. It feel like a new experience."[41] Celie herself has to learn to love without possessing: "Shug got a right to live too. She got a right to look over the world in whatever company she choose. Just cause I love her don't take away none of her rights."[42] The "final utopian vision" includes all the friends of the family who love each other, celebrating together on Independence Day with the reunion of Nettie and Celie at the center, a polyamorous party.

Intergenerational Sex

May/December relationships—usually between older men and younger women—are common in American culture. They also are not uncommon in gay relationships, as George Chauncey describes in his discussion of "wolves" and "punks."[43] In lesbian pulp, the intergenerational romance was a plot staple: the older coworker, the teacher, and the coach all serve as mentors in lesbian love. Perhaps the most famous lesbian pulp novel, Patricia Highsmith's *The Price of Salt*, features an intergenerational relationship.

The image of the predatory lesbian was often disavowed during women's liberation as a male fantasy and a suspect model of exploitive power, yet many southern lesbian feminists explored intergenerational sex in their writing. In *Rubyfruit Jungle*, when Molly Bolt learns that her coworker Holly is "kept" by an older actress, Kim, she is disgusted, but she discovers that Kim is both lovely and sympathetic. The host of a lesbian party is another matter. Molly imagines that she is "seventy years old, had her face lifted five times, . . . [and] sleep[s] in an alcohol bath," (156–57) and she complains to Holly, "I get pursued by the human pickle. Some friend you are, fixing me up with the geriatric ward" (157). The reality is almost as bad—not Chryssa's physical appearance, but how she treats Molly. Looking at Molly "with as much subtlety as a vulture" (162), Chryssa invites her to lunch and tries to buy her: "The questions from Chryssa—sly and charming but all leading to the same conclusion. . . . I nearly lost my restraint when she hinted she'd pay my way through film school, if only. . . . Why did that woman in her well-modulated voice try to buy me off? I know why, I know good and why. . . . How can I pay for school myself? A semester is $1,000. Goddamn being poor. I got to use my ass to save my head. Well fuck you, Chryssa Hart, I'm not taking your enticing money, and fuck me because I'm going to sit in that rathole and stay proud but poor" (167). Chryssa Hart is an unattractive predator eager to exploit poor attractive lesbians, and Molly feels as humiliated by her as she does by the male chauvinist pigs who prevent her budding directing career. It is noteworthy that among the novel's archetypal images of New York queer life, Brown includes "chickenhawks." Lesbian feminists often portrayed intergenerational romances as inherently exploitive and more common in gay culture, but Brown's casual reference to wealthy older lesbians like Chryssa suggests this was a recognizable feature of lesbian life as well.

June Arnold takes intergenerational sex in a different direction. Su steps out on her middle-aged lover not for a younger woman, but for the ninety-one-year-old Mamie Carter. Her description of the old woman's wrinkled body challenges the obsession with youth that supposedly undergirds intergenerational sex:

Su sunk her face into the ageless curve of her love's shoulder and smothered a giggle. . . . "Your silk is matched only by our exquisite ability to prolong swallowing, our mutual toothlessness allowing for such a long balance on the tip of flavor: I just never imagined that the delights of age would include the fact of endlessly drawn-out orgasms." . . . Su saw in her mind her coveted breasts, bound flat to her chest when she was in her twenties to produce a flapper fashion, hanging now from the base of the breastbone like soft toys, too small to rest a head upon, fit for a hand to cuddle very gently like the floppy ears of a puppy. Memory moved her hand to Mamie Carter's belly—skin white as milk, finely plucked like sugar-sprinkled clabber; memory dropped her hand to Mamie Carter's sparse hair curling like steel—there was strength between her legs and no dough there where the flesh was fluid enough to slip away from the bone and leave that tensed grain hard as granite and her upright violent part like an animal nose against Su's palm. The image of memory bruised.[44]

Arnold provides explicit descriptions of the aging body, with images that are discomfiting and unexpected. The comparisons of Mamie Carter's breasts to a puppy's ears and her clitoris to a dog's nose make her sexual organs seem cute and safe, even childlike, while also connecting her body to animal instincts. Similarly, the description of her body as a dessert—milk and "sugar-sprinkled clabber"—depict the aging female body as both delectable and commonplace. These safe, familiar images contrast with the taboo of this scene—old women are, apparently, capable of inspiring "long drawn-out orgasms." Arnold's fearlessness in this scene is distinctive in the archive of southern lesbian feminism.

Female Incest

Nowhere is the riskiness of southern lesbian feminists' engagement with transgressive sexuality more apparent than in its depiction of female incest. It was incest—shadowy, revolting, and vaguely titillating—that defined the southern gothic and enraged scholars in the nascent field of southern literature. In a tradition that began with Faulkner, portrayals of incest have confirmed the harshest stereotypes about deviant southerners, but also served thematic and literary purposes; the threatened incest between Bon and Judith in *Absalom! Absalom!*, for example, symbolizes the intimacy of racism in the South that separates members of the human family.

In the early days of women's liberation, incest between mothers and daughters was often celebrated. *Rubyfruit Jungle* features a mother and daughter, Polly and Alice, with whom Molly Bolt has sex, albeit separately (she also has sex with the mother's male lover). Polly and Alice have a close relationship, and in fact, Alice is convinced that her mother is sexually attracted to her. But rather than being upset about it, Alice thinks her mother's "hang-up" is hopelessly square.

> "You know Mom wants to sleep with me? . . . She won't admit it but I know she does. I think I'd like to sleep with her. She's very good looking, you know. Too bad it would freak her out. Incest doesn't seem like such a trauma to me."
>
> "Me neither, but then I can't really say much about that because I didn't grow up with my real parents. But I never have been able to figure out why parents and children put each other in these desexed categories. It's anti-human, I think."
>
> "Yeah, parents get freaked out about everything. Mom must have a heavy case of repression going, because she'll never deal with the fact that she digs my body." (209)

Molly advises Alice not to sleep with Polly, but not for moral reasons: "Just don't sleep with your mother. I'm not against incest if both parties consent and are over fifteen, but your mother's on her own weird trip" (209). When Alice and Molly have sex, it is without "weird trips" and "repression"; earlier, Molly had rejected the need for Freudian fantasies, and this is one encounter that delivers Foucauldian liberation from disciplinary structures: "Alice steamed and shook and sighed, and she hadn't one sexual quirk in her mind. She loved being touched and she loved touching back. Kissing was an art form to her. She was there, all there with no hang-ups and no stories to tell, just herself. And I was just me" (210). As members of the same generation, Alice and Molly dismiss the incest taboo as just another "sexual quirk" and approach sex with an unromantic interest in pleasure.

It is tempting to see this casual acceptance of incest as a footnote to the era of free love, when all sexual taboos were questioned, but Brown was not the only southern lesbian feminist to explore consensual incest in a positive way. Bertha Harris wrote the most comprehensive treatment in *Lover*, in which Veronica and Samaria, two widows married to the same man, become lovers and establish an all-female household in which sexuality circulates dangerously. Mother-daughter bonds become the framework for lesbian desire: "There is no intimacy between woman and woman which is not preceded by a long narrative of the mother," muses Flynn, as her "visitor" shouts "Motherfuck!" and "scald[s] her hand" in "boiling water" (173). This playful toying with the idea of incest, without ever naming it, marks much of the narrative—an homage to a southern grotesque past as well as a campy gesture to a lesbian feminist future. The closest Harris comes to saying the unspoken comes when Lydia, the movie star who has an affair with Flynn, warns off the rest of the family, which leads to a coded conversation:

"I hope you will not try to come between Flynn and I—except with great tact and delicacy of maneuver, of course."

"She is naked under that bathrobe. It reminds me that I am starving and exhausted," said Rose-lima. "You mean Flynn and *me*."

"I was under the expression that *I* was the first for Flynn," said Lydia Somerleyton, "and anyway, *you* and Flynn would be against the law, what they call *insight*."

"That's what I would call it, too," said Samaria. (157; emphasis in original)

Rose-Lima's correction of Lydia—"Flynn and I" should be "Flynn and me"—leads to Lydia's misunderstanding and malapropism. The playful substitution of "insight" for "incest" suggests Harris's use of the trope in *Lover*; female familial bonds—between sisters, mothers and daughters, even grandmothers and granddaughters—provide the motivation and model for lesbian desire. Flynn is obsessed with her mother Daisy, who has left the household for a man. The twins Rose and Rose-lima "pretend to be mama and the new husband" (20) and comfort Flynn in an elliptical and suggestive scene: "They held her tight and kissed her, and helped her cry for their mother. . . . Then they moved their sweet little hands down her body" (21). Daisy phones Flynn and describes a lesbian erotic dream she had about the two of them, to which Flynn replies, "That's one hell of a way to talk to your own daughter" (146). And at the end of the novel, Samaria has fallen in love with Flynn, her granddaughter. Harris is careful never to cross the line— Samaria moves out of the house to avoid Flynn; Flynn and the mother never enact the dream; even the threesome between the three daughters might be nothing more than innocent comforting. Embracing incest, one of the most lasting stereotypes of the backward South, was a risky strategy.

Blanche McCrary Boyd, whose investment in southern lesbian feminism was uneven, turned to incest to resolve her 1978 novel *Mourning the Death of Magic*, which follows childhood sweethearts Shannon and Galley and their diverging paths through the tumult of the 1960s. Galley, a fictionalized version of Boyd, has relationships with women and is in and out of mental institutions. After Galley attempts suicide, she discovers the source of her ongoing turmoil: she is in love with her sister Mallory, a lawyer and feminist involved in NOW. The final scene between the two is more evocative than lurid:

Certainty passed through Mallory like a shiver. She said, "Who do you love now?"

There was a silence. "You," Galley said.

"I know," Mallory said. And it was true, she did know. Had known for some time without realizing it. . . .

Mallory turned her sister clumsily by the shoulders and kissed her on the mouth. It was strange, soft, salty, kissing her sister.

There was a faraway sound, then Mallory felt light, a revelation. Lust began to open inside her like a door, like a fist unclenching. Her nerves seemed to hang outside her like a web, like lace. It was right, and it was inevitable. She felt a relief, a sadness, a pleasure she had not even known about.

After awhile Galley said, "Don't hurt me, okay?"

Mallory, who was too full of feeling to speak, shook her head that she wouldn't.

They went back to the house and sat together in the bright bedroom. Mallory took off Galley's shirt and then she took off her own. She turned off the lamp. She put her face gently against Galley's breast and licked the tightening nipple. "I don't know what this means," she said.

"I don't either," Galley said.[45]

This "resolution" of Galley's competitive relationship with her sister draws on a number of stereotypes: that homosexuality and incest go together (Mallory speculates just before this scene that Galley might be attracted to her[46]), that incest is endemic in the South (Galley is able to integrate into southern life after this sexual encounter, even running Mallory's political campaign), that feminists are all nascent lesbians (especially short-haired feminists like Mallory), and that sisterly incestuous desire is both the cause of and the natural conclusion to lesbian desire. That Galley's emotional problems seem to be cured by the consummation of her desire for her sister shows how deeply Boyd embraces the connection of transgressive sexuality and radical transformation.

Four years later, *The Color Purple* described Celie's abuse at the hands of her stepfather in devastating terms, but readers often overlook the ways that Walker depicts lesbian sexuality through implied incestuous bonds. When Shug and Celie first have sex, Celie describes it in maternal terms:

She say, I love you, Miss Celie. And then she haul off and kiss me on the mouth.

Um, she say, like she surprise. I kiss her back, say, *um*, too. Us kiss and kiss still us can't hardly kiss no more. Then us touch each other.

I don't know nothing 'bout it, I say to Shug.

I don't know much, she say.

Then I feels something real soft and wet on my breast, feel like one of my little lost babies' mouth.

Way after while, I act like a little lost baby too.[47]

This imagery continues in the parallel Shug draws between her relationship with Celie and Celie's relationship with her sister Nettie. Shug asks many questions about Nettie "'cause she the only one you ever love . . . sides me.'"[48] Arguably, this pairing makes the lesbian desire safe, just as the sexual abuse Celie suffers provides a "cause" for it. But it is noteworthy that a book so often credited with exposing the reality and the dangers of incest also incorporates imagery pairing maternal and sisterly incestuous desire as a positive alternative.

In June Arnold's final novel, *Baby Houston*, a celebration of her mother and the city of Houston, a daughter's desire for her mother is the prime mover of the narrative. The novel is narrated in the first person from the perspective of the mother, who describes her daughter's sometimes suffocating devotion to her. Hallie, the daughter, marries an abusive man, has children, and plans to move away. The dramatic final scene of section four, near the end of the novel, is the only time their erotic connection becomes explicit:

> No one would suspect her now, although she is thirty-five, if she decided to kill *me*: daughter who loved her mother to death.
>
> Now the thunder is in the room, lightning seems aimed at the house, at the kitchen where we stand. I am hugging her, holding her against my body as if we could insulate each other; I am frightened even as I understand that fear is a mask for loneliness.
>
> Holding the candle over the sink she returns my hug with her other arm; her front deflates against my chest; her back is as rigid as ever. I am stroking it. I am kissing her hair, her neck. I feel her youth transfer itself into my age. Thunder vibrates against my ears. Then there is another noise—the sound of a hundred hooves stamping on our roof. We are being pelted from above: hail.
>
> Although one room, one position is as dangerous as another, like babies we choose to huddle together in the bed, drawing the sheet around our shoulders, fixing the candle to a saucer and placing it on the dresser where we can see it. Fear unmasks itself. I am a fire of loneliness: no longer the gluey gray mud of yesterday, loneliness rages through my veins like hot rain, like flesh.
>
> I am kissing my daughter like a lover.[49]

The scene ends there, before the taboo is breached (the next section jumps forward years, revealing Hattie's departure to New York and Paris and her return to Houston for her mother's death). And it is described as an aberrant moment, fueled by loneliness, fear, and a rainstorm. Still, the longing that is expressed in this scene is the animating force of the whole novel: mother-daughter bonds are the model for lesbian desire.

These writers' sometimes cavalier, even celebratory attitude toward incest can be jarring, especially because work by Alice Walker and Dorothy Allison helped raise public awareness about the ubiquity and destructiveness of incest. Even queer theorists, with their enthusiasm for nonnormative sexualities including public sex, polyandry, and intergenerational sex, don't touch incest. So why did southern lesbian feminist writers take on such an explosive topic?

The theme of incest in the southern gothic is one factor. Incest was a common literary trope in both southern and queer pulp traditions, and for Brown, Harris, and Boyd, it was a textual strategy, not a real-world endorsement. None of them seem to have had sexual relationships with female family members. The incest trope for these three was a defiant embrace of their innate queerness in a heteropatriarchal society, a provocation. Brown, Harris, and (to a lesser extent) Boyd seemed to be amused by these transgressive literary gestures.

Harris's love for camp culture and gay pulp made her go furthest in her celebration of female-centric incest, but it was also part of a more sustained queer critique of heteronormativity, traditional reproduction, and "family values." As Elizabeth Freeman argues, Harris undoes patriarchal descent, constructing all-female genealogy, shifting from downtown New York to an imaginary all-female household, from lesbian grandmothers to lesbian daughters, all while making a mockery of any stable notion of origins: the novel "scramble[es] the logic of family lineage. . . . Harris's is a kin diagram turned rhizomatic."[50] Witness Veronica's disavowal as a mother to her two sons, by providing multiple and contradictory origin stories to free them and her from an Oedipal inevitability:

> I can't be your mother, because I am not. One more time, I'm going
> to explain. Then I won't ever again. Now listen: after the revolution-
> aries shot my parents and siblings, I wandered for a while, incognito.
> But the revolutionaries grew suspicious of my height, of my Floren-
> tine profile; and they quarreled over the royal body count. Some-
> body, according to some of them, was missing. I found two baby
> boys beside their mother, who was dying behind a haystack. The
> mother was an Irish dwarf, grateful for a chance to die in privacy. I
> strapped you to my back and continued my tortuous way. I escaped.
> You had grown fond of me—fond of my backbone, I suppose. I let
> you stay, even into my safety.
>
> "That isn't what you said, last time," said Bogart. "Last time you
> said we were the sons of a blimp pilot whose ship exploded in flames
> above the state of New Jersey—and that you had us as a widow, by
> caesarean, like Ceasar."

"No, that isn't what she said last time. Last time she said we were the sons of a great Canadian revolutionary. From Canada, the man who led the Canadian revolution to victory. 'Don't organize, mourn,' she said was our father's dying words."

"You pays your money, you takes your choice." (173)

Veronica's flippant conclusion that "the truth" doesn't matter ("you pays your money, you take your choice") suggests that all origin stories are equally irrelevant; what matters is their entertainment, their style, not their truth.

Lest we think Veronica is just being needlessly cruel, she herself is shrouded in mystery. She is a figure without origins, or with so many that any one genealogical version is suspect. After a deeply traumatic depiction of childbirth of both Daisy and Samaria (both "pulled through the lips of her vulva"), we witness a multiple, alpha-and-omega Veronica: "Veronica, however, came out of nowhere, and so she used to go exclusively with Veronica. They were childhood sweethearts. On February 15, 1947, Veronica gave Veronica a red heart-shaped box of candy and then they sat together in the porch swing that warmish February afternoon" (5). Harris goes on another two pages with these strange quasi-biographical details about Veronica, none of which clarify her character or even consistently fit together. She concludes, "Veronica began life as a religious poet composing ecstatic meters about drowned nuns. She began life as a bigamist, as a twin, as a married woman, as a lover. And still, at any moment, she can render herself again into an exact replica of all the creatures she started as" (7). Origins, in other words, are imaginary, the *result* of narrative, not the cause of it.

Ultimately, *Lover* positions lesbians as outside an oppressive gender binary. Flynn's grandmother, Samaria, states the escape explicitly: "The truth is I got myself back in spite of it. In spite of it, I could become a lover and could stop being a woman. What they said, *a woman*. That's why I am here, in spite of it, and not in a cage, like the rest of them, in a freak show. I am a lover, not a woman" (102–103). Harris's rejection of the term "woman" as oppressive opens up a wider range of erotic activity and sexual identity. She rejects traditional kinship bonds; in a sense, the system in which female incest is significant is moot in the world of *Lover*. In Harris's particularly queer lesbian feminist imaginary kingdom, familial bonds, like womanly identity, ultimately deconstruct themselves.[51]

For some other southern lesbian feminists, the embrace of female incest was a way to rewrite Freud's theories of "normal" psychosexual development.

Freud argued that small children sexually desired the parent of the opposite sex (boys, their mothers; girls, their fathers) and felt sexual jealousy toward the parent of the same sex. Freud thus makes incestuous desire the site of "normal" psychosexual development, and does so in a way that disallows any "normal" understanding of queer desire. When such notions of sexuality were commonplace, some lesbian writers—from Adrienne Rich to later feminist psychoanalytic theorists like Teresa de Lauretis and Diana Fuss—wanted to rewrite his notion of psychosexual development to include lesbian desire: if male heterosexual desire began with an intense attachment to the mother, then that model was also true for the lesbian child. Adrienne Rich's 1978 essay "Compulsory Heterosexuality and Lesbian Existence" argued that lesbian desire was rooted in the mother-daughter bond, which harked back to the physical connection of breastfeeding.

Southern lesbian feminists were making this argument even earlier. One example is Catherine Nicholson and Harriett Desmoines's 1976 essay "Sinister Wisdom."[52] In the prologue they link their intergenerational romance with the incest taboo: "Catherine is fifty-three; I'm twenty-nine. We'd been lovers nearly a year when we voluntarily left/were expelled from? a lesbian separatist collective[. . . .] After nights of confused anguish, I say to Catherine, we've broken a double taboo. There's a taboo against lesbian love, but there's also a taboo against cross-generational love. No, no[. . . .] The taboo underlying both is this: *it is forbidden for a woman to sexually love a woman old enough to be her mother . . . or young enough to be her daughter.*"[53] They refer to Freud to explain this taboo: "In the past of every woman, every mother-of-sons, lies a long-buried period of primary attachment to her own mother. The pre-Oedipal period is that time when the whole world seems a matriarchy, and the little girl is pleasurably at home in her body, content with its rightness, pleased with herself and with the mother who is the center of her world."[54] Patriarchy leads to a rupture and disdain between older and younger women, but the solution is clear (to them at least): "For a woman, to become whole is to untwist her past, to begin slowly the reconstruction of her mind and her body, her will and heart. To become whole is to spiral upward in a motion that is also return. Return to mother or to another mother, to an exchange of mothering. What has been used to denigrate lesbianism may constitute the healing power of lesbian love."[55] In this universalizing version of female sexual development, heterosexuality was unnatural for women; lesbianism was the most natural and holistic option for women's sexuality. Embracing the incest taboo, and inverting the Freudian pattern, becomes a dominant means of theorizing lesbianism. The "lesbian continuum" may have de-emphasized the logistics and physicality of lesbian sex, but it also provided a means of identification that did not involve deviance as a central value.

For southern lesbian feminist writers who engaged this trope, female incest was a symbol for women's liberation. For Brown, treating incest cavalierly demonstrates the feminist liberation of her respective heroines; for Harris, incest creates an all-female genealogical legacy that liberates itself from heteropatriarchal modes of descent; for Boyd, it extends her exploration of nonnormative sexual desire and provides an innovative resolution to a plot problem; for Walker, it provides a healing solution for Celie's empowerment and a means to a happy future; and for Arnold, it is a metaphor for lesbian desire, replacing the Oedipal triangle at the heart of Freudian psychology. The southern gothic, which made incest a central trope, was merged with the radical feminism of these writers to create a thoroughly transgressive sexual ethos—a queering of normative sexuality that risks reinforcing retrograde stereotypes about the "backward South" as it refuses to encode the transgressive in shadowy tropes or obtuse language. This body of work continues to challenge both literary scholars and queer theorists.

Prostitution

In the early 1980s Rita Mae Brown took on the disciplinary power of the South and sexuality directly, with a focus on prostitution. In her *Southern Discomfort*,[56] set in nineteenth-century Montgomery, Alabama (the first capital of the Confederacy), Brown tells the story of the South in microcosm through "two first class whores": Blue Rhonda Latrec and Banana Mae Parker. The prologue sets up the themes of this novel with admirable directness: "Blue Rhonda and Banana Mae looked at Montgomery, Alabama, in terms of sex. The town resembled a stud farm although everybody lied through their teeth about fucking. Maybe the real difference between Blue Rhonda, Banana Mae and the rest of Montgomery's citizens was that they told the truth. In this world, lying, fornicating and thieving are prerogatives of the sane. Small wonder that the two women, or any prostitutes, for that matter, were regarded as nuts."[57] Many other writers, before and after Brown, wrote about a queer South dominated by nonnormative sexuality, but few approached "fucking" so forthrightly. Brown is clear about the function of all this "secret" fucking: it constructs a disciplinary system that ties the culture together. All this "lying, fornicating and thieving" do not destabilize or undermine the southern patriarchal system; in fact, they are a key part of what makes it work.[58]

The "stud farm" is a metaphor for the entire South in *Southern Discomfort*. The whorehouses serve the wealthy male elite in Montgomery; public adherence to social norms of female "purity" and heteronormative families does not prevent men of privilege from visiting prostitutes. Indeed, Carwyn, the wealthy husband of the heroine, Hortensia Banastre, takes his paramour out in his carriage on Main Street. The prostitutes know every kink that prominent white men have, no matter what face they show to coworkers and family. Through prostitutes, Brown critiques the patriarchy in ways both entertaining and profane. Money defines sexual transactions between men and women, whether in marriage or in a brothel.

Whorehouses are allowed to exist because of the hypocritical privilege of white patriarchs. Yet Brown refuses to view prostitutes as victims. She insists on their agency; within an oppressive patriarchal system, they are heroes, with a surprising amount of freedom. In Reverend Linton Ray's morality campaign against prostitution, he brings a mob of outraged wives to burn down the whorehouses. At first, "every woman in the house was armed" (86), ready for a shoot-out, but to avoid the police, they ask another brothel to send them choir robes:

> "Where'd you get all these?" Blue Rhonda buttoned her purple robe with the pale-blue trim.
>   One of Minnie's employees whispered, "History night."
>   "Huh?" Rhonda fluffed up her sleeves.
>   "Peter Stove dressed up as a bishop. We had to sing while he desecrated the altar—if you catch my drift." She giggled.
>   "Peter Stove?" Blue Rhonda exclaimed.
>   "Ecclesiastical desires are a patent item," Leafy sniffed. (87)

Prepared to outsmart the mob, the prostitutes "sing like angels," and Bunny offers an invitation: "Fellow believers in the forgiveness of our Lord and Savior, Jesus, who died for our sins and rose again from the dead, please come in and join us for our weekly devotional" (88). This "Christian stardust" does the trick. Prostitutes use the existing Christian rhetoric to protect their own nonnormative livelihoods. Note that the white men in power who take advantage of this transgressive space are nowhere to be seen when the prostitutes are challenged—the brothels suffer the public shaming and the danger while the powerful simply exploit them.

This is not to say that such transgressive spaces don't allow occasional freedom from larger societal prescriptions—the prostitutes do survive the outside threat—but the brothel does not, in and of itself, challenge the hetero-normative status quo. When Hortensia Banastre, the wife of a powerful man in town, has a passionate sexual affair with a young African American laborer, Hercules, Blue Rhonda lets them use her apartment in the red-light district for their meetings. Everything about this relationship is a fantasy: that such a woman would risk such a liaison; that she could become pregnant, have a mixed-race child, and raise that child in her own house without being found out; that Hercules's untimely death results from a train accident (instead of being lynched). However, the scenario does allow Brown to draw a parallel between a woman who occupies the highest rung in southern society, Hortensia, and one who occupies the lowest, Blue Rhonda. Brown frames them as allies of sorts within southern heteropatriarchy:

> Hortensia turned to fully face Blue Rhonda. "I wish I had your courage."
> "What courage?"
> Rhonda was confused.
> "You do as you please and the hell with rules and regulations made by somebody else. Before he died Hercules asked me to run away with him. I said I'd have to think about it. I know now I never would have done it. I lacked the courage and I probably still lack it. I couldn't break the rules openly." She laughed at herself. "But I could break them in secret." Drew in a breath. "But then who doesn't?"
> "Don't be hard on yourself, Miz Banastre. I'm not so brave. I couldn't get any lower, if you consider where I came from. You had a lot to lose." (140)

Hortensia's transgressions are strategic, and her secrecy (and her lover's convenient death) saves her. Blue Rhonda may be more courageous and open, but she is also without privilege. For her, the lowest position in society is her only space of freedom, but it is hardly a transformative subject position. Here Brown may be critiquing the "downward mobility" of radical feminists who embraced terms like *slut* and *whore* as part of their activism, which was not exactly an optimistic statement about the future of revolution. Hortensia has tea in Blue Rhonda's house in private, but that does not change either woman's social position in public, nor does it affect the largely white male privilege that circumscribes both their subject positions.

Nowhere is the implicit link between transgressive sexuality and liberation more unstable than in Hortensia's incestuous relationship with her son Paris, who discovers the truth about her mixed-race daughter and then blackmails her. His price? She must have sex with him. His demand is depicted as proof of mental illness; her acquiescence is not. After all, sex is just sex in Brown's fictional universe, and just as the prostitutes' satisfaction of every imaginable kink of Montgomery's ruling classes is not shocking, so the heroine's ability to have enjoyable sex with her son is an unremarkable fact. Paris becomes obsessed with Hortensia, and in the end she shoots him dead to protect her daughter. It is a murderous denouement to the novel that leaves all the secrets of the novel intact. Hortensia's daughter is still a social outcast, publicly denied by her mother; Hortensia never tells her husband the truth about her affairs with her black servant and her son, and her privilege—and his—remains unchallenged. Brown had written many nonnormative sexual situations, but by 1982 she was arguing that transgressive sex is allowed only if it doesn't threaten the established order.

One more transgression appears at the end of *Southern Discomfort*. When Blue Rhonda dies and Banana Mae and Bunny prepared her body for burial, "they discovered she was a man. Her genitals were uncommonly small, but they were those of a man nonetheless" (276). In a last letter, Blue Rhonda had explained: "I was born James Porter with very little, as you know. I never felt like a boy and never want to be one. God played a joke on me and put me in a man's body, and not much of a man's body at that. I ran away from home when I was fourteen and passed myself off as a girl. I fooled you all, so I guess I did a good job. I didn't really want to fool anyone. I just wanted to be a woman and I think I was" (277). Brown's portrayal of trans identity, and trans sex work, is ahead of its time. Blue Rhonda has used her culture's twisted sexual politics to construct her own space of freedom as a prostitute. Despite the melodramatic plot of the privileged Hortensia, it is Blue Rhonda and her fellow prostitutes who are the real heroes of this novel, but they are heroes whose transgression supports, rather than challenges, the "stud farm" of southern power systems.

The politics of prostitution is also a central focus in Ann Allen Shockley's *Say Jesus and Come to Me*. When minister Myrtle Black befriends two prostitutes, she is "appalled at what she had heard from the women. Stories about police graft, payoffs in money and sex. The clientele of the prostitutes distressed her—pillars of the professional and religious communities."[59] As in *Southern Discomfort*, prostitution is enabled by the police department and the many men—including ministers—who frequent brothels. Prostitution exposes the hypocrisy of the patriarchy; southern chivalry is simply a tool for categorizing women into groups—"respectable," "whore"—and keeping them all in their subordinate places. Myrtle manages to save one prostitute from "the life," employing her at the church; the other remains a prostitute, but warns the church about a planned firebombing by one of the pimps. The reverend undertakes a systemic attack on a corrupt patriarchal system, denouncing from the pulpit "the Police Department, City Hall, pimps, dope pushers, and middle-class hypocrites"[60] and then organizing a cross-racial women's march "to protest vice, crime, and corruption in the city. A March of women of all colors, who would join hands to demonstrate against a male establishment of crooked and selfish lawmakers and lawbreakers."[61] The march ends when a car runs down Travis in the street, suggesting just how entrenched prostitution is in the larger functioning of the patriarchy. But for Shockley, the point of the protests is to create coalitions and alternative communities, as she does with her multicultural, gay-friendly church.

Rape

Just as the "transgressive" sexual act of prostitution sustains an oppressive system of power, rape, too, is a tool of domination under patriarchy in southern lesbian feminist texts. In this, the southern lesbian feminist archive was consistent with the broad critiques of sexual violence in women's liberation. To be forced into sex and hurt for a man's pleasure was the antithesis of everything feminism stood for, even for the most insatiable, irreverent, and campy southern lesbian feminists. In the later sex wars of the 1980s, some women defended many sexual practices that had been deemed antifeminist in the previous decade, including butch-femme role playing and S/M, but rape was never seen as acceptable. Previous violence might inform one's sexual practices, but consent was a bedrock principle, no matter which side one supported in the sex wars.

Southern lesbian feminist writers made the identification of rape as a tool of patriarchy central to their writing. To expose the ugliness of rape was to expose the nasty truth of patriarchy under the veneer of chivalry and benevolent paternalism. Indeed, a shocking frankness about how rape feels, how it wounds, is endemic in the archive of southern lesbian feminism. Many of the writers had been raped themselves, and they eschewed trigger warnings for uncomfortable directness about rape. Patricia Yaeger suggests that their focus on bodies, damaged and grotesque, is pervasive in southern women's writing: "Instead of the grotesque as decadent southern form, I want to examine the importance of irregular models of the body within an extremely regulated society and to focus on figures of damaged, incomplete, or extravagant characters described under rubrics peculiarly suited to southern histories in which the body is simultaneously fractioned and overwhelmed."[62] The disciplining of queer women's bodies is written in particularly frank terms in the archive of southern lesbian feminism.

This stems from the long history of rape as a means of intimidation and control in the South. The "Southern rape complex," Deborah Barker explains, "assumes a black male rapist, an innocent white female victim, and a white male vigilante: the innocent white victim is transformed into a symbol of a threatened southern culture."[63] Rape accusations against black men were a key tool of Jim Crow oppression, as the epidemic of white male violence against black women and unruly white women was obscured. White men thought they had the right to take black women's bodies at any time, but even the hint of black men assuming the same privilege with regard to white women resulted in the sexualized castration/lynching spectacles of the twentieth century. Black women in the South were accustomed to rape as a tool of terror and intimidation, not only by white men but also sometimes by black men (modeling white privilege). In *The Color Purple*, Celie's abuser was not a white man, but a man she had accepted as her father. Her rape occurs after Celie's mother had refused her husband's advances; it is described on the novel's first page in graphic, direct language: "He never had a kine word to say to me. Just say You gonna do what your mammy wouldn't. First he put his thing up gainst my hip and sort of wiggle it around. Then he grab hold my titties. Then he push his thing inside my pussy. When that hurt, I cry. He start to choke me, saying You better shut up and git used to it."[64] Much has been written about Walker's depiction of sexual abuse, but what is most noteworthy here is the language—purely descriptive, violent, devoid of titillating images or metaphor. The shock of perfectly frank language refuses to let the reader avoid the logic of this patriarchal system, white and black. Later violence in the novel—the beating of Celie by Mister, the beating of Sofia by Harpo and later by a group of white men, Mary Agnes's rape by her uncle—is as logical an extension of this system as Celie's initial rape. Though some critics have protested Walker's negative depictions of black men, she is depicting and protesting a patriarchal system, primarily white, in which men were encouraged and sometimes required to be brutes. Mister's rehabilitation at the end of *The Color Purple* suggests that "rape culture" can be repudiated and dismantled, but only if one diagnoses its ills unflinchingly.

Also notable is the novel's first-person point of view. Robin E. Field argues that this was a first in narratives about rape: "For the first time, we are placed *within the victim's consciousness*, via the use of a first-person narrative voice. It is not the rapist narrating his actions, or a (seemingly) impartial omniscient narrator, or even a sympathetic female friend of the victim. Instead, the rape victim herself gains control of her story, and through her own voice readers learn about her reality of traumatic sexual assault. The use of this first-person narration necessarily shifts the focus of the story to the very personal aspects of rape."[65] If this was not the first instance of first-person narration of rape, it was certainly the most widely read. This point of view underscores the agency and value of the survivor, and it has been employed in other key southern lesbian feminist texts as well.

Poor southern white women, too, were familiar with the workings of rape as a tool of patriarchal oppression, but this came as a surprise to white women of a certain class; their own "purity" was a justification for the excesses of Jim Crow, after all. When white women challenged patriarchal authority, rape was used against them almost immediately; "nigger lovers," especially, did not deserve chivalry. Many southern lesbian feminists first came to political activism through the civil rights movement and anti-Klan activism, and the use of sex as a weapon against them was instantaneous. Cris South's description of a brutal rape in *Clenched Fists, Burning Crosses* makes it clear that sexual violence is tied to other forms of violence, and that rape is a tool of terror, along with beatings and lynching. When a Klansman beats Jesse outside her printshop, "she didn't see the fist coming. She felt it instead, bony and unyielding against the side of her face. The blow slammed her back and shoulders into the dumpster. Her head cracked against the cold metal. There was blood in her mouth, a ringing in her ears. Her face felt numb; there was no pain in her jaw, only blinding jolts in the back of her head. Tom jerked her to him, his breath warm on her cheek. 'You're not talking so big now, are you? Go on. Fight back. I like that.' All clarity vanished as he hit her again. Dazed, Jesse tried to kick him, to break his grip with her hands."[66] Pounding her with his fists leads, inexorably, to another pounding, and his strange sadistic sexual language quickly leads to a sadistic gang rape:

"I don't want you to kill her," Edgar said as he pushed Tom away.
"I want a crack at her."

"We'll all get a crack at her, old buddy. Don't you worry about that."

"Now's the time then. Why don't you go first, Tom? After all, you been doing all the work. What about you, Hank? You gonna get in on the fun?"

Jessie heard the voices dimly but the words made no real sense to her. Names. She heard names.

There was laughter, then hands grabbed her and pulled her onto her knees. Someone locked rough fingers into her hair and pulled her head up. She felt cloth brush her face and heard the sound of a zipper sliding down its short track. She tried to raise her arms to ward off what she suddenly knew was about to happen, but she couldn't move. Keeping her eyes closed, she fixed her spinning thoughts on some blank space she found in her mind. Hold on. *Hold on.* Choking her, Tom came with the same violence that was in his fist when he hit her. She tried to spit when he withdrew, but she was too weak for even that.

She tried to concentrate on the cold, damp grass against her buttocks as they pushed her down onto the ground and pulled her jeans to her ankles. Pain shifted, changed, lessened, increased, as one man finished and another took his place. She didn't know how long it lasted or how many times. At one point, she was aware of the heavy pressure of a body on top of her but felt nothing between her legs. Her wonder was brief; she could find no answers. She felt them shift in turn. Time seemed to stop, isolating each thrust into an eternity of fear and agony.

Then a voice spoke close to her ear. "You just got a second chance. You remember what we told you."[67]

The detail of the attack is hard to read; the narrative blacks out and disso-ciates during the rape, as it would have for the protagonist. The men be-lieve they have done her a favor by "just" raping her. The assumptions of rape culture are explicit: all women need to be taught their place through violence. The fact that she survives and triumphs over her attackers by the end of the novel does not erase the violent reality of this disciplinary rape.

The rape scene in Dorothy Allison's *Bastard out of Carolina* is by far the most detailed and wrenching depiction of rape in the archive of southern lesbian feminism. Allison makes us experience the pain of Bone's rape, as well as Daddy Glen's obvious sexual pleasure in her humiliation and suffering.

"You're not going anywhere." He laughed. "You think you're so grown-up. You think you're so big and bad, saying no to me. Let's see how big you are, how grown!" His hands spread what was left of my blouse and ripped at the zipper on my pants, pulling them down my thighs as my left hand groped to hold them. I tried to kick, but I was pinned. Tears were streaming down my face, but I wasn't crying. I was cursing him. . . .

"*You fucker!*" I punched up at him with my almost useless right arm.

"You little cunt. I should have done this a long time ago. You've always wanted it. Don't tell me you don't." His knee pushed my legs further apart, and his big hand leisurely smashed the side of my face. He laughed then, as if he liked the feel of my blood on his fist, and hit me again. I opened my mouth to scream, and his hand closed around on my throat.

"I'll give you what you really want," he said, and his whole weight came down hard. My scream was gaspy and low around his hand on my throat. He fumbled with his fingers between my legs, opened me, and then reared back slightly, looking down into my face with his burning eyes.

"Now," he said, and slammed his body forward from his knees. "You'll learn." His words came in short angry bursts. "You'll never mouth off to me again. You'll keep your mouth shut. You'll do as you're told. You'll tell Anney what I want you to tell her."

I gagged. He rocked in and ground down, flexing and thrusting his hips. I felt like he was tearing me apart, my ass slapping against the floor with every thrust, burning and tearing and bruising. . . . He started a steady rhythm, "I'll teach you, I'll teach you," and pounded my head against the floor. . . . He reared, up, supporting his weight on my shoulder while his hips drove his sex into me like a sword. . . .

He went rigid, head back and teeth showing between snarling lips. I could feel his thighs shaking against me as my butt slid in the blood under me. . . . He went limp and came down on me, rag-loose and panting. His hand dropped from my mouth, but the urge to scream was gone. Blood and juice, his sweat and mine, my blood, all over my neck and all down my thighs, the sticky stink of him between my burning legs. How had it all happened so fast? I tried to lick my lips, but my tongue was too swollen. I couldn't feel my tongue move, just my lips opening and closing with no sound coming out. Red and black dots swam up toward the ceiling and back down toward me.[68]

This scene is one of the novel's most notorious, figuring in most of the extensive scholarship about *Bastard out of Carolina*. Though most articles refer to the incest, few discuss the specifics of *how* this scene is constructed; usually, scholars quote passages about her rage and avoid the graphic details of the rape itself. Even Ann Cvetkovich, who otherwise discusses incest and trauma with admirable directness, cites with approval Allison's description of this scene: "In an interview with Amber Hollibaugh, [Allison] says, 'I wanted you to know that kid's rage, shame and confusion, but I didn't even want you to know how he put his dick in.'"[69] Yet what is most striking is how explicitly the scene describes the rape. Unlike Cris South, who has her narrator black out the details of the rape, Allison doesn't provide any such relief to Bone or the reader. We may not "know how he put his dick in," but we know exactly how Bone felt when he did.

Allison insists that we see rape as a specifically sexual form of misogynist violence that isn't titillating, but revolting. Daddy Glen's efforts to enhance his own pleasure in Bone's violation intensify the physical pain she endures: "He rocked in and ground down, flexing and thrusting his hips. I felt like he was tearing me apart, my ass slapping against the floor with every thrust, burning and tearing and bruising." And Allison makes us see Glenn's climax; if Bone doesn't understand what is happening, Allison makes sure the reader does: "He went rigid, head back and teeth showing between snarling lips. I could feel his thighs shaking against me as my butt slid in the blood under me. . . . He went limp and came down on me, rag-loose and panting." His physical response—rigid, shaking, panting—contrasts with the blood, bruises, and tears of Bone's physical response. His pleasure in her pain is clear not just in his physiological responses but in his "sex talk," which reads like a primer in rape culture ("You've always wanted it," "I'll give you what you really want") as he educates her about the reality of the patriarchy: shut up, do what you're told, suffer all violence in silence and be grateful for it. His chilling statement at beginning of the rape, "Now you'll learn," marks rape as a pedagogical tool to give Bone what she "deserves" and, in Daddy Glenn's mind, really wanted. Bone's own internal monologue highlights both the self-justification and stupidity of these rationalizations of violence.

There is nothing titillating or delightfully transgressive in either of these rape scenes. Rape isn't queer because it doesn't undermine the normative in patriarchal society; it is a primary disciplinary tool for the patriarchal normative. Some sex is clearly irredeemable, even for Allison, who insists on a place for the grotesque in literary expression.

The Southernness of the Queer: Southern Lesbian Feminist Legacies

The archive of southern lesbian feminism explores transgressive sexuality in explicit detail, from the titillating to the horrifying. In all cases, these writers eschew allusion and shadowy metaphor for an often uncomfortable specificity. This tradition provides a key link between the queer grotesque visions of the Cold War southern gothic and broader heteronormative critiques of queer theory. Southern lesbian feminists' frank depictions of specific sexual acts and gender identities purposely transgressed both community standards and political efficacy. Taken collectively, the archive of southern lesbian feminism is an often overlooked but essential part of the genealogy of queer theory.

4 Women's Space, Queer Space

Communes, Landykes, and Queer Contact Zones in the Lesbian Feminist South

. . . .

The middle-aged man sitting in the row in front of me shoved his wife's arm and pointed at two women. "See?!" he said, conspiratorially, derisively. I looked at my friend Cheryl and raised an eyebrow. Where did he think he was, anyway? The Southeastern Conference (SEC) Women's Basketball Tournament audience is filled with lesbians—butches, femmes, sportsdykes, some distinguished by a modified mullet, others by their no-makeup, tennis shoes, and jeans uniform, but all united in their obsession with women's basketball.

Of course, the tournament audience includes others besides lesbians; like most queer spaces in the South, lesbians share the space with many other groups—retirees, parents and their tween daughters, and random diehard SEC fans who love their team or really hate their rivals. Yet the SEC Women's Basketball Tournament is a roving capital of the southern sisterhood, and it is anything but subtle, but if you ask the fathers and the busloads of white-haired retirees about all the lesbians they will look at you blankly, whether they noticed them or not.

This is because "the South" has always been an imagined community, based in wish fulfillment and aspiration, that depends upon deliberate unlooking. It excludes populations that, collectively, comprise a majority of the population. It excludes black southerners, who understandably have a more ambivalent relationship to the "sense of place" invested in their subordination. It excludes the many immigrant groups that have made the South their home over the generations—Chinese, Lebanese, Italians, and more recently, Indians, Vietnamese, Africans, Hispanics. It ignores queer southern communities in towns both small and large. In other words, the "sense of place" so beloved by traditional southern literary critics overlooks the actual people in that place.

This tendency to disavow the full complexity of diverse communities in the South has a long, shameful history. The Confederacy imagined a southern aristocracy based on honor and culture, obscuring a white supremacy dependent on stolen slave labor. Post-Reconstruction politics did more than rewrite the cause of the Civil War—it also remade the space of the South: Confederate memorial statues were erected, often in town squares or in prominent public locations, as Jim Crow laws limited the spaces and places African Americans could live, work, and recreate.[1] The fact that these public Confederate monuments still dominate southern spaces, and that their removals provoke intense debate and outcry, suggests how effectively this southern space made inequity seem natural.

The ubiquitous notion of a static, conservative South has led to many unwarranted assumptions about LGBTQ communities and their incompatibility in the South. Gay liberation was framed as an urban phenomenon; gay people leave their inhospitable small towns and regions and build a critical mass in major cities like New York and San Francisco, where their visibility and numbers result in political clout and political influence. Greenwich Village in New York and the Castro in San Francisco were two models; pioneer Harvey Milk encouraged queers across the country to join him in paradise.

This metronormativity has been questioned in studies of rural and southern queer spaces like John Howard's *Men Like That*, Mary Gray's *Out in the Country*, and Scott Herring's *Another Country*. Howard's groundbreaking book challenged the linking of gay identity and urban life, insisting that this bias "at times has denied agency to rural folk, [and] has assumed that nonurban dwellers can't attach meanings to, can't find useful ways of framing, their nonconforming attractions and behaviors."[2] He argues that "in Mississippi, spatial configurations—the unique characteristics of a rural landscape—forged distinct human interactions, movements, and sites," and that the urban model "incompletely and inadequately gets at the shape and scope of queer life."[3] He suggests new models for understanding that queer life, decoupled from both identity and a fixed sense of place.

Scott Herring concurs. He provides a detailed overview of the growing scholarship on queer rural communities, concluding that "these artists and authors pay heed to the 'non-metropolitan' as a dynamic space of inquiry and sexual vitality. Complicating geophobic claims that ruralized spaces are always and only hotbeds of hostility, cultural and socioeconomic poverty, religious fundamentalism, homophobia, racism, urbanoia, and social conservatism, their works question knee-jerk assumptions that the "rural" is a hate-filled space for queers as they archive the complex desires that contribute to any non-metropolitan identification."[4] Herring's own work focuses on contemporary artistic portrayals of the rural queer in periodicals, photography, memoirs, and graphic novels.

This work on rural queerness is enhanced by feminist and queer geography, which has provided new paradigms to theorize how ideologies order and impede our understandings of space and how different configurations can remake that sense of space. Jack Geiseking explains that "space is not absolute or fixed in the Kantian sense but constantly produced in how it is all at once created, conceived, and lived."[5] Our "natural" notions of space, in other words, are not innocent; instead, as the Women and Geography Study Group argues, "dominant senses of place reflect, in both their form and their content, the meanings given to places by the powerful."[6] They continue, "A consequence of the way in which very specific senses of place are constructed through the particular images and values attached to them by the socially and culturally powerful, is that senses of place are often highly controversial. Other groups may challenge the senses of place produced by the powerful, and cultural geographers therefore argue that senses of place are often also sites of contestation."[7] This focus on space as a site of contestation serves as a dominant focus of feminist and queer geography. "Space" isn't natural, and it isn't neutral.

Doreen Massey lays out the terms for understanding space beyond the fixed narrative of the powerful. She argues that space is heterogeneous, inhabited by diverse groups of people who often disagree about its functions and purpose. Multiple and relational, space is also open-ended and unfixed. As she explains,

> What is special about place is not some romance of a pre-given
> collective identity or of the eternity of the hills. Rather, what is
> special about place is precisely that throwntogetherness, the un-
> avoidable challenge of negotiating a here-and-now. . . . There can be
> no assumption of pre-given coherence, or of community or collective
> identity. . . . In sharp contrast to the view of place as settled and
> pre-given, with a coherence only to be disturbed by "external"
> forces, places as presented here in a sense necessitate invention;
> they pose a challenge. . . . They require that, in one way or another,
> we confront the challenge of the negotiation of multiplicity.[8]

Massey's insistence that there is no "pre-given coherence" to a space challenges a fundamental assumption about the fixity of the South and rejects the idea that there is some coherent essence of southernness. It constructs space that is always being created in the present moment, negotiating often contradictory perspectives.

Indeed, Massey's notion of "throwntogetherness" allows for radical reimaginations of space: "What I'm interested in is how we might imagine spaces for these times; how we might pursue an alternative imagination. What is needed, I think, is to uproot 'space' from that constellation of concepts in which it has so unquestioningly so often been embedded (stasis; closure; representation) and to settle it among another set of ideas (heterogeneity; relationality; coevalness . . . liveliness indeed) where it releases a more challenging political landscape."[9] The idea of "alternative imagination" of space is a dominant theme in feminist and queer geography. Geiseking privileges the "action of queering: refusing the normative and upsetting privilege for more radical, just worlds, even those not yet imagined,"[10] to "uproariously alter the everyday spatialities of heterosexuality."[11] These disruptions include interventions in "the built environment" and the "landscapes" we construct to represent "nature."

Though studies of this utopian "act of queering" tend to focus on contemporary, urban interventions, the act of queering was central to utopian reimaginations of rural space in early women's liberation. Creating autonomous women's space and queer space was a central focus of women's communes and the landyke movement, which had particular resonance in the archive of southern lesbian feminism.

Landykes, Communes, and Lesbian Idealization of the Rural

Early women's liberation was long engaged with challenging the patriarchal hierarchies of space, both public and private. Many early protests—the sit-in at *Ladies Home Journal*, for example, and the burning of undergarments at the Miss America pageant—were forms of performance art that sought to make visible the seemingly "natural" public spaces allowed to women. These demonstrations intended to smash the public/private distinction that had isolated women and made their concerns a personal failing rather than a structural injustice. The creation of temporary spaces of freedom within a larger heteropatriarchal society—like gay bars and women's music festivals—were another strategy to reconfigure space.

Some lesbian feminists opted for more permanent means of escape that involved experiments in living that were, fundamentally, experiments of spatiality. Grete Rensenbrink explains that "separatist communities emerged in urban areas, especially San Francisco and New York, and increasingly on rural land communes across the United States."[12] These separatist communities often functioned as "collectives" in urban areas; some of the most important manifestos of the early women's movement emerged from collectives, which formed and reformed with alacrity in the early 1970s. Women lived and worked in the same space, breaking down the notions of public and private, masculine and feminine. Collectives broke down hierarchies within private and public lives, as well. Members often rejected the distinction between intellectual labor and physical labor; in press collectives, for example, women both wrote articles, short stories, and poems and physically printed these pieces—sometimes on mimeograph machines and later on letterpresses they bought and taught themselves how to use. There was deep suspicion about "leaders" of these groups; decisions were collectively and democratically reached. Cooking, cleaning, home repair—all were burdens to be shared equally in the collective. Collective members tried to remake space to construct new revolutionary models. They also tried to remake economic models. Frequently, only a few of the members of these collectives had "straight" jobs, which were used to support the entire community. Collectives experimented with different models for self-sufficiency to free themselves from the obligations of capitalist patriarchy. Very few women stayed in these collectives for long; manifestos often had more staying power than the intentional communities that produced them.

Some collective experiments sought physical separation from mainstream society. Research has shown the "the country was an 'ideal' or 'fantasy' place for lesbians to live,"[13] because it seemed to allow for a reinvention of space from the ground up. Sine Anahita explains, "In the early 1970s, the landdyke movement was created when a radical branch of second-wave feminism converged with ideas from the hippie back-to-the-land and other social movements. . . . From the outset, landykes articulated the connections between ecological and feminist principles. Early activists sought to create a network of land-based communities where ecofeminist principles could manifest in everyday acts to prefigure a lesbian feminist, nature-centered, postpatriarchal future."[14] This geographical experiment allowed for more democratic and communal constructions of space to teach, inspire, provide refuge, and influence the larger culture with guerrilla-type actions. Rose Norman, Merril Mushroom, and Kate Ellison, editors of a special issue of *Sinister Wisdom* on the landyke movement in the South, explain that "landykes were creating something larger, beyond a couple or a family. They attempted to live out egalitarian and ecological principles, which they saw as the core of female culture. They attempted this within sometimes stark financial, cultural, and psychological limitations."[15] While the landyke movement was national, the editors suggested that the South has always contained a large share of these experimental communities.[16]

Such movements are controversial and have been denounced as essentialist, white-identified, privileged, and unrealistic, but participants portray them differently. Some are unapologetic in their insistence on a women-only space and cling to essentialist notions of women's innate difference and superiority, but others see the landyke movement as an essential part of their development that allowed for creative rethinking of what is possible in culture, politics, and living. Sarah Shanbaum explained: "We created a closed and separatist environment, and in that closed and separatist environment, we learned and we became strong, and then we broke that like an egg, and went out into the world, and did what it was we wanted to do."[17] Seeing separatism as a necessary phase that led to a broader inclusiveness is common for participants, and it is a pattern that we see in the archive of southern lesbian feminism as well.

Women's space and women's land were essential for the utopian possibilities they fostered. Greta Resenbrink argues that "separatists embraced prefigurative politics, seeking to live the future in the present and working to create communities and local cultures that anticipated a utopian dream."[18] As one landyke participant explained in the documentary *Lesbiana*:

> We were actively rethinking the world. Each time I walked out of the bar, I felt like I was crossing a zone from a fictional world—the life in the bar—into reality—life in the city. And that is how I developed this notion of reality versus fiction. Meaning that women's reality was perceived as fiction by men, and what we called reality, was in fact the accumulation of masculine subjectivity that has been working for centuries establishing laws, traditions, etc. And we called that "reality," but it was nothing more than the male version of reality carried through the centuries. During that time, I was writing two pages. On one page I was trying to figure out the male system, a horrible system, detrimental to women: patriarchy. I was trying to figure out its strategies and its tactics, and how it evolved and was persistent to this day. And on the other page, I was writing about desire, utopia, beauty, pleasure, and everything I was discovering with other women. This is how I stayed in touch with the reality of patriarchy and still I could take flight, into love, lust, sisterhood, and all the discoveries I was making at that time.[19]

The creation of a utopian, liberated space, both actual and imagined, was a key part of early women's liberation. It is why the arts were so enmeshed with political activism; why "consciousness-raising" moved from physical gatherings to novels; why women's press collectives were seen as political activism. Physical and imaginative space were mutually interdependent, and a compelling imagined space might end up having more impact than a physical space.

Many writers in the southern lesbian feminist archive were invested in communes and collectives. Bertha Harris went with a group of lesbian friends (including anthropologist Esther Newton and her then-lover Louise Fishman, the painter) to an upstate New York property owned by Jill Johnston,[20] which served as a weekend getaway and part-time retreat that Harris would later memorialize in *Lover*. Blanche McCrary Boyd joined a commune in Vermont (not an exclusively lesbian commune, though she transforms it into one in *Terminal Velocity*); Rita Mae Brown was part of a women's collective, the Furies, in Washington, D.C., and when she eventually moved to Virginia (after the sale of *Rubyfruit Jungle* to Bantam Books) she didn't establish a commune, but she did buy land.

In *Rebels, Rubyfruits, and Rhinestones*, James T. Sears describes a seamless transition of southern queers from their small southern towns to New York City and back to intentional communities in the South—a fluid circulation that negated neither urban gay communities nor southern identities.[21] The Pagoda community in St. Augustine, Florida, was one of the most famous,[22] but many smaller ones thrived under the radar across the South. Dorothy Allison belonged to a women's collective in Tallahassee, Florida. Catherine Nicholson lived in a collective in Charlotte, North Carolina, but was kicked out for her intergenerational romance with Harriet Desmoines; photographs of the *Sinister Wisdom* group, taken at Nicholson's house on Country Club Drive (with many of the women topless), suggest a faux commune had formed there. And Catherine Ennis, who was so cautious that she wouldn't do readings of her lesbian novels too close to her hometown, appeared in the *Ponchatoula Times* in the mid-1980s with her "artisans" collective; the photograph suggests a lesbian commune flying under the radar.[23] In smaller communities this sort of caution wasn't uncommon. Other communes—usually those in urban centers or college towns in the South—were more open and combative, though often no more visible. The Atlanta Lesbian Feminist Alliance (ALFA), which operated for two decades in the largest urban center in the South and hosted a number of lesbian writers, including southern lesbian feminist writers, was largely unknown in Atlanta proper. The Feminary collective in Durham, North Carolina, was well known within lesbian feminist circles but fairly anonymous inside the Research Triangle. More recent communes include one in Alabama and Camp Sister Spirit in Mississippi.[24]

Despite their many differences in locations, visibility, and intentions, all these communes and collectives served an important function in the archive of southern lesbian feminism. Southern lesbian feminists were deeply invested in the spaces and places of the South. Whether they stayed in the South or fled to New York or San Francisco, they engaged imaginatively and combatively in the remaking of southern place to create a South they did not have to leave. Southern lesbian feminists—white, Latina, and African American—reconsidered their own "sense of place" in regard to their sexual identities and regional inheritance.

Southern lesbian feminist writers reinvent southern space as an imagined kingdom of racial impurities, sexual perversity, and political radicalism. In their imaginary sites of southern space, they include utopian imaginings, communes and collectives, and queer contact zones within the larger communities.

Utopian Imaginings, Speculative Fiction

Joanna Russ was the patron saint of the 1970s feminist speculative novel—a science fiction genre that posited an all-female world free of the patriarchy. A successful science fiction writer before the feminist movement began, Russ was an early critic of misogyny in science fiction, and she wrote one of the most famous feminist speculative novels of the 1970s. Her 1975 *The Female Man* featured women in four parallel universes; one of them, Whileaway, had a complex all-female society. Other novels in this genre included Daughters, Inc.'s *Riverfinger Women* by Elena Nachmann (later Dykewomon) and, arguably, *Lover* by Bertha Harris, whose all-female alternative universe was more aesthetic than otherworldly. All imagine women's worlds as less violent, more equitable, more diverse, and more in tune with the wider natural world than the patriarchy.

Sally Gearhart's 1978 novel *The Wanderground* is part of this tradition, though its insistence on the natural affinity of women and Mother Nature has led to its characterization as an early text of ecofeminism. A southern expatriate, Gearhart grew up in Virginia, attended Sweet Briar College as an undergraduate, and received a master's degree from Bowling Green State before getting her Ph.D. from the University of Illinois. She is one of the few academics in the archive of southern lesbian feminism; at San Francisco State University, she became the first openly lesbian woman to be tenured at a major university and helped to establish one of the first women's studies programs in the country.[25]

The Wanderground was published by the feminist Persephone Press; Rita Mae Brown blurbed it approvingly. The novel's focus on nature reflects Gearhart's southern roots and her queer reinvention of neo-Agrarianism. In connected sketches/stories, Gearhart describes a world in which the misogyny of "the city" led to extreme restrictions on women's freedom, profession, and dress; some women escaped the cities to establish female-only communities. Each story features one woman; sometimes the characters reappear but generally they do not, emphasizing collective rather than individual agency. Communes have a symbiosis with nature that verges on the mystical, and women can communicate telepathically—"mindstretch"—across great distances in groups of two or more. Mindstretch is described thus: "Always open, ever enfolding one another, the channels came together, joined in knowing, making a third entity between the two, yet one at home with them both. The holdings lengthened. Voki felt a familiar center: Artilidea's point of absolute balance, the source from which the old women's life energy seemed to come. As she sought her own balance in her own source she knew already Artilidea's center to be for that time her own and her own for that time to be Artilidea's. The knowing of that knowledge was the earthtouch, the strength-giver, the doubt-dispeller, the lover-loved."[26] A belief in the communion of women, which creates a different energy and a nurturing communication, circulates throughout the novel. Gearhart emphasizes differences between women; she allows them to be prickly, possessive, stubborn, and even wrong, but those differences can always be transcended.

Communion extends beyond women to the natural world. The "hill women" can communicate with animals, asking for their help and even singing together. Some can "windsurf," or fly. They possess a host of magical powers that the men in the city do not, because they live in harmony with nature and don't try to dominate, kill, or control. As one of the guides says to a young woman learning the history of the hill women: "You can do this too, when you learn to separate and see. We can do anything that the old machines could do. And with a good deal less effort. . . . That's the mistake the men made, sisterlove, and made over and over again. Just because it was possible they thought it had to be done. They came near to destroying the earth—and may yet—with that notion. Most of us like to think that even long-ago women could have built what's been called 'western civilization'; we knew how to do all of it but rejected most such ideas as unnecessary or destructive" (145). The queer feminist perspective here is consonant with the landyke movement, but there are also traces of the Agrarians' rejection of capitalism and the gospel of "progress." Harmony with nature is paramount. Where Gearhart differs is in her indictment of both capitalism and patriarchy as impediments to harmony with the land.

The hill women's union with nature is absolute, so much so that nature embraces and protects them. In one mindstretch, women, pine trees, and a panther (Huntsblood) sing a mythic story of love together, creating a distinctive artistic experience:

> Gently, with bare suggestions, Troja shifted the beat to another
> subtle plane. As she slowed the poundings and directed the rhythms,
> she began her humming—a steady single tone. A chorus joined her
> in thirds and sixths—simple things at first for ones so young in
> singing. . . . Now the pine tree joined in the singing. Far away from
> the voices she rustled her needles and swayed her passengers under
> the downpour of sounds. Huntsblood was in ecstasy. His head was
> erect, his eyes closed, his voice an amazing soft obligato. His paws
> pumped on Blasé's breasts in alternate half-time pressures. . . . The
> chorus filled the air, one none had ever heard before or would ever
> hear again, the blending of those particular voices above those
> particular rhythms, with those particular variations, each with the
> other. (74–75)

That harmony, in which women, animals, plants, and the earth itself exist in cooperation, is expressed through aesthetic as well as practical means. Their communion creates art that includes all living beings in partnership. Nowhere is the dream of "women's culture" better symbolized.

The earth itself protects the hill women from the aggression of men in the cities. A hill woman explains: "'Once upon a time,' began Bessie, 'there was one rape too many. Once upon a time . . . the earth finally said 'no.' There was no storm, no earthquake, no tidal wave or volcanic eruption, no specific moment to mark its happening. It only became apparent that it had happened, and that it had happened everywhere'" (158). What happened is simple—men could no longer have erections outside the cities, and so could no longer rape in the countryside. One harrowing flashback describes groups of men in trucks hunting women to assault. After chasing down two women, a rapist is thwarted because he can't get an erection, and the men are then chased back to their vehicles by women united in support of their sisters. Rape is an ongoing horror in the novel, its threat a constant of patriarchy.

The Wanderground often constructs its utopia through essentialism; one character, Bertha, muses on an "essential fundamental knowledge: women and men cannot yet, may not ever, love one another without violence; they are no longer of the same species" (115). It also contains some of the prejudices of lesbian feminist separatists, particularly in its rejection of hyperfeminine gender performance as oppressive. Ijeme's description of a "city woman" teeters on disgust: "a thickly painted face, lacquerstiffened hair, her body encased in a low-cut tight-fitting dress that terminated at mid-thigh; on her legs the thinnest of stockings, and the shoes—were they shoes?—Ijeme could not believe they fit the same part of the anatomy that her own boots covered. How could she walk in these spindly things? And with the flimsy straps that fastened them to her ankles and feet? The dangles that hung from the woman's ears jangled in tune with her bracelets. She clutched a cloth-covered purse to her side" (63). The high femme look—makeup, minidress, heels, jewelry—is rejected as "unnatural" in favor of the androgynous gender performance favored by separatist lesbian feminists. With regard to clothing and culture, *The Wanderground* demonstrates the essentialism that was becoming axiomatic in lesbian feminism.

But the novel complicates that essentialism as the queer erupts in the role of gay men. When hill women go undercover in the cities they are assisted at every step by "the gentles," gay men who give them information and support them in a hostile environment. Indeed, Bertha's rumination about men being a "different species" is prompted by her successful telepathic communication with a gentle. At the end of the novel, the hill women discover that the gentles have created a masculine version of mindstretch to communicate with animals. This knowledge shakes the hill women, prompting one of the gentles to respond, "Does it occur to you that we might have some humanity too? That as a special breed of men we may be on the brink of discovering our own nonviolent psychic powers?" (179). *The Wanderground* isn't willing to accept men in women's communities, but it does contain fierce debates about separatism and concludes that the hill women cannot withdraw completely from other communities and contexts. When the number of hill women in the cities drops, men are able to commit rapes outside the cities. The ecological balance requires that some women engage with the patriarchal system, even if only as undercover agents.

Gearhart's conclusion, that women's communes must have broader coalitions and goals, resonates throughout most of the archive of southern lesbian feminism. Utopian spaces cannot be fully autonomous; they must interact with the outside world in order to transform it, even as communes function as sanctuaries. This theme continues in novels that explicitly discuss women's collectives and communes.

Separatist Communes

Several novels in the archive of southern lesbian feminism are set in separatist communes, making queer space central to the characters' evolution. One of the earliest and most celebratory is June Arnold's 1973 novel about the Fifth Street Women's Building takeover, *The Cook and the Carpenter*; she relocates the action to a small town in Texas. It begins with a long rumination about the landscape of Texas—a framing of the heteropatriarchal status quo that the novel directly challenges. The carpenter, who lived from ages nine to eighteen in Houston, reflects:

> Nine years for Texas is a quarter-hour for every square mile. The carpenter knew na had foolishly wasted most quarter-hours on the same quarter-acres, not even counting the disproportionate time allotted to the milli-mile, nan bed. . . . Na could say only that na knew quarter-acres of Houston, Galveston, Fort Worth; Sugarland and Sweetwater; Kemah, Corsicana, Amarillo; Edith, Alice, Beulah; etc. etc.—separate squares inside which na knew certain repeated figures of the patchwork quilt of unrelated pieces that was Texas: an expanse which agreed to act as a whole only where specific issues needed covering.
>
> The land lay flat and silent, melted down from the few distant hills by a fierce August sun. The carpenter walked around to the east side of the porch and started the sander up again. I don't know Texas, but if "it" has the denier of violence, it probably is true. That thread joins cotton to calico in every state of the world.[27]

Arnold situates her story within the imagined geography of Texas, a site that is really a "patchwork quilt of unrelated pieces that was Texas." "Texas" is an ideology rather than a real place, a coalition of local communities that seem to have little in common but "act as a whole" under particular circumstances, which enforcing an inequitable status quo and uniting against outsiders.

Arnold's provocative last sentence places Texas within another imagined community—the global plantation system. Cotton and calico are symbols of the system of terror, slave labor, and systematic violence that governed plantations "in every state in the world." Recent scholarship connects the U.S. system of slavery to a system across the Americas, including South America and the Caribbean, and one with global colonial reach in Asia and Africa.[28] "Cotton and calico" continue to inform that system of hetero-patriarchy that dominates the lives of people in the South.

Arnold shows us that system in glimpses, in the men who threaten to break into the commune, and in the men in the bar who play a practical joke that causes the carpenter to fall and get their second black eye in Texas (8). The carpenter reflects on the complicated workings of power, what we might call, in contemporary parlance, microaggressions: "Na knew Texas too well to expect its people to be open except to each one's own class, race, sex, national and business equal. Others had to translate their own meanings from the doubletalk, flattery or sarcasm which was the rule. Straight language and level guns were no longer around when the carpenter had been young; now Texans had civilized themselves up to the practical joke, taken from animated cartoons" (7–8). The "doubletalk" later erupts into actual violence, but these early, circuitous warnings help create a climate a fear to control the subordinate. Violence unveils itself systemically, in the drunken misogy-nist who attacks the members of the commune at their carnival and has to be subdued by the carpenter, and in the police who beat them and arrest them, call them "perverts," and strip-search them in cells. Only at the end of the novel do we see the full violence of "cotton and calico," but the land-scape of imagined violence haunts the members of the commune.

In such a landscape, actual and superimposed with patriarchal ideology, how can one fight back? The opening pages of the novel uncover existing networks of resistance. A community member, whom we learn from con-text is African American, has learned of a planned attack on the commune because their husband overheard the white men they were serving. Pretend-ing to sell eggs, they warn the commune members and "walked then back down the driveway, carelessly holding nan empty basket, having stayed no longer than five minutes, just the right amount of time to make a usual de-livery of eggs" (6). This dodge hides resistance within the safe shape of servitude, allowing for counternetworks of knowledge to thrive covertly under the dominant system.

The opening pages thus present dominant, imperialist Texas and then shift to describe alternative spaces and knowledge—or more precisely, over-looked presences and camouflaged spaces. The servants, usually overlooked, evade the surveillance of the violent racist patriarchal state; in this way,

Arnold suggests that subordinates—African Americans, females, queers—negotiate space to create alternative networks of potential resistance, sometimes through strategic coalitions.

That coalition is threatened not just by white men but also by an African American man: "When Will come home na told me what the men had said and all, and I told na there was nothing right about it and I was going to warn you folks over here. Na liked to have jumped out of nan skin. 'You say one word, girl, and I'll lay you upside the house lopsided,' and na come at me like a crazy man. I said, 'The side of this house is big enough for both of us, Mr. Williams, and I ain't afraid of you and I ain't afraid of those men neither.' Well, na hollered and cried and begged and called me baby and I said na was the baby and na didn't need to know every move I made noways and I come over here on my way to work" (5). The language identifies the subordinate African American man within the networks of patriarchal disciplinary violence. Even covert resistance is dangerous and risks punishment, from both dominant and subordinate subjects. Thus, in one layered opening scene, Arnold represents subordinate and queer space, infused with the complicated dynamics of race and gender, and suggests both the desperate need in "Texas" for a radical remaking of hierarchical space and the dangers of such a revolutionary project.

The underground warnings continue when the black press shows up to warn of the raid and especially encourages Leslie (an African American member of the commune) to leave before the white policemen arrive. When Stubby loses custody of their children and then steals them back, the commune hides the children in the black community, counting on its invisibility to the police. There are already fissures within the Texas community, sites of difference and resistance underneath the "deep in the heart of Texas" lore. Indeed, at the end of the novel, the commune members mock this nostalgic view of Texas by ironically singing patriotic songs: "Oh beautiful, beautiful Texas . . . The most beautiful land that I know / The land where our forefathers / Fought in the Alamo . . . You can live on the plains or the prairie / Or down where the sea breezes blow / And still be in beautiful Texas/ The most beautiful land I know" (141). And then they end with a statement on the surveillance state, in a Texas jail: "The eyes of Texas are upon you / All the livelong day / the eyes of Texas are upon you / You can not get away" (141). Underground networks continue to influence the work of the carpenter; open rebellion is punished, and always threatened with violence. But the commune seeks to transform the violent hierarchies of "beautiful Texas" to create a free state, liberated from patriarchy.

It is apparent from the opening passage of the novel that the first strategy to remaking space is linguistic. Arnold uses the gender-neutral pronouns *na* and *nan* to open up an imaginative space in which characters are not defined by gender.[29] Adults do not use their given names; instead, they are identified by the work they do. One gets a sense of their gendered and racial identities only from how outsiders interact with them.

All members of the community consciously and constantly question the assumptions that guide their interactions with each other and the world. The carpenter sees all their work—even the menial labor of woodworking—as part of a larger cultural reimagining: "Reporting, observing, recording, detached—the carpenter in nan earlier work had felt isolated most of the time, even though na had not clearly understood how isolated. Na had become a carpenter to become involved, to break away from detachment, not understanding at all how privileged being a carpenter was, or how the structures which were built by nan hands paralleled the structures previously set up in nan mind" (9). The carpenter's desire to break existing structures and create new ones in which they are central fuel much of their own experience on the commune. They seek freedom through reconstructing space, both metaphorically and materially. "It was the carpenter's fantasy about naself, the one thing na most wanted to be—a non-be, in a sense, completely fluid. . . . The reason na had become a carpenter was the lust of nan hands to touch, grasp, caress, move or change the shape of whatever was accessible. To see what structures could be dissolved but also to restructure in wood and nails—geometrically, to organize space, interrupt air" (86). We might refer to the carpenter's ideal identity as nonbinary, and indeed, the use of the gender-neutral pronoun "na" is an attempt to imagine a world outside the gender binary. Yet even this utopian and "separatist" political commune is never completely apart from the larger Texas landscape, nor does it want to be. The commune is constantly looking for ways to connect with the larger community—creating a public resource for the whole community in the school takeover; meeting with Hispanic groups; connecting with women in different classes and ethnic communities; reaching out to other potential allies. Its utopian thrust is not insular but revolutionary.

In the linguistic and physical space of the novel, living spaces are communal. Children do not stay with their biological parents, and the hierarchies between children and parents are challenged. Children are allowed their own autonomy and must interact with parents as independent beings, with the right to their own sexuality. Even falling in love is a communal event; when the cook reveals the carpenter's private declaration to the group, the carpenter feels exposed and betrayed but must keep pushing against her discomfort with groups.

> Then the cook spoke. "Something really beautiful happened to me this afternoon, something I want to share with the group. A person I've known and loved as a friend for two years did something that took more courage than I have—we all know how afraid we all are of being rejected. This person came up to me and said, 'I love you,' meaning 'in love.' Because na had the courage to grow."
>
> The carpenter's ears felt boxed with echoes. Na heard nan own sacred urgent embrace coupled with the story of the child who cried to announce that nan need was to win, and both things described by the phrase, "guts to take a new step." A hundred miniature alarms ringed the carpenter's brain. . . .
>
> Then through the ringing one word came clearly, "mind." The carpenter shook nan brain to dismantle the clocks and listen; the cook's voice was pointing at the carpenter's head and was hoping that the other person did not mind na (the cook) saying this, that na (the cook) was sure the other person (now clearly the carpenter) did not—"none of us came all the way to Texas to protect our privacy, the one thing we all know kept us locked up in the hope chests of the system back there." (22)

The cook's characterization of privacy as the thing that kept them locked in the "hope chests of the system" insists on a fundamental reinvention of societal structures. Seemingly, private acts have serious cultural and political consequences; saying "I love you" becomes a model of revolutionary potential. Later, when Three (the cook's ex-lover) arrives and takes up with the carpenter, even that shift is seen publicly and no one can complain or denounce it, because rejecting privacy involves rejecting marriage as a form of ownership. When Three says to the carpenter, "Our most serious revolutionary is into possessing nan lover? You want to own me!" (108), it is the most devastating accusation they can make in the liberated space of the commune.

In Arnold's vision, transforming the commune, the larger culture, and the consciousness of the participants are inseparable aims. "The two things we are trying to do—set up a counterculture and make a revolution . . . it's hard to do at the same time" (49), the carpenter explains. The process continues experimentally. The carnival that the commune memebers host on the day of the planned attack confounds community members' expectations.

When one woman visits the "women's health" booth, she objects to its lack of support for "family values":

> "Well, I think you're in the wrong town. Our young people still get married, thank heavens." The voice recited this indignation as a matter of form; above, the eyes were green with curiosity. "You mean you examine people—girls—you give medical examinations and things like that?"
>
> "We have classes to teach people how to examine themselves, too." Carter smiled deliberately, exaggerating naself. "Why, I bet you couldn't draw an accurate picture of female genitals with everything in the right place—clitoris, vagina, urethra, both sets of lips—they call them labia, you know." (33–34)

Sex keeps appearing as a disciplinary tool; the eyes "green with curiosity" frame the experiment of the commune in purely sexual terms. When Tiny insists on seeing the carpenter's drawing of female genitalia and they refuse, the encounter erupts into violence.

The focus on transgressive sexuality comes to the fore when the commune challenges patriarchy by taking over an abandoned school and claiming it as a community center on behalf of the people of the town. This is their most public defiance of the status quo, but in their planning they struggle with *how* to make sexuality a centerpiece of their work:

> "Whatever we call this center, I know what it is: it's a revolution against the slave-family, the slave-house, the slave-bed and the whole copulating system."
>
> "Leslie?"
>
> "I think we should think about it first before we come out strong against marriage and the family. The black people in town . . . marriage is a kind of status thing with us because we've always been put down for not getting married and not having stable families and all." (92)

The different contexts in which sexuality functions become central to the debate, but so too does the question of intersectionality; members of the community are not just white, and the community as a whole works to include race, ethnicity, and class in its understanding of gender. They fail, as the experiment itself inevitably fails, but the struggle is central to the utopian remaking of space. When Leslie says, "Right now I feel like a tangle of bits of string. Now am I supposed to identify with the oppressed gay people or the oppressed black people. . . . I could divide myself up by race or class or sex or money or age or past or future. Shit, man, I'm a fucking rat's nest of oppressed parts" (100), that struggle is central to the remaking of space.

The commune members issue a press release as part of their action in an attempt to protect themselves through publicness; with this, Arnold presents a case study in the dangers of using the media for revolutionary purposes. From the commune's long list of demands, all the media focuses on is the gay and lesbian community center; the commune is only queer in the mainstream imagination. The violent takeover of the commune—described in excruciating detail—is grounded in homophobic slurs that justify the violent suppression of women's rights.

Despite the action's failure to transform the broader culture, however, the commune does make a difference. The effort to construct different patterns for living defies the system they resist; in jail, the unified consciousness they have been working toward finally coalesces: "They were joined to each other like the petals of a five-point flower, dependent upon the joining for any life at all. An extreme consciousness of physical self was the center of their flower, awareness of individual body outlines which exaggerated the previous absence of such a separation into forms of flesh. . . . The space they had created (up until now) for themselves had formed a vacuum wherein they could scatter and diverge, where shape was unnecessary; a totally safe, conflictless space within which all tensions, attacks, storms were between/among their own members" (140). The utopian remaking of space and place the commune in *The Cook and the Carpenter* works toward isn't just impractical dream making; it has concrete value as a site of resistance in the "act of queering." Though the cook and the carpenter leave the commune at the end of the novel, it is clear that what they learned in the commune will continue to inform their revolutionary practices, wherever they settle.

Arnold's novel, the most direct celebration of landyke space set in the South, was published in 1973, when Arnold and women's liberationists still believed that communes could transform the wider culture. Other commune novels in the archive of lesbian feminism are set outside the South and range from satire to nostalgia. Florence King's 1982 novel *When Sisterhood Was in Flower* has been largely forgotten, even by fans of her 1975 *Southern Ladies and Gentlemen* and 1985 *Confessions of a Failed Southern Lady*. The book is out of print, which is unfortunate because it is a fascinating and revealing cultural artifact that combines the writer's witty hostility toward the feminist movement with quirky commitment to equality and liberated space.

When Sisterhood Was in Flower was framed as a satire of the women's liberation movement. A note in the 1982 Viking edition says that "a portion of this book originally appeared in *Penthouse* in slightly different form."[30] At a time when the lesbian sex wars were raging, Dorothy Allison was being publicly pilloried, and Barbara Grier would soon be denounced for selling an excerpt of *Lesbian Nuns* to *Penthouse*, King's decision to publish in *Penthouse* is telling. The opening of the novel establishes her literary bona fides. After an epigraph from Henry James's *The Bostonians*, King writes "Call me Isabel. The story of how I was shanghaied into the feminist movement begins in Boston in the politically pulsating year of 1971" (1). "Call me Isabel" is a send-up of the opening sentence of *Moby-Dick*, suggesting another epic journey in largely uncharted territory and a dramatic self-reinvention of the narrator; the name Isabel suggests Henry James's heroine Isabel Archer from *Portrait of a Lady*, a naïve woman abroad who is exploited by seeming friends in an unfamiliar culture. The novel's setting and epigraph suggest it is an updated version of *The Bostonians*, which critiqued the nineteenth-century feminist movement and included southern expatriates. Finally, the verb *shanghaied* equates feminism with white slavery, titillating the reader with sexual innuendos ("pulsating").

King circulates some of the most common stereotypes of the women's movement—that is it humorless, collectivist, focused on absurd causes and politically correct prescriptions—and spoofs the trends Arnold considers so earnestly. Feminist Polly Bradshaw first appears on her talk show advocating a birthing bucket filled with elephant dung; the other feminist causes that continue to surface throughout the novel are equally ridiculous. Polly's anti-intellectualism and utter lack of a sense of humor lead to painful group planning sessions. A trial of a manufacturer of female blow-up dolls accused of sexism generates double entendres and the dismissal of the spectator gallery, the clerk, and the bailiff for raucous laughter. And a collective approach to producing scrapple ends with an entire birthing bucket of scrapple rolling down the street and smashing into a police car.

King mocks feminist print culture with equal verve. Isabel is irked by the large book contracts feminists are receiving in 1971, so she joins a women's commune to gather material for her own prospective advance. When she is invited to edit *The Enchanted Clitoris*, a feminist periodical, Isabel discovers feminists' crimes against good writing. Isabel is not permitted to reject anything or improve anyone's writing: "Everyone has a right to his or her own English. . . . If you correct someone else's writing, you set up a structured relationship" (125). The sex toy advertisements that appear in *The*

Enchanted Clitoris seem to undermine its feminist ideals. King's satire of feminism—especially its radical, collectivist wing—is wicked, and her "royalist" narrator embraces both individualism and intellectualism.

But despite her disdain for the collectivist impulses of the women's commune, King does explore her own version of women's land and queer space. Isabel meets Polly Bradshaw through a violent remaking of space: the flimsy particleboard wall that separates their apartments is torn in two by a wayward bomb-making operation in the basement: "What really riveted my attention was the fiberboard wall that separated me from my next-door neighbor. It was starting to take on all the elements of a Regency novel: a ripping noise like the heroine's bodice, a corner-to-corner slit like the villain's grin, a buckling like the old baronet's knees, and a waft of powder filling the air as though from a dowager's dusted bosom. And of course, since no Regency is complete without the collapse of an olde English sea wall, the two-by-four studs snapped in half and Gioppi's chintzy room-divider gave up the ghost" (14). Space is fragile and malleable; the disruptions of 1960s radicalism suddenly brings a southern conservative and a New England reformer together—now as roommates. No matter much Isabel disdains the era's social movements, she embraces these egalitarian juxtapositions.

When Polly Bradshaw, WASP scion, inherits a house, a migration and another transformation of space occurs, to great comic effect. Though the house is in California, it evokes the southern gothic:

> It was the biggest house I had ever seen, with all sorts of Queen Anneish things dripping and hanging and thrusting all over it. There were three full stories, plus an attic, veranda, turret, and widow's walk. The back practically hung out over the sea.
>
> We all got out and said "Well, here we are" several times. Then a silence fell, which Gloria promptly filled.
>
> "It looks like the house in *Psycho*." (85)

The size of the house—"eight bedrooms, drawing room, parlor, dining room, cellar, attic, eat-in kitchen, walk-in pantry, wrap-around veranda, three-car garage, and a detached workshop" (91)—places it within a southern plantation imaginary, and the cast of eccentric characters would not be out of place in a Capote novel: Gloria, the druggie/medievalist (whom they found on a beach in Massachusetts and brought with them to California); Agnes, an escaped survivalist wife who steals more than 6,000 cigarette coupons (who saw Polly on the news in California and ran to their motel room, tapping "SOS" in morse code on the door); Martha, the southern wife of a man who divorced her in favor of a blow-up doll named Delilah, whom he named as his heir in his will (who was brought to the commune by the feminist lawyer who handled her case); Edna, Isabel's aunt who has had a decades-long affair with her boss, an Episcopal priest (and came to visit her niece). The comic touch of the novel makes these characters lovable.

King satirizes the remaking of the space as the "Don't Tread on Me" women's commune. The pigpen, the garden, the group cooking projects—all are depicted ridiculously. But later, the safe space of the commune is violated by Agnes's violent husband; he takes her hostage in a scene that doesn't mince words about his misogyny or his violence. As the television news reports:

> "The terrorist's name is Boomer Mulligan, president of a group
> that calls itself 'Stop Women's Lip.' I have a copy of their latest
> newsletter, *The Wife Beater*, which contains an interview with
> Mr. Mulligan telling of his plan to capture his runaway wife, Agnes,
> who fled to the commune. Mr. Mulligan, who is a survivalist, is
> armed and dangerous and has told WNLA that he has placed explo-
> sives around the house and yard. . . .
>   "Can you tell us how your wife feels?"
>   "She's okay, dumb as ever. Never mind her. . . . This is my wife
> and I'm gonna fuck her." (175, 177–178)

Boomer embodies violent patriarchy, raping his wife to exert his dominance. Though King's novel is a satire, it still critiques the misygony endemic in patriarchal culture.

In the end, the house's very gothic qualities allow the women to save themselves—Gloria crawls through the attic, gets the drop on the survival-ist, and subjects him to the fate of Edward II, using a hot curling iron in-stead of a poker. Boomer's scream "was an unearthly sound, like something coming out of a misty bog, so shrill and full of agony that it was impossible to tell whether it was the voice of a man or a woman" (179). Gloria's protection of their commune unmans the misogynist, and his inability to control the women's space leads to a queer spectacle: "Naked except for his Australian hat, Boomer lay on his stomach groaning and coughing at once. His eyes were open in an expression of dumb shock, as though he could not believe what had happened to him. Neither could the horrified newsmen. It took a seasoned Edward II scholar to remain blasé at the sight of Gloria's curling iron sticking out of his ass" (180). Gloria's revenge against a rapist and an abuser is radical, and it is celebrated in the novel. As much as Isabel loathes feminism, by the end of the novel, feminism is resurgent and relevant. The case of Agnes, a battered wife who escapes her husband with two black eyes, only to be recaptured and raped by him, suggests that feminism is more than the hysterical rantings of frigid women.

Feminism provides the solution to a number of the commune members' woes: Isabel's aunt Edna can marry her minister paramour because his wife leaves him for a lesbian lover; Gloria, a drug addict medievalist, trains to be an Episcopal minister, a job that is possible only because of feminism; Agnes is free from her abusive husband and finds work as the minister's secretary; and Polly and Martha start a business together. Collectivism and leftist slogans are rejected, but the characters of individual women are fostered through women's liberation. In the end, Isabel invites all members of the commune to return with her to Virginia and set up a southern version of their commune that presumably will be more decadent and less collective than the California version, but feminist nonetheless. Like Arnold, King returns imaginatively to the South, but for King's characters, the South is the solution to their collective problems rather than the site of their defeat. Her vision of liberation is more individual than communal, but it allows her to imagine a space within the South that can embrace the misfits and outsiders of the feminist commune.

King's satire of lesbian communes is hilariously sharp but ultimately kindhearted. Blanche McCrary Boyd's 1998 novel *Terminal Velocity*, by contrast, is both serious and melancholy. It takes a nostalgic look at the commune: its experimentation with drugs and sex, its radical remaking of relationships, and the danger it posed to established mores. Boyd introduces the commune in the opening pages of the novel as an enterprise already doomed, depicting the dissolution of paradise before discussing its function and purpose.

> In 1970 I realized that the Sixties were passing me by. I had never even smoked a joint, or slept with anyone besides my husband. A year later I had left Nicky, changed my name from Ellen to Rain, and moved to a radical lesbian commune in California named Red Moon Rising, where I was playing the Ten of Hearts in an outdoor production of *Alice in Wonderland* when two FBI agents arrived to arrest the Red Queen.

> The Red Queen was my lover, and her name, I thought, was
> Jordan Wallace. It turned out that she was Nancy Jordan, and a flyer
> about her was hanging in post offices all over the country.[31]

This passage is a model of concision. It also takes all the drama out of the plot of the novel. We already know who Jordan really is, and we also know that the radical experiment of Red Moon Rising is a failure, because Boyd begins with its invasion by "the Man." It is as if June Arnold began *The Cook and the Carpenter* with the raid on the school and never used *na* at all. Even Florence King, whose sarcastic opening lets us know that the "kidnapping" of Isabel is temporary, doesn't give away the most dramatic parts of her plot in the opening paragraphs; as a writer of genre fiction, she knew that the curling iron needed to be a surprise.

So why does Boyd take the suspense out of her plot? Possibly it is because of her own ambivalence about women's liberation, and the landyke movement specifically. When *The Revolution of Little Girls* was published in 1992, it was marketed as if it were a newcomer's debut, with no reference to Boyd's previous publications. *Revolution* was my first introduction to Boyd; I had no idea that she had published two novels in the 1970s, because she will not allow them to be reprinted. (She did agree to republish her 1978 collection of essays, *The Redneck Way of Knowledge*, with an introduction by Dorothy Allison.) Boyd spent most of the 1970s in an alcohol- and drug-induced haze, and she associates her early novels with an addiction she struggled very hard to overcome; I suspect that she connects her embrace of extremes to the radicalism of early women's liberation as well. The radical reimagining of the commune, including its rejection of all conventions and rules, led Boyd into risky behavior that she seems to regret.

As much as *Terminal Velocity* is a memorial of the utopianism of women's communes, it is also a dirge. In Boyd's telling, the transgression of boundaries was idealistic but doomed, and it leaves the novel's narrator, Ellen Burns, with years of regret. The structure of the novel sustains this vision; only part one focuses on the experimentation of the commune, and that is framed by the imminent loss of paradise. Part two follows the two lovers as fugitives from the FBI and depicts Ellen's total breakdown; part three skips ahead years to Ellen's meeting with Jordan's daughter. Less than half of the novel focuses on the communal experiment, which is seen mainly in flashbacks. Boyd never wants the reader to get caught up in the idealism of the commune.

Only within those parameters, safe in the knowledge of its imminent demise, does Boyd present the theory and practice of the lesbian feminist commune, which is countercultural, not explicitly political. Two members of the commune, Jordan and Ross, leave the California commune for a political action in Boston, but such explicit political activism is rare. Mainly, they stay at the California commune and get high on "a mixture of acid, psilocybin, marijuana, nitrous oxide, and white wine."[32] Though their experiments with drugs are depicted as consciousness raising, it becomes clear that for Ellen, drug use is part of a loss of control. The remaking of space here is mainly internal, not external; the commune pretends to be a collective endeavor but it is actually an expensive retreat made possible by a large inheritance.

But it is sex that becomes the main focus of Red Moon Rising's radicalism. Sex was part of the communal remaking of space and place in *The Cook and the Carpenter* but not the primary focus. Here, making a revolution is the same as making a counterculture:

> "The Western Revolution will not be economic," Ross said. "We're postscarcity in the West. One upheaval will be social and sexual, aimed at the very root of the patriarchy, which is, inarguably, sexism."
>
> "I suppose you've heard," Amethyst said, "that the personal is political. Which means everything is political. Who you sleep with is political."
>
> He seemed to hear part of this. "Vat? Who I am sleeping?"[33]

That final bewildered response—"Vat?"—is typical of how *Terminal Velocity* treats women's liberation theory as nonsensical, overblown jargon that doesn't explain the experiment actually going on. It was not politics but sex that radicalized a former Duke sorority girl and made her an outlaw and fugitive.

Artemis Foote and Jordan Wallace induce Ellen's transformation through their sexual charge, their playful engagement with the mainstream, and their awakening of uncontrollable sexual urges. Sex, in a very real sense, causes a psychic split in Ellen. She loses her public, conventional persona—Ellen Sommers—to the suppressed parts of herself and becomes the anarchic and reckless "Rain Burns." When Rain describes sex with Jordan as an out-of-body experience, it is threatening, not liberating: "I was making a growling sound from deep in my chest. The floor and the walls were growling too, and the earth seemed to be rising through the floor. Then light shot through me, light split me up the center, shrieked through my mouth, and I seemed to be hurtling through space. Great shudders racked me as I reentered the atmosphere, *don't let me break apart.* . . . The earth spread itself out before me, and I saw the ridges of the Sierra Nevada covered with snow, the ocean in Mendocino, a house in a clearing, the tiny sliver that was two naked women lying in a bed."[34] Sex is shattering, a notion the queer theorist Leo Bersani would endorse. But the larger framing of the novel shows that this dissolution of a grounded identity and grounded space is madness, not only for Ellen/Rain but also for Jordan and Artemis. Indeed, the association of radical feminism with mental illness was made in the notorious *New Yorker* profile of Shulamith Firestone that used her mental breakdown as a metaphor for the breakdown radical feminism as a whole.[35] To imagine a radical transformation of the heteropatriarchy, Boyd suggests, is to court madness.

The self-smashing sex of *Terminal Velocity* is not only ungrounding but also antithetical to the grounded space of the South. Ellen's southernness is framed in opposition to her newfound radicalness. California is the radical place, as far from southern tradition and landscape as one can imagine. Her southernness is opposed to her lesbianism—nowhere does Ellen/Rain imagine that these two poles can be merged. After her mind-blowing sex, Ellen feels homesick, not for her husband or for Boston, but for the South of her childhood: "So I told her about Charleston, about smells as earthy and salty as cemeteries and the ocean, where the air is heavy and moist, pressing down, and mosses drape the shaggy oaks like scenes in horror movies. I told her I'd grown up in a bad Southern movie, a B movie with characters too weird to believe. I told her I still thought of myself as a person from another country, a defeated, annexed country, and that if I spoke with my real accent she wouldn't even understand what I was saying."[36] Note the Fugitive-like commitment to place in this description that draws on stereotypes of the South—cemeteries, moss, an annexed nation—and yet contrasts this imaginary South with the falsity of her California sojourn; only her southern accent is real. The commune, by contrast, is a dream that quickly becomes a nightmare.

The commune can provide no permanent haven; indeed, it seems to hasten the narrator's fractured breakdown. The commune and the South are binaries in the novel. This may be why, even in the section on the commune, so much of the exposition is framed by Ellen's immanent departure. The very structure of *Terminal Velocity* suggests that a utopian reinvention of space is impossible. When on the run with Jordan, Ellen is caught shoplifting, and she asks the store owner: "Am I in Denver?" "I guess it's hard not to know where you are," he said. "I'm from South Carolina."[37] Ellen doesn't know where she is, and though her response "I'm from South Carolina" seems like it doesn't follow, it is an attempt to reground herself by claiming her identity as a southerner. She is institutionalized by force, and upon her release she moves to Los Angeles and writes for a Confederate sitcom called *Rise Again* in an ironic attempt to remake her southern identity. After witnessing the suicide of her lover Jordan, Ellen returns to South Carolina to try to ground herself in the space of the South. But it is clearly not a radical South; communes do not thrive in the South that Boyd imagines.

Boyd is invested in making sense of communes and the radical feminist movement. She draws many of the same type of characters and situations that appear in the novels of Arnold and King—the dogmatic Marxists, the group meetings where one character criticizes another, the evangelical belief in the power of sex to transform the community. Bertha Harris, too, looms over the novel; when Ellen takes drugs and has a sexual experience with the earth in the garden, Boyd references the famous scene from Harris's *Confessions of Cherubino*. The commune's staging of a musical, *Alice Does Wonderland*, a delightful reworking of the famous porn movie *Debbie Does Dallas*, is also an homage to Harris, whose all-women's commune in *Lover* performs *Hamlet* outdoors. Even the smoked glasses Ellen wears at the end of the novel reference Harris, who was famous for wearing these glasses in New York in the 1970s.[38] I suspect that the super-rich Artemis Foote, from a well-to-do Texas family, bears more than a passing resemblance to June Arnold. The attraction and hatred Ellen feels toward her, and the sexual revenge she takes on her, may relate to Boyd's own resentment of Arnold, who refused to let Boyd republish her first novel *Nerves* with a mainstream press in the 1970s, but Boyd creates a reconciliation between the two characters at the end of the novel.

The novel's final scene—eight years later, when Ellen takes Jordan's daughter to meet Artemis Foote in England—attempts to make sense of the legacy of communes. It recognizes the potent emotional forces that communal experiments unleashed and suggests that they could not contain such power. Ellen, finally sober, needs to keep the anarchic power of utopian communes at a safe remove. In her telling, the last scene is a melancholic, regretful benediction to a movement that is over.

Beyond Communes: Queer Contact Zones
in the Lesbian Feminist South

Pensacola, Florida, is part of what's known in the South as the "redneck Riviera." It caters largely to inhabitants of the deep South, who can make it to Florida's white sand in six hours from Louisiana, Arkansas, Tennessee, Mississippi, Alabama, and Georgia. Add to that a major Navy base in Pensacola, and you know what kind of place Pensacola is—conservative, patriotic, defiantly southern.

Unless you arrive in Pensacola on Memorial Day. Then you see something unexpected: a "tent city" with rainbow flags, SEC flags, and national flags of other countries (like Australia). Alumni from different schools share pleasantries (we heard many "Hotty Toddys" by our tent, which flew the only Ole Miss/pride flag combination we saw on our part of the beach). Strangers wander by offering jello shots, and sometimes just shots directly into your mouth. Queers young and old drag huge coolers of beer down the beach to their tents, just as they would at football tailgates in the fall. It is a defiantly queer version of southern decadence. For those who live in gay neighborhoods in New Orleans or Memphis or Atlanta or Miami, this is simply an extension of a gay party scene; at night, circuit parties dominate at bars and on the beach. For others, those who live in small towns or rural outposts, Pensacola Pride is a magical occurrence, not unlike the discovery of Oz. During the last week of May, queer southerners take over the city of Pensacola and hold the beach for a week, marking their territory. When the week ends it disappears, and the redneck Riviera reasserts itself. Most straight southerners, even the progressives, have never heard of Pensacola Pride. But almost every queer southerner I know has.

· · · · · ·

Though women's communes still exist, they are no longer the potent cultural force they once were. But queer space continues to thrive, in spaces that aren't visibly queer. We are still developing the language and the methodology to recognize and analyze a more fluid notion of queer space; to do so, we need to rethink some of our bedrock assumptions about queer communities. The metronormative narrative focuses on "gay ghettos" in cities like San Francisco, Chicago, and New York, but even urban areas with a concentration of queer voters were never solely gay spaces. Greenwich Village was known as a haven for anarchists, radicals, and other outsiders long before it became a center of gay life (indeed, that is one reason it became such a center). The Castro was an Italian neighborhood before it became a refuge for hippies and queers, and though it has maintained its reputation as a gay neighborhood, gentrification has transformed it significantly. This is true of every gay neighborhood in every major city.

Considering lesbian spaces complicates the metronormative model even more. Lesbian spaces in urban areas have always been visibly heterogeneous. Manuel Castells's classic study of urban life argues that lesbians tend to be less territorial in their constructions of queer space, building coalitions with other groups and considering issues beyond queer identity; "Lesbians," he explains, "tend to be politically much more radical and willing to make the connection of personal issues to the transformation of society, to be the marching wing of the women's liberation movement."[39] Other geographers have challenged this idea, arguing that "lesbians do create spatially concentrated communities but that 'the neighbourhood has a quasi-underground character; it is enfolded in a broader countercultural milieu.'"[40] Despite these differences, both arguments get at a similar idea: lesbian space tends to be shared, in coalition or in tandem with other groups. The Mission District in San Francisco, long a Hispanic neighborhood, was simultaneously, from the 1970s until the 1990s, also a radical lesbian neighborhood. The Squirrel Hill District in Pittsburgh was a lesbian neighborhood in the early 2000s, but it was also a long-standing Jewish neighborhood that included Orthodox communities. Perhaps because they lacked the financial clout of upper-crust gay men, lesbian communities have been more intersectional in their creation of queer space—their own spaces do not preempt or exclude other uses of space.

In rural areas, simultaneous use of space is mandatory for all queers, who can rarely construct a critical mass to exert political clout. Mary Gray explores this idea in *Out in the Country*, as a queer youth group "do some drag at Wal-Mart," transforming "Wal-Mart into a meeting space, drag revue, and shopping excursion all rolled into one."[41] Gray terms such use of space "*boundary publics*: iterative, ephemeral experiences of belonging that circulate across the outskirts and through the center(s) of a more recognized and validated public sphere."[42] For Gray, the space of Wal-Mart, or a Methodist youth group, "is not definably or definitely queer, but its open-endedness allows for queer definitions and understandings to be written into the space."[43] Such boundary publics are adaptable, flexible, and ephemeral: "These worlds nest and intersect, but they also layer and enmesh multiple publics in indissoluble ways. Rural queer youth recycle the spaces around them, then occupy them for as long as they can. It is temp work at best."[44] Gray's boundary publics make visible the creation of queer spaces in the South, which are generally invisible to the mainstream, temporary or fluid, and hiding in plain sight. Like Pensacola Pride, they are permanent fixtures that last for only one week every year in cities otherwise known for their conservativism; or, like Ajax Diner in Oxford, Mississippi, they emerge only at a certain time of night, and go unnoticed by the Republican southerners who walk right past; or, like the Code Pink queer parties in Oxford, they erupt for one night only. Southern queer space is rarely permanent, but it is still potentially transformative.

In a presentation at the 2007 Faulkner conference (a lesbian reading of Faulkner's *Absalom! Absalom!*), I called these contested spaces "queer contact zones." *Contact zone* is a term invented by Mary Louise Pratt to discuss cultural encounters between different cultures, in an attempt to move beyond the notion of the frontier (and its hierarchy of civilization and savagery).[45] I used the term to discuss eruptions that exist within and in opposition to hierarchical southern space, arguing that Judith and Clytie created a subversively queer space on Sutpen's Hundred in *Absalom, Absalom!* Judith and Clytie, marked as a couple by Rosa's lesbian panic, create a society counter to white supremacy by recognizing illegitimate, mixed-race siblings as part of the family:

> Fragile and transitory, these . . . contact zones construct refuges
> from the South's hegemonic metanarrative. . . . Male narrators . . .
> see this dynamic queer refuge as a symbol of the South's decay, an
> apocalypse in which "the Jim Bonds are going to conquer the
> western hemisphere," until "I who regard you will also have sprung
> from the loins of African kings" (302). For Judith, though, who gave
> her life to save Charles Bon's descendants, Jim Bond's eventual
> triumph would simply extend the logic of the queer contact zone
> across the Southern landscape. She considered her dead fiancé's
> mixed-race grandson as not only family but legitimate heir, the
> proper representative of the mulattas, queers, spinsters, and maroons
> of her family tree. Judith's Hundred, and the other lesbian contact
> zones of Southern literary traditions, are integrated into the larger
> Southern community, providing a refuge from heteronormative
> restrictions for gay and straight alike.[46]

This queering of the plantation space is a direct challenge to the hazy glow of nostalgia that undergirds so much mainstream southern myth making. And while it doesn't transform the larger society, it does provide an alternative from which other challenges might potentially grow (as I discuss in chapter 2). I suggest that the dream of women's land and queer land in the South continues, both in actual spaces and in the literary imagination. Unlike communes, which are meant to be permanent outposts, these spaces are often transitory, frequently invisible, and usually a contact zone for all kinds of cultural outsiders, who discover their strength in coalition.

Dorothy Allison never completed her novel about her own experience in a lesbian commune, but the legacy of communes and utopian spaces is seen in her writing. In *Bastard out of Carolina*, Bone's aunt Raylene creates a commune of one. She lives in a rented house, but unlike her siblings, she stays in the same place. Her home was "easy to get to on the Eustis Highway but set off by itself on a little rise of land. . . . From the porch that went around three sides, you could watch the river and the highway that skirted it. Raylene kept the trees cut back and the shrubs low to the ground. 'I don't like surprises,' she always said. 'I like to see who's coming up on me.'"[47] Raylene's home suggests a strategic outpost—one she can defend, if necessary. It is significant that Bone's rape takes place not at Raylene's, as the movie version suggests, but at another aunt's house that had been the site of another horrifying scene of domestic violence. Raylene's home is a communal space to escape from, and heal from, the violence of the dominant culture.

Raylene "kept her gray hair cut short, and wore trousers as often as skirts," and her friends were "the widowed choir director and two of the local schoolteachers" (179). The queer encoding of these details is clear; for those paying attention, her queer identity, revealed at the end of the novel, is not a surprise. But her way of surviving in a hostile climate is distinctive: she supplements her small pension with gardening and scavenging: "Aunt Raylene's house was scrubbed clean, but her walls were lines with shelves full of oddities, old tools and bird nests, rare dishes and peculiarly shaped rocks. An amazing collection of things accumulated on the river bank below her house. People from Greenville tossed their garbage off the highway a few miles up the river. There it would sink out of sight in the mud and eventually work its way down to Aunt Raylene's, where the river turned, then rise to get caught in the roots of the big trees" (181). Employed by Raylene, Bone "dragged stuff up from the river—baby-carriage covers, tricycle wheels, shoes, plastic dishes, jump-rope handles, ragged clothes, and once the headlight off a Harley-Davidson motorcycle" (182). Raylene is delighted by her work: "I can clean and patch the clothes up. We'll just soak the dishes in bleach and give the rest of it a scrubbing. Saturday morning we'll put out blankets and sell it off the side of the road" (182).

Raylene creates a new version of the independent yeoman farmer, whom Jefferson thought was the backbone of democracy. Only in this case, she earned independence by making value out of the detritus of capitalism. Like the trash of the river, Allison's people are seen as throwaway lives, and none more so than a gender nonconforming white trash queer like Raylene. Yet she has made an autonomous space on the margins, transforming the discarded refuse of the society into an independent life. She has also created a hidden queer space on the margins, providing Bone with the only refuge from the cycle of abuse she witnesses and experiences. Raylene's house is a Southern prototype of the lesbian commune, a commune anchored by lesbians but not exclusive to them. That queer contact zone is a legacy of the landyke movement, enacting a more inclusive version of alternative space. Queer contact zones appear in a number of southern lesbian feminist texts, inviting cultural outsiders to create a more inclusive South.

The queer contact zone is also central to Fannie Flagg's *Fried Green Tomatoes*. Idgie Threadgoode is the youngest member of a large, prosperous southern family in Whistle Stop, Alabama, whose refusal to wear a dress to her sister's wedding marks her as a butch—though she is never identified as such. Indeed, the normalization of Idgie is one of the most notable, and even radical, things about *Fried Green Tomatoes*. Idgie's brother Buddy supports her when she refuses to wear a dress to her sister's wedding. As an adult, Idgie is accepted as a man in the town—hanging out at the brothel on the river, going on hunting trips, appearing in the "womanless beauty pageant," and teaching her son, Buddy Junior, to be tough and respectful.

Idgie and Ruth are depicted, unambiguously, as in love. It is Idgie's mother who tells her, "Go and get that girl. You won't be any use to anyone until you do."[48] When she returns to Whistle Stop, Ruth essentially asks for Idgie's hand in marriage.

> Ruth went into the parlor with Momma and Poppa and closed the door. She sat across from them with her hands in her lap, and began, "I don't have any money, I really don't have anything but my clothes. But I can work. I want you both to know that I'll never leave again. I should never have left her four years ago, I know that now. But I'm going to try and make it up to her and never hurt her again. You have my word on that."
>
> Poppa, who was embarrassed at any sort of sentiment, shifted in his chair. "Well I hope you're aware of what you're in for. Idgie's a handful, you know."

Momma shushed him. "Oh Poppa, Ruth knows that. Don't you dear? It's just that she has a wild streak. . . . Poppa and I just want you to know that we think of you as one of the family now, and we couldn't be happier for our little girl to have such a sweet companion as you."

Ruth got up and kissed both of them. (199)

Flagg queers the most private traditional spaces—the home, the parlor—in which the femme Ruth asks for their daughter's hand in marriage. It is typical of the novel that Idgie and Ruth are accepted as a married couple without ever being named as such. When Buddy Junior is born, Idgie's mother exclaims, "Oh look, Idgie, he's got your hair!" (192). And it is Idgie's father who told her she had a family to support and gave her the money to start the Whistle Stop Café. Flagg constructs an imaginative space in which being gay simply is not an issue; nothing inhibits the integration of a lesbian couple into this small southern community.

Indeed, Idgie and Ruth create a queer space that unites the larger community and mitigates (but doesn't solve) community injustices. The Whistle Stop Café provides a home for Idgie, Ruth, and Buddy Junior; it also provides a boundary public in which all kinds of community members can interact. Sipsey, an African American friend who worked for Idgie's mother, cooks for the café, and her adopted son Big George kills the hogs and prepares the barbecue. Sipsey, George, and George's wife and children are part of a larger familial/communal unit that includes Ruth and Idgie, related not by blood but by affiliation. Buddy Junior "belongs" to his racist, misogynist father by law, but to Idgie by love; George is given away by an anonymous woman at the train stop to Sipsey, who takes him home and becomes his mother. The devotion of this communal unit is at the center of the novel. Though the "they're part of the family" dodge was a common way for well-to-do white families to describe their black "help," this communal unit goes well beyond genteel fictions. George's family has autonomy and cultural agency, and is not simply subordinate to the white family; we see the generations of Sipsey's grandchildren and great-grandchildren operating within predominantly African American communities—especially church—without the mediating force of white patronage. The relationship between Sipsey, George, Ruth, and Idgie is mutually supportive, and they take considerable risks to their own safety in order to protect each other. Flagg reveals at the end of *Fried Green Tomatoes* that Sipsey killed Frank, Ruth's ex-husband, to prevent him from taking Ruth and Idgie's son. The fact that

Sipsey took such a risk—which certainly could have provoked her lynching, had it been discovered—suggests the depth of her devotion to Ruth and Idgie; that she and George covered up the murder with a cannibalistic barbecue of Frank—a symbolic skewering of the racist, sexist southern patriarch—and told no one, not even Ruth and Idgie, suggests the limits of this communal relationship. But Idgie also takes risks, in turn, to protect them. When George and Idgie are accused, decades later, of Frank Bennet's murder (after the discovery of his car), Idgie refuses to run away or establish an alibi because she knows what will happen to George if he is accused, as a black man, of murdering a white man. She risks her own safety to try and protect George from a racist, murderous justice system.

Both George and Idgie are saved by the preposterous lies of another outsider community—the drunks, gamblers, and whores of the river camp community—and this suggests the potential power of resistance of alternative spaces in a hegemonic South. The river community—run by Eva Bates, whom Idgie's brother Buddy loved and who initiated both Idgie and Buddy Junior into sex—connects respectable and unrespectable Whistle Stop. The Whistle Stop Café is another distinctively queer contact zone in Whistle Stop. It operates within the South's Jim Crow strictures, which inhibit its democratic functioning, so it must, by necessity, struggle against both racial and sexual hierarchies. Idgie and Ruth insist on serving the African American community (across the tracks in Troutville). When African Americans come for barbecue, Idgie reveals the delicate balance the café must maintain to succeed as a public space of interaction.

> Idgie sighed and shook her head. "Let me tell you something, Ocie. You know that if it was up to me, I'd have you come on in the front door and sit at a table, but you know I cain't do that. . . . There's a bunch in town that would burn me down in a minute, and I've got to make a living. . . . But I want you to go back over to the yard and tell your friends, anytime they want anything, just to come around to the kitchen door." . . .
>
> Sipsey mumbled under her breath, "You gonna get yourself in a whole lot of trouble wid them Ku Kluxes, and I'm gonna be gone. You ain't twine see me aroun' no more, no ma'am." (53)

Sipsey's warning is prescient; Grady, the town sheriff, warns Idgie against breaking Jim Crow laws: "Nobody wants to eat in the same place that niggers come, it's not right and you just ought not be doin' it" (53). That's when

Idgie breaks one of the cardinal rules of southern obfuscation by calling out Grady as a Klan member:

> She continued, "Yeah, Grady, it's funny how people do things they ought not to do. Take yourself, for instance. I guess a lot of people might think that after church on Sunday you ought not to go over to the river and see Eva Bates. I reckon Gladys might think you ought not be doing that." . . .
>
> "Oh come on, Idgie, that's not funny."
>
> "I think it is. Just like I think a bunch of grown men getting liquored up and putting sheets on their heads is pretty damn funny. . . . The next time those 'some people' come in here, like Jack Butts and Wilbur Weems and Pete Tidwell, I'll ask 'em if they don't want anybody to know who they are when they go marching around in one of those stupid parades you boys have, why don't they have enough sense to change their shoes. . . . Oh hell, Grady, y'all ain't fooling anybody. Why, I'd recognize those size-fourteen clodhoppers you got on anywhere." (54)

Speaking the unspeakable, Idgie challenges one of the key constraints that allow the "natural" system of the South to continue. Defeated, Grady says, "I'll talk to the boys. . . . You keep them out back now." This leads to one of the few moments in her nostalgic, affectionate portrait of small-town southern life when Flagg critiques the doublespeak and hypocrisy of the South.

> "Ruth, I wish you could have seen that big ox, down at the river for three days, drunk as a dog, crying like a baby, 'cause Joe, that old colored man that raised him, died. I swear, I don't know what people are using for brains anymore. Imagine those boys: They're terrified to sit next to a nigger and have a meal, but they'll eat eggs that came right out of a chicken's ass. . . . It just makes me so mad sometimes."
>
> "I know honey, but you shouldn't get yourself so upset. That's just the way people are and there's not a thing in the world you can do to change them. That's just how it is."
>
> Idgie smiled at her and wondered what would happen if she didn't have Ruth to let off steam with. . . .
>
> After that day, the only thing that changed was on the menu that hung on the back door; everything was a nickel or a dime cheaper. They figured fair was fair. (55)

Ruth's repetition of that deadly justification of the status quo—"that's just how it is"—prevents a direct and dangerous challenge to segregation. They stop right at the line, and their lowering of prices for coming to the back door is a symbolic protest that in no way changes the system. That is the price for the boundary public they establish, which is carefully contained by the larger power structure.

It could be argued that Idgie is too accommodating—that her defiance of Jim Crow should have been more direct—but given the violence that met civil rights activists a couple of decades later, direct defiance probably would have led to the burning of the café. The mystifying fact that Idgie's best friend is a Klan leader is likely what saved it from arson in the 1930s; when Klan members, prompted by Frank Bennet, visit the Whistle Stop Café with torches, it is only Grady's intervention that saves both George and the café: "Quietly, two black pickup trucks had parked in front of the café and about twelve members of the Klan, dressed in full regalia, had slowly but deliberately gotten out and lined up outside the café. . . . One had a sign that had written on it, in bloodred letters, BEWARE OF THE INVISIBLE EMPIRE. . . . THE TORCH AND THE ROPE ARE HUNGRY. Grady Kilgore stood up and went over, looked out and picked his teeth with a toothpick while he scrutinized the men in the pointed hoods. . . . [Grady] said with certainty, 'Thems not our boys'" (203–4). The menace in this encounter is unmistakable, and it is a surprising eruption of violence, but this is how Flagg's fiction works—it circulates common nostalgic stereotypes about the South's "sense of place" and then slips in scenes that suggest a darker complexity. Grady's handling of the situation isn't particularly comforting, since it suggests a similarly repressive control of space by the Klan/police. He explained:

> "They was just a bunch of old boys out to throw a little scare in you, that's all. One of them was over here the other day for something or another and saw you was selling to niggers out the back door and thought he'd try to shake you up a little bit. . . . I just told them that these are our niggers and we sure as hell don't need a bunch from Georgia coming over her telling us what we can and cain't do."
>
> He looked Idgie right in the eye. "And I'll guaran-damn-tee you they won't be back," and he put his hat on and left. . . . What Idgie and Ruth didn't know was that although these Georgia boys were mean, they were not stupid enough ever to fool around with the

Klan in Alabama and were smart enough to leave in a hurry and stay gone. (204–5)

There is a strange element of bragging here—our Klan is tougher than your Klan—but even more surprising is that Flagg acknowledges the influence of the Klan at all. Of course, this is a kinder, gentler, Whistle Stop Klan—one in which Grady, the Klansman sheriff, takes care of "our niggers." He gets Big George's son out of jail; he helps Idgie give food to Troutville during the Depression, stealing food and throwing it out of the train; he is part of the Dill Pickle Club with Sipsey, the only African American member. Such imaginative depictions of queer contact zones are both utopian and realistic—one never totally escapes the specter of violence in these fictional reimaginings of southern space.

It is the liminal places like the Whistle Stop Café that inspire Flagg's affection and nostalgia, and she recognizes how temporary and essential such places can be. Dot Weems wrotes the obituary for the Whistle Stop Café in the final issue of *Weems Weekly* in 1969: "Now that I look back, it seems to me that after the café closed, the heart of the town just stopped beating. Funny how a little knockabout like that brought so many people together" (385–86). In that construction the Whistle Stop Café becomes a free(r) zone where more egalitarian interaction of outsiders is possible, but within carefully circumscribed limits in which queerness is tacit and unspoken.

In Alice Walker's *The Color Purple*, queer space evolves. Early in the novel, space is a matter of dispossession. Celie is denied privacy and agency; her bedroom, a room connected to the larger house by a walkway, is invaded by her (step)father, repeatedly, when he rapes her. Danielle Russell explains that "the precarious situation of the sisters is exacerbated by, and reflected in, their position within the house. . . . Physically detached from the family dwelling, what should be a sheltering space becomes a site of exploitation; bedroom as private sanctuary is obliterated by the stepfather's intrusion."[49] When Celie is married off to Albert without her consent, she works in a new space, in the fields and the kitchen, with no control over that space. Her person, her labor, all are controlled by her husband, who makes it clear that she has no say about anything, including whether his mistress can share their home. Celie's situation is extreme but not unique. African American women in the novel are denied agency and control of space, and this is especially true for women who violate sexual taboos such as Celie (because of her multiple unmarried pregnancies) and Harpo's mother (because she had an affair and was killed by her boyfriend). When Sofia's parents won't let her marry Harpo because of his mother's reputation, he has a nightmare: "Harpo be trouble with nightmares. . . . She got Harpo by the hand. They both running and running. He grab hold of her shoulder, say, You can't quit me now. You mine. She say, No I ain't. My place is with my children. He say, Whore, you ain't got no place. He shoot her in the stomach."[50] The haunting refrain "Whore, you ain't got no place" describes the fate of most of the women in *The Color Purple*, forced by violence from their homes into other spaces equally dangerous.

The novel also makes it clear that the wider culture in which African Americans live is even more constrained and dispossessing. Encounters in the public space of the South, which range from rudeness to utter brutality, include the beating of Sofia in the town square (for sassing the mayor's wife) and her enslavement as a further punishment, and the lynching of Celie's father because of the success of his farm and store. The white men who commit these acts are not the kindly Klan members of Flagg's imagination, but killers of extraordinary depravity, epitomized by the white sheriff who rapes his own niece, Mary Agnes. In this Jim Crow space, any zone of black freedom must be purchased at a high cost. As Celie's stepfather explains, "The key to all of 'em is money. The trouble with our people is as soon as they got out of slavery they didn't want to give the white man nothing else. But the fact is, you got to give 'em something. Either your money, your land, your woman or your ass. So what I did was just right off offer to give 'em money. Before I planted a seed, I made sure this one and that one knowed one seed out of three was planted for *him*. Before I ground up a grain of wheat, the same thing" (188; emphasis in the original). This colonization— of space, down to the last seed—was the conscious intention of Jim Crow, to construct African Americans as subordinate subjects of a white-controlled space. In such an environment, a liberatory queer contact zone might seem impossible, yet over the course of the novel, Walker delineates how such pockets of resistance are constructed and sustained. Just as relationships between characters evolve and change over the course of the novel, so, too, do spaces. Sofia and Harpo's house is the site of their epic battles and of Harpo's attempts to break his wife through violence. After Sofia leaves him, it becomes a juke joint, a sinful alternative to the local church and a space where Mister, Celie, and Shug appear in public, where Harpo and Sofia bring their lovers. But the origin of the space is telling, as we learn from the announcement of Shug's performance: "Harpo and Swain got Mr. ___ to give 'em some of Shug old announcements from out the trunk. Crossed out The Lucky Star of Coalman Road, put in Harpo's of _____ plantation. Stuck 'em on trees tween the turn off to our road and town" (76). The land that both Harpo and Albert work was originally a plantation, suggesting a liberation of the land (Albert's father owns it) and the ongoing legacy of plantation violence.

Once Celie discovers that Nettie is alive, more liberatory uses of space emerge. African uses of space suggest ongoing legacies of Africa in African American experiences and provide a model for subversive queer contact zones. Nettie's immersion in Africa provides proud models of spatiality: "Did you know there were great cities in Africa, greater than Milledgeville, or even Atlanta, thousands of years ago? That the Egyptians who built the pyramids and enslaved the Israelites were colored? That Egypt is in Africa? That the Ethiopia we read about in the Bible meant all of Africa?" (138). She also finds the different patterns of living in Africa more sympathetic. Her "hut is round, walled, with a round roofleaf roof. It is twenty steps across the middle and fits me to a T. Over the mud walls I have hung Olinka platters and mats and pieces of tribal cloth" (164). Closer to the natural world, Nettie's hut is a space of independence and growth.

The ongoing relevance of these African patterns in the African American South is clear when Shug reveals that she too wanted a round house: "Her bed round! I wanted to build me a round house, say Shug, but everybody act like that's backward. You can't put windows in a round house, they say. But I made me up some plans, anyway. One of these days . . . she say, showing me the papers. It a big round pink house, look sort of like some kind of fruit. It got windows and doors and a lot of trees round it. What it made of? I ast. Mud, she say. But I wouldn't mind concrete. I figure you could make the molds for each section, pour the concrete in, let it get hard, knock off the mold, glue the parts together somehow and you'd have your house" (215–16). Shug's desire for a round house suggests an archetypal memory of African patterns of living, and her longing for more harmonious living connects her creation of space to her pantheistic religious belief: "Us talk about houses a lot. How they built, what kind of wood people use. Talk about how to make the outside around your house something you can use. I sit down on the bed and start to draw a kind of wood skirt around her concrete house. You can sit on this, I say, when you get tired of being in the house. Yeah, she say, and let's put awning over it. . . . By the time us finish our house look like it can swim or fly" (209). Though, as Danielle Russell argues, "the blueprint for Shug's dream house remains a mere vision," it prepares the reader for the "spirit of accommodation, cooperation, and creativity [that] will be sheltered in the home Celie prepares for her long-lost family."[51] These domestic reconstructions of space, harmonious and "natural," without servitude or hierarchy, inspire the regeneration of queer space in *The Color Purple*.

Celie's childhood home undergoes the most dramatic transformation in the novel. It is first the site of her abuse, and then finally becomes a refuge in which her lover, her ex-husband, her ex-husband's son and wife and son's ex-lover, and at last her own children can live free of Jim Crow discrimination. When Celie returns to that home with Shug, she discovers a space that resembles the Garden of Eden in its beauty:

> Well, it was a bright spring day, sort of chill at first, like it be round Easter, and the first thing us notice soon as we turn into the lane is how green everything is, like even though the ground everywhere else not warmed up good, Pa's land is warm and ready to go. Then all along the road there's Easter lilies and jonquils and daffodils and all kinds of little early wildflowers. Then us notice all the birds singing they little cans off, all up and down the hedge, that itself is putting out little yellow flowers smell like Virginia creeper. It all so different from the rest of the country us drive through, it make us real quiet. . . . All round the house, all in back of it, nothing but blooming trees. Then more lilies and jonquils and roses clamming over everything. And all the time the little birds from all over the rest of the country sit up in these trees just going to town. (184–85)

Celie's land creates an oasis within an otherwise oppressive Jim Crow South, a queer contact zone which is "different from the rest of the country." The power of Celie's queer contact zone, liberated from man-made oppressions and man-made ideologies, sets up her triumphant reclaiming of the space after her stepfather's death. She is shocked by her sudden inheritance, in a space that had defined dispossession: "I never had no house, I say. Just to think about having my own house enough to scare me" (251). But after Shug smudges the house—"She took some cedar sticks out of her bag and lit them and gave one of them to me. Us started at the very top of the house in the attic, and us smoked it all the way down to the basement, chasing out all the evil and making a place for good" (252–53)—Celie remakes her land as a queer contact zone, a reprieve from the oppression of the South. All the queer extended family is welcome, and the final vision of unity—her sister and the sisters' southern/African blended family—suggests a fluid remaking of the Jim Crow South by the African American community. In *The Color*

Purple, that lesbian contact zone isn't cross-racial. It also isn't separatist; it includes men and women, polyandrous unions, and ex-lovers and friends. Though white southern lesbian feminists imagine a cross-racial utopia in their southern spaces, African American lesbian feminists are more skeptical about transcending that line.

Many queer contact zones, as depicted in the archive of southern lesbian feminism, manage to survive because of secrecy. They aren't solely queer; they incorporate others, even those hostile to their greater purpose, which shields them from attack and destruction. These sorts of flexible queer spaces—which survive through camouflage—are diametrically opposed to the metronormative gay urban ghettos that tend to dominate queer literature. Such secrecy may be a necessity in rural spaces because of a lack of critical mass of gay political power.

But there are also more direct challenges in the archive of southern lesbian feminism, queer contact zones that are out and proud. In Sheila Ortiz Taylor's 2006 novel *Outrageous*, a belated conclusion to the trilogy she began with Naiad Press in 1982 with *Faultine* and a homage to her own southern rebirth, lesbian Chicana poet Arden Benbow arrives at Midway College in 1973 (just as Ortiz Taylor herself did at Florida State). Arden and Topaz, her African American best friend and nanny, arrive in a blue hearse pulling a U-Haul trailer to find a house for Arden's lover, Alice, and their six children. Arden is smitten by the landscape: "Along either side of the highway, waist-high grass of an improbable green defined each curve, a green she had never known in the seared southern California rolling hills she had always adored, in the land of her mother and her mother's mother and her mother's mother's mother. She perhaps felt, despite her *Californio* lineage, her devotion begin to waver, to wander toward this new, lovely one, she who shimmered in moist heat and seductive promise: *La Florida*."[52] Ortiz Taylor is playing with a common trope here—the feminization of landscape, to be possessed and conquered by male explorers. Arden's embrace of Florida as a "new green world," a Garden of Eden curved like a woman's body, in "moist heat and seductive promise," sets up the novel's queering of space. Arden "allow[s] herself the innocence of falling in love with a state, a geography, a demography" (3), an attraction that initially makes her feel unfaithful to her lover. The erotics of landscape continue to inform her encounters with the South (even as that attraction is sorely tested over the course of the novel). Arden's decision to embrace the "fecund Florida soil" encourages a fanciful gesture: "She gazed up into an old live oak tree draped in Spanish moss, through which morning sun streamed, steamed and shimmered. How could she possibly resist stretching high into the blue Florida sky to pull down a strand of the moss and wind it into her long California hair?" (33). The fact that she gets chiggers from the moss and has to cut her hair into a short, dykey hairdo only emphasizes the lesbian body of Florida.

The climax of this paragraph presents the most radical queering of southern space: *La Florida*. Though Arden is consistently framed by white southerners as an alien invader, *La Florida* reminds us that the white Confederate version of "cotton and calico" is a relatively new invention. Long before that version took hold, all of the South was *La Florida*, colonized under Spanish rule and inhabited by mestizo subjects who looked like Arden Benbow, not Scarlett O'Hara. Whatever the colonial, racist, and sexist legacies of *La Florida*, it represents a queered geography that could embrace Arden Benbow like a lover.

But the space Arden soon encounters is considerably less welcoming. Arden and Topaz, a Latina and an African American man, violate the disciplinary rules around racial segregation that still govern public spaces in the South. As Topaz puts it, when he is being eyeballed by a trucker in a diner, "He thinks you're a white woman—or should I say lady—and he *knows* I'm a black man, and he assumes that everybody is heterosexual, despite compelling evidence to the contrary. Now he's wondering exactly where his responsibilities lie" (6; emphasis in the original). Only the timely intervention of the waitress—who "caught the gaze of the truck driver and gave her beehive an almost imperceptible shake, transmitting the ancient coded warning from the southern female to the southern male that meant: *Now you behave yourself, hear?*" (6; emphasis in the original)—saves them from a public and possibly violent altercation.

Ortiz Taylor emphasizes the comic possibilities of this misrecognition even as she highlights the threat of violence beneath the dominant culture's policing of diversity. When Bobbi June, a realtor and the wife of the dean, takes them to breakfast, she is able to handle the cross-racial relationship but is thrown by Arden's "ring finger, that carefully pared, colorless and totally naked ring finger" (16). The shock of their "living in sin" causes her to feel "something like fear for them. She thought of the gazelles in last night's TV nature film just before the lion broke through the grass and chased them out into the open" (16). The ghosts of racial violence continue to structure the Floridians' responses to Arden, who remains optimistic and willfully innocent of these complicated disciplinary strains. Bobbi June's misinterpretation sets her up for an even graver revelation:

"So Bobbi June, I might save us all some time by saying I really think the children would be better off living in the country some-where. . . . And of course there's Alice," said Arden.

"Alice is your girl," added Bobbi June, dabbing at her imperiled eyeliner with a paper napkin.

"Alice is an adult." Dr. Benbow set down the pepper and looked offended.

"I meant Alice is your maid, honey. That's what I meant. That's what we mean when we say 'your girl.' It's just our way of talk-ing." . . .

"Actually," said Mr. Wilson, "*I'm* the maid."

"Alice is my lover," said Dr. Benbow. (17; emphasis in the original)

Bobbi June is pummeled by her assumptions. The disclosure that the black man is the "maid," not the live-in partner, reasserts racial hierarchies (even as it flips gender hierarchies), but the large family plus lesbian lover places Arden in an opaque category for which the realtor has no name. When Arden assures her "our concept of family is exactly the same, yours and mine" (18), Bobbi June cannot process it.

The incredulous response to this out lesbian who willfully violates the "tacit understanding" that often functions for queers in southern commu-nities continues as Arden meets her colleagues. At the college opening re-ception the faculty are treated to a "mauve apparition": "Arden Benbow in a mauve tuxedo, trimmed, if Bobbi June was not mistaken, in pearl gray velvet piping with tie and matching cummerbund, the whole set off by gray patent leather opera pumps. On her arm came Mr. Topaz Wilson in a black tuxedo and looking very distinguished with a paisley gray, navy and crim-son tie and cummerbund. Arden's hair was of course still sticking straight up from where she got bit by the chiggers last week, but somehow the crown of it seems soft and inviting and part of her stunning outfit itself" (52). The mauve apparition is an ongoing joke in the first part of the novel—the queer outside agitator naively entering a world she doesn't understand. Arden is often flummoxed by "these strange codes and customs and assumptions. If only she had a map to these, a guide to the South that identified and trans-lated signs, gestures, glyphs, tropes, metaphors and other curious habits of being. She felt like a blind creature set down in a strange world" (71). This motif of "mapping" a purposely opaque geography of "the South" suggests that *Outrageous* itself is a queer map of the South, not only for this lesbian Californian Latina but also for many other kinds of outsiders.

Arden sets out to adapt this existing southern space to her own ends. Her first attempt involves the purchase of an old plantation on the outskirts of town. Topaz is horrified.

> "You mean this house which was raised up by black slaves and possibly Indians as well, to whom—who knows? You might even have been related. You mean you want to live with your innocent babes and your devoted spouse in this dilapidated monument to the most vicious impulses of European patriarchy?"
>
> "And what better place!" declared Arden, as if Topaz had proved her very point. "We'll take back this monument and claim it in the name of La Malinche." (21)

Arden's insistence that she has moved to *La Florida*, not the Confederacy, writes Midway into a global, multicultural, and multiracial South. La Malinche, the native interpreter who served Cortes, was denounced by generations of nationalists as a whore and a traitor; in *Borderlands/La Frontera* Gloria Anzaldua reclaimed La Malinche as a patron saint of the mestizo, a subversive figure who inhabits the spaces in between.

Arden's encounter with the plantation rewrites one of the most ubiquitous tropes in southern literature. Nowhere is southern nostalgia more disingenuous than in its romanticizing of the plantation. Plantations were anything but natural—they grew large amounts of one crop intended for the factories of the North; they displaced native populations, and depended on the stolen labor of slaves who were terrorized, sexually and physically, by overseers and other white members of the planter class. Yet the "idyllic" plantation remains a key part of southern nostalgia that still circulates through southern spaces; even Blanche McCrary Boyd, whose book *The Revolution of Little Girls* is set on a former plantation, was not immune to its attraction. Well-ordered, hierarchical, "gracious," the plantation creates a landscape that seems to epitomize the truth of the southern sense of place. It is for that reason that restaurants, condos, housing developments, wedding venues, and resorts across the South continue to refer to Tara, or "High Cotton," or other markers of *Gone with the Wind* exuberance.

So when Sheila Ortiz Taylor has Arden buy a plantation in *Outrageous*, it is a clear shot across the bow, and *how* she does it says a lot about the southern lesbian feminist campaign to queer southern spaces. Witness, for example, the exchange that occurs after Arden invokes La Malinche:

"Who's Malinchey?" asked Bobbi June. "Is she from around here? Who are her people?"

Topaz knew in his bones Arden was going to answer this question, that for her no question was negligible. "Malinche is dead," he offered, hoping to put an end to it but not expecting to.

"Dead?" said Bobbi June. "Oh I am so sorry for your loss."

"History is not dead," said Arden, a little circle of pink appearing in each of her brown cheeks. "Malinche was the Aztec princess who interpreted for Cortes. She's the goddess of language and patron saint to all women poets, the first activist, sometimes called La Chingada, which in English translates as—"

"Malinche'd want screens on her damn windows and Alice will too," Topaz interrupted. "Trust me." (22)

Ortiz Taylor contrasts Arden's teacherly zeal with Bobbi June's conventionality and Topaz's practicality, for humorous effect. But Bobbi June isn't simply a foil here; she becomes Arden's friend and ally.

Besides, Bobbi June's questions—Is she from around here? Who are her people?—are surprisingly prescient. In place of neo-Confederate hegemony and nostalgia, Ortiz Taylor constructs a geography in which queer *La Florida* will rise again. Arden remakes the landscape of the South into a mythic land, using indigenous mythologies that place her own identity at the center. Contemplating the plantation, "She dreamed of Aztlan, the mythic lost land of the Aztecs, her people, their dear homeland that might be in New Mexico, Arizona, Utah or. . . . some people—respectable scholars, as she recalled—had even placed it somewhere in Florida. Had they not? Yes, she was almost positive, quite positive, they had. One crack-brained theory put it in Wisconsin. Clearly that was absurd. But Florida. Now that was really quite plausible. Likely, even. Aztlan. And she, Arden Benbow, had returned to claim on behalf of all the earth's dispossessed the archetypal homeland for her people" (30–31). Arden writes another genealogy onto the South. By placing Aztlan, the legendary home of the Aztec people, in Florida, Arden places herself at the center, then invokes mythic female heroines and goddesses from that tradition: La Malinche, Tonantzin, Coatlique. In a land obsessed with history, Arden trumps them all by reaching to an older tradition that is actually indigenous to the landscape.

Yet, Arden doesn't entirely discard the neo-Agrarian fantasy of the South, either. When she visits the land, she muses, "We could raise all our own food right here, be self-sustaining" (22). She has a rapturous vision of the landscape: "Arden studied admiringly the three live oaks and stand of pines running along the western property line. A hawk high up in the blank afternoon sky lazily caught updrafts. Arden had found, just this side of that first oak tree, a perfect spot for her windmill. In her poet's mind the blades already revolved slowly, pumping fresh spring water toward the tender plants of her garden. Children, her own and dozens she had yet to meet, bent to the joyous labor, the sound of their garden tools working through the earth symphonic, their voices bright with expectation" (23). The idyllic images of plantation life at the beginning of *Gone with the Wind* might have inspired this agrarian idyll. Of course, Arden's imagined free labor, communal work, and community garden free that idyll from the legacy of servitude.

Ortiz Taylor doesn't let the reader forget the real history of the plantation and its forced labor. Inside the property is a "peninsula" owned by Miss Hattie. As Bobbi June explains: "Hattie White. Children are all grown and scattered to the winds. Got their college, then nothing could hold them back. . . . 'Course mostly she eats straight from that garden of hers. . . . That little house of hers was part of the original plantation, Daddy says, slave cabin most likely. But after the war Mrs. Faircloth, she up and give Miss Hattie's mama that house free and clear, to stay in her family right along. Now it belongs to Miss Hattie" (24). The history of slavery is explicit, but it is Hattie, the descendent of slaves, who has inherited the legacy of the independent yeoman farmer; like Raylene, she eats from her garden and lives self-sufficiently. She also watches, recognizing Topaz as a "lady boy" (93) and observing the happenings at the big house with great amusement. An alliance with Arden develops after Arden sees a fire and puts it out, saving Hattie's house. Hattie returns the favor when she takes the rap for the Midway students' marijuana. When Arden encourages her student athletes to garden on her land, they take advantage of her by planting marijuana. On a tip, the white sheriff comes to take Arden away and rid the college of a troublemaker, but Hattie steps up, claiming that the land the marijuana is on belongs to her, and insists on being arrested. Defeated, the sheriff leaves, and an alliance of black and mestiza have defeated the white power elite.

Arden changes the name of the plantation to Crossroads Gardens, and it becomes a place for new counteralliances to combat the white southern patriarchy. Arden discovers that she and the diverse others who inhabit her town are able to create a more open and flexible space. As she says after the fallout from her mauve apparition episode: "I'm going out to find our people tomorrow. . . . If they're here, I'll find them" (55). One key ally comes through the WIP movement. Arden visits the "alternative" bookstore, where she is told about Full Court Press, overseen by the cynical but lovable Boss Granny. Arden is "searching her map for Sumatra, then County Road 7 . . . territory Butch fondly referred to as East Jesus" (71). The lesbian press is difficult to find—another example of the complicated and hidden geography of queer *La Florida*. But Arden prevails: "Finally, eureka, Arden found herself on the map. In an eighth of an inch more she'd run into County Road 7. She eased the hearse back onto the road and soon passed a country church with a battered electric sign saying in red plastic letters, 'Fearing God is the beginning of wisdom.' On the opposite side of the road, another sign, this one professionally lettered on wood, said FULL COURT PRESS AND WRITERS RETREAT, PRIVATE PROPERTY, POSTED" (71). Here, Ortiz Taylor contrasts the conventional Bible Belt of "East Jesus" with the queer South, both found on the same road. At Full Court Press, Boss Granny is a loveable tyrant, boss of her own queer domain. She rules Sumatra as well: "They don't mess with me in Sumatra because I help prop up their sorry ass little town. I'm the greatest single user of UPS. I donate to the library, such as it is, and I employ construction workers, plumbers, electricians, you name it, all local. When Boss Granny roars, Sumatra listens" (74). Even her knowledge of prevailing southern gun culture protects her lesbian empire; when Arden asks what "posted" means on her sign, Boss Granny replies, "Posted means if you're on my property, then I can damn well shoot you dead, no questions asked. That's the South for you. Don't you just love it!" (75). Boss Granny's embrace of the gun serves as a warning to her neighbors—this is not a pacifist lesbian nation.

Boss Granny provides a key moment of support at the end of the novel when she funds an endowed professorship. But individuals linked to the more mainstream South are also allies in *La Florida*. Many are involved with Arden's first reconfiguring of space in Crossroads Plantation, including Bobbi June, who sells her the property; Butch, who oversees the construction; and Altron, the drywaller who transforms the sewing room into a Spanish-style bathroom with elegant arches. Altron, like Arden, is an artist, and he inspires her ruminations on space: "And as she feathered the compound over the tape with her joint finishing knife, she thought about sheetrock, about the way it shaped and defined space for the inhabitants, how it could be both ephemeral and lasting, like poetry itself. Next thing she knew she was writing a poem about sheetrock and poetry right up there on the sheetrock itself, using Altron's thick, red pencil and it was coming like crazy, straight out, the way she liked it" (114).

An unexpected alliance occurs midway through the novel when Arden, homesick for Mexican food, tries to make tortillas at home and fails miserably. Butch says casually,

> "I was fixin' to say, Miss Arden, that if your heart is dead set on tortillas tonight then you might just pick you up a dozen or so from the Menudo Palace. They don't close weekdays till three, and I think you could just about make it if you leave now."
>
> "Menudo Palace? Here? In Midway? Where I live?"
>
> "Between the dry cleaners and the food stamp store. You know, catty corner to the Unocal? We got a lot of migrant workers hereabouts."
>
> "Butch, Butch," she said, reaching for her wallet and her keys, "what other reservoirs of knowledge are you keeping from me?"
>
> (144)

The owner of the Menudo Palace is from her grandfather's home in Mexico; Arden discovers a hidden community and a cause. She supports a demonstration by migrant workers, and although the photograph of her riding on a motorcycle at the head of the union march might be the final straw for the university administration, her participation extends Arden's *La Florida* alliances to include her own mestiza background. The fact that it is a white gallant southern man, Butch, who connects her to this community suggests that the counteralliances of *La Florida* are flexible, unexpected, and inclusive.

There is, without question, a conservative hegemony against which Arden must struggle; Dean Billy Wayne Kilgore and English chair Booth Hazard, who can't fire a minority hire, try to sabotage her career, first by requiring all athletes to take a poetry class with Benbow, then by more pernicious means that involve the local sheriff. But *La Florida* undermines the notion of outside agitators and true southerners, because Arden discovers a host of local allies; even the athletes who are forced into a poetry class with Arden in an attempt to break her spirit become converts and troublemaker allies. Ortiz Taylor portrays a coalition of old-time residents, migrants, and outsiders that successfully counteracts the hegemonic controls of a patriarchal southern order. The plantation ethos is thoroughly decimated by the end of the novel, on the very ground of the original southern hegemony. With lover, nanny/best friend, and six children reunited, Arden remembers the flag still flying in front of Crossroads Gardens (the red flag she carried at the front the of the migrant workers' march), and she awakens to lower it for the night:

Outside on the front porch, she stood in her pajamas, yielding to the moist embrace of the night, the bright, nearly full moon. There was wind up there tonight. Dark clouds streaked past the luminous face, while here below everything remained still. The flag hung in the silence, as if about to speak. Then off in the woods she heard an owl call. A moment passed, and then a second owl answered. The hunters were out tonight, she knew, working the clearings in pairs, vigilant for carelessness or need.

Arden reached up to release the rope, lowered the flag into her arms, folded it carefully, musing all the while on time and work and geography and on love, that strange foreign language. (187)

Ortiz Taylor depicts a queer Garden of Eden, always at risk of predators "vigilant for carelessness or need." But Arden's own vigilance that night—the care with which she protects the emblem of her queer space—makes the reader trust in the survival of Crossroads Gardens.

· · · · · ·

The B.T.C. Old-Fashioned Grocery is the cornerstone of Water Valley, Mississippi's revival: featured in *Garden and Gun*, *Southern Living*, *O*, the *Oprah Magazine*, and a host of other regional and national publications, the B.T.C. is an exemplary local-foodie destination. It also serves as a crossroads for that other South. Started by Virginia transplant Alexe van Beuren, the B.T.C. contains a café overseen by Mississippi native and lesbian Dixie Grimes, the Dixie Belle Café, which welcomes cross-dressing construction workers, professors, indie-rock vegan bassists, activists, artists, and writers, who interact with retired insurance agents, garden club members, local teachers, and Bible school leaders over Miss Vetra's fried chicken. It is a queer contact zone that provides a haven for local youth who don't fit in the Bible Belt South, connecting them with all kinds of expatriates and outsiders—Democrats, academics, queers, scalawags, carpetbaggers, and townabouts. Many longtime Water Valley residents hate the B.T.C. for these very reasons, but it continues to thrive on business from locals, overflow from Oxford, Mississippi, and tourists who view it—rightly—as the legitimate heir of that most famous southern intersectional restaurant, the Whistle Stop Café.

Chef Dixie Grimes grew up in Oxford, Mississippi; she has a Mississippi lilt that is unmistakable—her name is Dixie, for goodness' sake. Her southern credentials are unassailable, and she has a gay pride flag on her workstation in the kitchen. Not everyone likes that, but they all want her hand-cut fries and onion rings, her creative sandwiches and delectable plate lunches. The Mississippi legislature may try to turn back the clock and send queers back into the closet; HB 1523 would make queers and other sexual dissidents second-class citizens. But Dixie is undaunted. In May 2016 she led Oxford's first gay pride parade, throwing Mardi Gras beads and gay pride flags to the crowd. Queer contact zones are not hidden—not anymore. We plant our flags and claim our southern space. In the name of Dixie.

Conclusion

Lesfic: Alternative Publishing, Activism, and Queer Women Writers

· ·

Sheila Ortiz Taylor's 2006 *Outrageous* included a warm tribute to Barbara Grier, as Boss Granny explains to Arden Benbow why Full Court Press was a success: "I have a clear market in mind, the large, voracious market of lesbians out there wanting to read about themselves, who aren't particularly educated but know what they like and don't mind spending their money to get it. Why shouldn't people like that be able to buy the kind of books they want?"[1] Arden's response captured Grier's motivation: "So really . . . really you're an idealist."[2] Though Boss Granny whooped at this characterization, Ortiz Taylor knew it represented the deepest aspirations of the WIP movement.

When Ortiz Taylor wrote *Outrageous*, the world in which Grier operated had already changed dramatically. Of course, many of the writers featured in *The Lesbian South* continue to publish, including Ortiz Taylor, Minnie Bruce Pratt, and Mab Segrest. Florence King published a column for the *National Review* for years, "The Misanthrope's Corner"; though she largely disavowed her alliance with the WIP movement, she is still best known for *Southern Ladies and Gentlemen* and *Confessions of a Failed Southern Lady*. Rita Mae Brown has created a long, lucrative career as a writer of popular novels, including a series of mysteries cowritten with her cat, Sneaky Pie Brown. Though transgressive sexuality makes an appearance in a number of her novels (including *Sudden Death*, her exposé of lesbians on the pro women's tennis tour, written after she was dumped by Martina Navratilova), it no longer defines her public persona. Alice Walker continues to be a bracing public presence, even as she has moved away from fiction in recent years. Fannie Flagg remains an enormously popular novelist of the South, though she included no lesbian characters in her fiction after *Fried Green Tomatoes* until her 2010 novel *I Still Dream about You*—and then only in a subplot that was little more than an aside. Dorothy Allison is still a literary star, but she hasn't published a novel since *Cavedweller* in 1998. In 2018, her long-promised speculative novel *She Who* was listed as "forthcoming" on her website.

Other institutions survive. Charis Books and More, the feminist bookstore founded in the Little Five Points neighborhood of Atlanta in 1974, is one of only a small group of feminist bookstores in the country. The lesbian feminist community that once dominated the Little Five Points area is gone; ALFA closed its doors in 1994, and the neighborhood is quickly gentrifying. But Charis remains an outpost of queer energy in its new location at Agnes Scott College, where one can still buy used Naiad Press paperbacks and used LPs of "women's music." *Sinister Wisdom* is still publishing; now led by editor and poet Julie Enszer, it is one of the few remaining institutions creating lesbian feminist community, and true to its roots, it has published three special issues on lesbian feminism in the South, all of which have been essential to the writing of this book. These special issues, based largely on oral histories, were organized at the lesbian writers' retreat Womonwrites, which still meets at a state park in Georgia every May and offers a series of workshops for women writers. The many feminist periodicals that reviewed books are mostly gone, but *Lambda Literary*, a print journal founded in the 1980s that has evolved into an online resource guide, continues to be a central focus for queer publishing, with its daily reviews and its annual awards for almost every category of queer writing imaginable, including lesbian poetry and fiction.

Even some of the original lesbian presses continue to exist. Naiad Press turned over its writer contracts to the newly formed Bella Books, and when former Naiad employee Linda Hill became a partner, Barbara Grier gave her the coveted Naiad mailing list (evolved from the original mailing list pilfered from *TL*) and sold her the backlist "at approximately five cents per volume."[3] Bella Books still operates out of Tallahassee; it keeps some Naiad books in print and continues to publish lesbian romances, mysteries, and coming-out novels. Bella Books publishes southerners Mary Griggs, K. G. MacGregor, and many others.

The survival of these writers and institutions is remarkable, considering how dramatically the literary landscape has changed. The feminist culture of letters that enabled and nurtured the southern lesbian feminists discussed in this book was unraveling by the end of the 1990s, when mega-bookstores Borders and Barnes and Noble were putting independent bookstores, including gay and feminist bookstores, out of business. The rise of Amazon and ebooks further undermined the viability of small niche bookstores. At its height, there were more than 200 gay and feminist bookstores around the country; today, only a handful remain. Barbara Grier's decision to retire in 2001 seems remarkably prescient. The deaths of many influential bookwomen—Bertha Harris in 2005, Barbara Grier in 2011, Catherine Nicholson in 2013, Florence King in 2016—can easily lead one to nostalgia for a lost era. Certainly, the political and cultural conditions that produced the WIP movement no longer exist.

It is easy to mourn the demise of the WIP movement, a network of authors, bookstores, publishers, and readers that fostered so much innovative writing. Yet today there is more lesbian fiction—known affectionately as "lesfic"—available to women, in both large cities and small towns, than anything the WIP movement achieved in its heyday. An Internet search of the term *lesbian fiction* may yield 56,799 results on a given day. The volume of lesbian writing is breathtaking, but making queer publishing culture visible is extraordinarily challenging.

Grier's populist vision for lesbian publishing supported by genre fiction, especially romance, dominates lesfic. Bold Strokes Books, founded by Radclyffe (the pen name of a former surgeon), emphasizes lesbian romance but publishes a wide range of genres, including, in its own terms of categorization, speculative fiction, series, intrigue and thriller, erotica, fantasy, action and adventure, paranormal and urban fantasy, and general fiction. Bold Strokes Books also hosts writing retreats for aspiring writers through the Flax Mill Creek writing retreat.[4] With more than 120 authors, it is a worthy successor to Naiad Press; indeed, Naiad was the model for Radclyffe's own writing.

Bywater Books was cofounded by mystery writer J. M. Redmann and named for a New Orleans neighborhood. Kelly Smith, who formed Bella Books (and was ousted at Barbara Grier's suggestion) became Bywater's editor in chief.[5] Its president, Michelle Karlsburg, is also a publicist for queer writers based in New York. Bywater styles itself as the more literary of the lesbian presses, but it doesn't publish anyone like June Arnold and Bertha Harris; its fiction is closer to the "real novels" that Barbara Grier championed. Katherine Forrest, who transformed Naiad with *Curious Wine*, now publishes with Bywater, and the press also features a number of southern lesbian writers including Ann McMan (who lives in North Carolina), Alabama natives Bett Norris (who lives in Florida), and Wynn Malone (who lives in Kentucky).

Bella, Bold Strokes Books, and Bywater are some of the biggest publishers of lesfic. But established lesbian presses, with southern roots or otherwise, are not the only places that queer women are publishing. Younger writers are less likely to identify as solely lesbian and often write gay male erotica and focus on trans issues. Some publish with presses that are often more identified with gay men, like Lethe Press, or with "slash" erotica (male/ male erotica that is primarily consumed by, and often produced by, straight women), like Arsenal Pulp Press, based in Vancouver. In Arkansas, Sibling Rivalry Press specializes in queer poetry and also publishes chapbooks, memoirs, and essays by lesbians and gay men. Queer coalitions provide other venues for queer women writers focused on erotica, BDSM, and political issues like homeless queer youth. The older identity-based publishing forums of gay and lesbian literatures still exist, but more flexible and diverse forms of erotica are everywhere, and younger writers are moving in and out of "set" genres and forms to create remarkable writing portfolios.

The most dramatic change has been the rise of self-publishing; authors can publish inexpensively and sell directly to readers, bypassing gatekeepers. Laura Antoniou, for example, makes her living as a full-time writer, without a day job or an academic position to sustain her. She began writing male/male erotica columns on safe sex for the *Person with AIDS* newsletter in the 1980s, then graduated to making $50 per story. Antoniou is the author of the Marketplace series of novels about an S/M secret society, which focuses on a wide range of sexualities, kinks, and identities. The series is categorized as erotica, though the sexual descriptions are part of a larger cultural critique and an imaginative reinvention of sexual identities into a freer, more hybrid erotic exchange. For her most recent book, Antoniou initiated a kickstarter campaign that raised $30,000, allowing her to publish beautiful, hand-bound editions for her dedicated readers, whom she refers to as patrons of her art. She has created a viable means of support for herself as a writer and artist without ever reaching the notice of more mainstream literary venues.

Queer publishing, then, continues to thrive, under the radar, as it has since the days of Cold War pulp paperbacks, out gay pulps, and lesbian feminist publishers. But abundance brings its own challenges. How do authors find readers, and how do readers discover the books they really want to read? There is no national association of feminist and gay bookstores for touring authors to visit to meet with readers directly, no network of feminist presses that publish books outside the mainstream, and no feminist periodicals to review them. As one aspiring writer told me at the New Orleans Saints and Sinners Literary Festival in 2016, "There is no gatekeeper. No one reviews the books anymore. I don't know how you find an audience." Though writers have become extraordinarily adept at marketing their own work, it may be that you don't find an audience anymore; the audience finds you.

As Antoniou's example makes clear, readers have taken charge, most notably in the plethora of groups, websites, and guides online. There are many online blogs about lesfic, including my favorite, *The Lesbrary*. Pinterest has a robust community, and #lesfic is an active hashtag on Twitter. One can spend many hours Googling *lesfic* and still not reach the end of the list of blogs, author websites, and reader discussion boards; searches in every social media platform keep turning up new sites, self-published authors, and publishers. Lesfic may be derided as trash, ignored, and patronized, but as Barbara Grier understood, readers know what they want. Indeed, these readers often become writers, and they support lesbian writers both virtually and in person.

In the absence of a national network of bookstores, queer book festivals have emerged nationwide to fill the void. The Left Coast Lesbian Literary Conference happens every fall in Palm Springs, California. The Rainbow Book Fair in New York City brings together a wide range of queer writing. Queer book fairs are held in the South, too. The Miami Book Fair brings a host of queer writers to its annual conference, and the Saints and Sinners Literary Festival in New Orleans is one of the best known queer book conferences in the South, uniting southern queer writers like Dorothy Allison with New York writers like Andrew Holleran and Felice Picano.

The association most clearly indebted to the WIP movement is the Golden Crown Literary Society (GCLS), founded in 1999, which hosts an annual conference in a different city every July, featuring panels of lesbian writers discussing topics as diverse as creating video games from your fiction and creating tension in romance novels. Bella, Bywater, and Bold Strokes have large displays of books for sale, but self-published entrepreneurs abound. The first writer I met at GCLS in Alexandria, Virginia in 2016 was Ali Spooner, who began her writing career by self-publishing and then joined epublisher Affinity Books. Ali was wearing a t-shirt depicting the cover of one of her books; in fact, she had a t-shirt with a different book cover for every day of the conference, and if she met someone who had read all her novels, that reader was rewarded with one of the t-shirts. Self-promotion is prevalent, as writers show up with their self-published novels. The sister of an author gave me a t-shirt that said "Buy my book" and had the scan code on it, front and back. Everywhere, authors are touting their books, reading from their books, referencing their friends' books, and hoping for a "Goldie," the annual award GCLS created because it felt the Lambda Literary Awards didn't pay enough attention to lesbian romance. GCLS has created its own literary association of the rock stars of lesfic who are unknown in more traditional literary venues.

A new network, then, has formed; these queer literary festivals give lesbian readers direct access to lesbian writers, with tourism thrown in. What makes this network different is the lack of engagement with the literary that Arnold and Harris championed on the one hand, and the absence of the merging of queer politics and queer publishing that so animated the WIP movement on the other. Barbara Grier's triumph means that "literary" lesbian authors like Sarah Schulman, Jeannette Winterson, and Dorothy Allison operate in one sphere—of AWP and New York publishers—and lesfic authors operate in another. Bywater positions itself as the more literary of the lesfic presses, with higher-brow offerings and cover art, but it also publishes romances, and its fiction isn't experimental, as Daughters was. The productive tension between pulp and avant-garde is largely absent from the current lesfic scene; the literary and lesfic do not meet.

The largely apolitical tone of lesfic is another key difference. It's not that some authors don't incorporate politics; Bett Norris, for example, focuses on the civil rights movement in her debut novel *Miss McGhee*, and speculative fiction, as a genre, is always fertile ground for cultural critique. But the widespread engagement with radical politics that so animated the writers in *The Lesbian South* isn't readily visible in the alternative forum of lesfic. Romance stories about white women dominate lesfic, and conversations about race and about sexual ethics are in a nascent stage at the GCLS conference. At the 2016 meeting it often seemed like romance writers and readers were celebrating the current state of lesfic, and conversations about race, diversity, and sexual ethics were happening among other participants. Those conversations about objectifying women and including more diverse lesbian characters replay the debates of lesbian feminism in the 1980s. Participants aren't arguing for more writers of color, but for more characters to be included by white writers. Concerns about lesfic book covers that objectify women—the topic of a panel dominated by Bywater authors—had no traction for the majority of authors, who simply want to sell their books and are happy to have scantily clad women help them do so (just as Cold War lesbian pulps did).

Perhaps this lack of interest in politics is understandable in an era when marriage equality has become mainstream. But queer activism continues to be widespread, especially in the South. Marriage equality has provoked a vicious backlash in southern states, and organizations like the Campaign for Southern Equality are resisting this backlash with lawsuits, rallies, and pride parades, with the vigorous support of allies in local communities. The Campaign for Southern Equality has had enormous success challenging anti-LGBT measures in Mississippi, with Roberta Kaplan winning high-profile cases. This activism is coalitional, with Black Lives Matter and progressive religious organizations joining with queer activists to resist institutional racism, sexism, and homophobia. Social media, not print, has dominated the activist strategies. Queer southerners are increasingly eager to stand and fight where they are. That real-world activism seems disconnected from lesfic.

In the current moment, remembering the queer South of the archive of lesbian feminism is more important than ever. The legacy of the southern lesbian feminist tribe and the independent presses that sustained them could inspire the next generation of queer southerners as they create a queer South that is not simply imaginative and virtual. The audacious, challenging vision of a queer South that the southern lesbian feminist tradition championed has never been more relevant—or more necessary. Their bold revision of "the South" into a multicultural, kinky, liberated space is still in progress, but the energy they unleashed and the taboos they challenged inspire a queer South that is still in a process of becoming.

Acknowledgments

Many have supported the publication of *The Lesbian South*, including friends, family, and colleagues too numerous to name. At Brigham Young University, an irreverent band of feminist rebels first discovered the power of consciousness raising in Cecilia Konchar Farr's living room. Those Monday Feminist Home Evenings began an interest that culminated most recently in *The Lesbian South*, and I am fortunate to have many of those people still in my life, including Cecilia Konchar Farr, Missy Bradshaw, Becca Walquist, and Benjamin Carr.

Many thanks to my students at the University of Mississippi, both undergraduate and graduate, whose smart conversation informs this book. My summer research assistants Josh-Wade Ferguson and Travis Smith searched periodicals tirelessly for reviews. The College of Liberal Arts at the University of Mississippi supported the writing of this book with summer research grants and a sabbatical in the spring of 2016; English department chair Ivo Kamps has supported my research with travel money and course releases over the years, and my colleagues in the English department have created a supportive research community over many years, for which I am grateful.

Correspondence with June Arnold's daughters, Roberta and Fairfax, enlightened this project; their generosity has been remarkable. Ann Allen Shockley graciously corresponded with me as well. The LGBTQIA archives at the San Francisco Public Library house the Naiad Press archive, and librarian Tim Wilson has been remarkably generous in his help. The Sallie Bingham Center for Women's History and Culture at Duke University houses the papers of Dorothy Allison, Mab Segrest, Blanche McCrary Boyd, Catherine Nicholson, Minnie Bruce Pratt, and ALFA, and an extensive collection of feminist periodicals; the professionalism and generosity of their staff, especially Kelly Wooten, was exceptional.

Many thanks to Annette Trefzer and Katie McKee, whose careful readings of early drafts made this a better book. Thanks to Michael Bibler, Julie R. Enszer, and Jessie Wilkerson for reading chapter drafts, and to the outside reviewers and UNC editor Lucas Church, who provided careful feedback. Special thanks to Ellis Starkey for their meticulous copy editing and source checking and to Kevin Cozart for his photographs and conceptual design.

Finally, my gratitude and love to my wife Dixie Grimes, who read numerous drafts and always believed that this book would come together, even when I wasn't sure. I am more fortunate than I can say to have her as my partner.

The Lesbian South Timeline

1966   Barbara Grier becomes book review editor of the *Ladder* and
       publishes the column *Lesbiana* as Gene Damon.
       June Arnold publishes *Applesauce*.

1969   Bertha Harris publishes *Catching Saradove*.

1970   Barbara Grier becomes editor of the *Ladder* and remakes it as a lesbian
       feminist journal.
       June Arnold participates in the Fifth Street Women's Building takeover in
       New York City.
       Rita Mae Brown organizes the Lavender Menace at a NOW meeting in
       New York City.

1971   June Arnold and Parke Bowman found Daughters, Inc. in Plainfield,
       Vermont.
       Rita Mae Brown publishes *The Hand that Cradles the Rock*.

1972   Bertha Harris publishes *Confessions of Cherubino*.

1973   Barbara Grier founds Naiad Press.
       Pat Parker publishes *Pit Stop*.
       Daughters, Inc. publishes its first novels, including *Rubyfruit Jungle* by
       Rita Mae Brown, *Nerves* by Blanche McCrary Boyd, and *The Cook and the
       Carpenter* by June Arnold.

1974   Ann Allen Shockley publishes *Loving Her*.

1975   Barbara Grier visits New York City to speak at the Gay Academic Union
       Conference, and meets Bertha Harris and June Arnold.
       Sagaris Feminist Institute held in Vermont. Rita Mae Brown and Bertha
       Harris are instructors; Dorothy Allison takes a writing class with Harris
       and arranges to work for Charlotte Bunch at *Quest* magazine.
       June Arnold publishes *Sister Gin*.
       Florence King publishes *Southern Ladies and Gentlemen*.

1976   The first Women in Print Conference, organized by June Arnold,
       is held in Nebraska and attended by Barbara Grier, Catherine Nicholson,
       and Bertha Harris.

Catherine Nicholson and Harriet Desmoines found *Sinister Wisdom* in Charlotte, North Carolina.

Daughters, Inc. publishes Bertha Harris's *Lover* and Rita Mae Brown's *In Her Day*.

Rita Mae Brown publishes *A Plain Brown Rapper* with Diana Press.

1977   June Arnold sells *Rubyfruit Jungle* to Bantam Books and is denounced by the feminist community. She moves to Houston.

Rita Mae Brown and Barbara Grier sue Diana Press for failure to pay royalties.

Blanche McCrary Boyd publishes *Mourning the Death of Magic* with Macmillan.

1978   Pat Parker publishes *Womanslaughter*.

Rita Mae Brown publishes *Six of One* with Bantam Books, beginning her career as a bestselling novelist.

1979   *Feminary: A Feminist Journal for the South, Emphasizing the Lesbian Vision* is born.

1980   Ann Allen Shockley publishes *The Black and White of It* with Naiad Press.

1981   Minnie Bruce Pratt publishes *The Sound of One Fork*.

1982   June Arnold dies.

The Barnard Sex Conference, which features Dorothy Allison, begins the lesbian feminist debate known as the "lesbian sex wars."

Alice Walker publishes *The Color Purple*.

Florence King publishes *When Sisterhood Was in Flower*.

Ann Allen Shockley publishes *Say Jesus and Come to Me*.

Sheila Ortiz Taylor publishes *Faultline*.

Rita Mae Brown publishes *Southern Discomfort*.

1983   Dorothy Allison publishes *The Women Who Hate Me*.

Alice Walker publishes *In Search of Our Mothers' Gardens*.

1984   Cris South publishes *Clenched Fists, Burning Crosses*.

1985   Mab Segrest publishes *My Mama's Dead Squirrel*.

Minnie Bruce Pratt publishes *We Say We Love Each Other*.

1987   June Arnold's *Baby Houston* is published posthumously.

Catherine Ennis publishes *South of the Line*.

Naiad Press reprints Ann Allen Shockley's *Say Jesus and Come to Me*.

Fannie Flagg publishes *Fried Green Tomatoes at the Whistle Stop Café*.

1988   Dorothy Allison publishes a collection of short stories, *Trash*, and a collection of essays, *Skin: Talking about Sex Class and Literature*.

1989   Pat Parker dies.
        Minnie Bruce Pratt wins the Lamont Prize for *Crime against Nature*.
        Sister Gin reprinted by the Feminist Press.

1990   Florence King publishes *Confessions of a Failed Southern Lady*.

1991   Minnie Bruce Pratt publishes *Rebellion*.

1992   Dorothy Allison publishes *Bastard out of Carolina*, which becomes a
        finalist for the National Book Award for fiction that year.
        Blanche McCrary Boyd publishes *The Revolution of Little Girls*.

1993   Bertha Harris's *Lover* is reprinted by New York University Press.

1994   Mab Segrest publishes *Memoir of a Race Traitor*.

1995   *The Cook and the Carpenter* is reprinted by New York University Press.
        The Redneck Way of Knowledge is reprinted by Vintage.

1997   Blanche McCrary Boyd publishes *Terminal Velocity*.

1998   Dorothy Allison publishes *Cavedweller*.

2005   Bertha Harris dies.

2006   Sheila Ortiz Taylor publishes *Outrageous*.

2011   Barbara Grier dies.
        Fannie Flagg publishes *I Still Dream about You*.

Notes

Introduction

1. Rule, "For 'Writer/Publisher Relationships,'" 47.
2. Rule, 49–51.
3. Rule, 50.
4. Howard, *Men Like That*, 142. Emphasis in the original.
5. Kreyling, *Inventing Southern Literature*, 34.
6. Kreyling, 25.
7. Bone, *Postsouthern Sense of Place*, 4–5.
8. Kreyling, *Inventing Southern Literature*, 31.
9. Kreyling, 35.
10. Peckham, "Reconstructing Self," 207.
11. Duck, "What Was the 'New Southern Studies'?"
12. Duck, n.p.
13. McKee and Trefzer, "Global South"; Smith and Cohn, *Look Away!*
14. "As both Kreyling and Barbara Ladd have noted, even efforts to incorporate African American and female writers into the category of 'southern literature' tended not to disrupt the principles of the old paradigm (Kreyling, *Inventing Southern Literature*, 76–125; Ladd, "Literary" 1631), Duck, n.p.
15. Jon Smith's *Finding Purple America* is one of the more uncompromising articulations of this perspective.
16. Duck, "Southern Nonidentity."
17. Duck, 329.
18. She explains her central term: "'Southscape' has both subjective and objective elements, but primarily it acknowledges the connection between society and environment as a way of thinking about how raced human beings are impacted by the shape of the land. . . . It is invested in understanding the persistent conceptual power of the South as a spatial object and ideological landscape where matters of race are simultaneously opaque and transparent" (Davis, *Southscapes*, 2).
19. For example, see Baker's *I Don't Hate the South* and Robinson's *This Ain't Chicago*.
20. Richards, *Lovers and Beloveds*; Bibler, *Cotton's Queer Relations*; Herring, *Another Country*; Gray, *Out in the Country*.
21. Romine, "Southern Affects."
22. Hemmings, *Why Stories Matter*, 3–5.
23. Hemmings, 5.

24. Halberstam, *Gaga Feminism*, 2.

25. Halberstam, 3.

26. Hemmings, *Why Stories Matter*, 13.

27. Minnie Bruce Pratt, interview by Kelly Anderson, March 16–17, 2005, Jersey City, NJ. Voices of Feminism Oral History Project, Sophia Smith Collection, Smith College, Northampton, MA.

28. Hemmings, *Why Stories Matter*, 13–14.

29. Gilmore, *Feminist Coalitions*; Hewitt, *No Permanent Waves*.

30. Valk, *Radical Sisters*.

31. See Gilmore, "Dynamics of Second-Wave Feminist Activism"; Wilkerson, "Company Owns the Mine"; Blair, *Revolutionizing Expectations*; Allured, *Remapping Second-Wave Feminism*.

32. Cvetcovich, *An Archive of Feelings*; Stone and Cantrell, *Out of the Closet*. For more on queer inquiry into archives, see Stone and Cantrell, "Introduction: Something Queer in the Archives," in *Out of the Closet*, 1–24.

33. Enszer, "'Black and White of It,'" "'Fighting to Create,'" and "Whole Naked Truth."

34. That decision was influenced by my book on Christopher Isherwood. I was first introduced to Isherwood through his 1976 memoir *Christopher and His Kind*, in which he rewrote his experience in Berlin in the 1930s through gay liberation. I found that the Christopher of his letters and diaries at the time was dramatically different from the Christopher he reinvented for a contemporary audience. And I was much more interested in the inconsistent, sometimes unsure, and culturally grounded figure I pieced together than the more consistent gay liberation superhero he created—even if that superhero had way more sex and way less doubt than the Christopher I discovered (or, if you prefer, created).

35. See Echols, *Daring to Be Bad*.

36. The Combahee River Collective in 1977 made the most famous statement of this problem: "Although we are feminists and Lesbians, we feel solidarity with progressive Black men and do not advocate the fractionalization that white women who are separatists demand. Our situation as Black people necessitates that we have solidarity around the fact of race, which white women of course do not need to have with white men, unless it is their negative solidarity as racial oppressors. We struggle together with Black men against racism, while we also struggle with Black men about sexism" (Combahee WomenRiver Collective, "Combahee River Collective Statement," http://circuitous.org/scraps/combahee.html).

37. For more information, see Vance, *Pleasure and Danger*, and Duggan and Hunter, *Sex Wars*.

38. Hesford, *Feeling Women's Liberation*, 239. Emphasis in the original.

39. Morris, *The Disappearing L*, 2, 3.

40. For more on pinkwashing debate, see Schulman *Israel/Palestine and the Queer International*. For more on homonationalism, see Duggan, "New Homonormativity." Debates around queer history, by scholars like Heather Love, Ann Cvetcovich, Carla

Freccero, Valerie Minor, and others have focused on two main issues—one ideological, the other epistemological. One is what Love calls the "progress" narrative—the assumption that everything before Stonewall was closeted, destructive, and abject. Rethinking that relationship to the past, whether through erotic metaphors or the embrace of negative emotions, becomes a key focus. Another issue is the question of whether one can ever "know" the past, or whether our relationship to that queer past is always mediated by our own desires or concerns. Theorists more invested in poststructuralism (like Jonathan Goldberg) maintain that it is impossible to know the past, while others (like Valerie Traub) insist that attention to actual archives and information can yield real information about that past.

41. Warner, "Queer and Then."

Chapter One

1. Some examples include Hesford's *Feeling Women's Liberation*; Flannery's *Feminist Literacies*; Enszer's "Whole Naked Truth of Our Lives"; and Hogan's *Feminist Bookstore Movement*.

2. Grahn, *Simple Revolution* and Cordova, *When We Were Outlaws*.

3. Harker and Farr, *This Book Is an Action*, 11.

4. Foster, *Sex Variant Women*.

5. For more on the Daughters of Bilitis, see Gallo's *Different Daughters*.

6. Passet, *Indomitable*, 10.

7. Passet, 43.

8. Grier, *Lesbiana* 2, 35.

9. Grier, 35–36.

10. See Keller, "'Was It Right?'"; Foote, "Deviant Classics"; Nealon, *Foundlings*, chap. 4.

11. Passet, *Indomitable*, 85.

12. Passet, 44.

13. See Harker, *Middlebrow Queer*, chap. 4.

14. Harker, chap. 5.

15. Grier, *Lesbiana*, 38.

16. Grier, 38–39.

17. See Gunn, *Golden Age of Gay Fiction*, and Gunn and Harker, *1960s Gay Pulp Fiction*.

18. Passet, *Indomitable*, 84.

19. Grier, *Lesbiania*, 42.

20. Grier, 44.

21. Grier, 76. Emphasis in the original.

22. Grier, 44–45.

23. Grier, 75. Emphasis in the original.

24. Passet, *Indomitable*, 44.

25. Passet, 105–6.

26. Passet, 101.

27. Passet, 102.

28. Arnold and Arnold, "Art *Is* Politics," 35.

29. Arnold and Arnold, 36.

30. Arnold and Arnold, 38.

31. Enszer, "Whole Naked Truth," 104.

32. Glimpses of Bertha Harris's life may be found in North Carolina newspaper articles in the 1960s and 1970s. For one example, see "Writer's Conference."

33. Radicalesbians, "The Woman-Identified Woman."

34. Grahn, *Simple Revolution*, 135.

35. Travis, "Women in Print Movement," 276.

36. Travis, 276.

37. Adams, "Paper Lesbians," 193.

38. Grahn, *Simple Revolution*, 142.

39. Whitehead, *Feminist Poetry Movement*, xv.

40. Whitehead, 8. Emphasis in the original.

41. Dorothy Allison to Walter Kendrick, 17 May 1990. Dorothy Allison Papers.

42. Harris, "More Profound Nationality," 77; hereafter cited parenthetically in text by page number.

43. "Frontiers." Author's ellipses in brackets.

44. Brown, "'Violet Hill Elementary School.'"

45. Arnold, "Cook and the Carpenter."

46. Galana, "How to Make a Magazine."

47. "Feminist Press."

48. "Frontiers."

49. Enszer, "Whole Naked Truth," 105.

50. Arnold, "Feminist Presses," 18; hereafter cited parenthetically in text by page number.

51. "Lesbians and Literature," 28. Emphasis in the original.

52. "Lesbians and Literature," 28–29.

53. "Lesbians and Literature," 29.

54. Harris, "What We Mean to Say," 6.

55. Harris, 6. Emphasis in the original.

56. Harris, 6. Emphasis in the original.

57. Bertha Harris to Barbara Grier, 25 February 1975. Barbara Grier–Naiad Press Collection.

58. Enszer, "Whole Naked Truth," 72.

59. Grahn, *True to Life*, 10.

60. Grahn, 10.

61. Onosaka, *Feminist Revolution*, 46.

62. Hogan, *Feminist Bookstore Movement*, 42.

63. Hogan, 30.

64. Gould, "Creating a Women's World," 10–11, 34, 36–38.

65. Gould, 34.

66. Harris, introduction to *Lover*, xvii–lxxviii. esp. xxvii–lxxviii.

67. Desmoines, "Retrieved from Silence," 63.

68. Desmoines, "Notes for a Magazine" (July 1976), 3. Emphasis in the original.

69. Hodges, "Lesbian Writing and Publishing."

70. "Lesbians and Literature," 30.

71. "Lesbians and Literature," 30.

72. Arnold and Harris, "Lesbian Literature," 45.

73. Clausen, "Politics of Publishing," 97.

74. Clausen, 107.

75. Hodges, "Letter from the Editor."

76. Desmoines and Nicholson, "Letter to Beth."

77. Desmoines, "Notes for a Magazine" (Spring 1977), 100. Emphasis in the original.

78. For more on *Feminary*, see Cantrell, "Subscribe to *Feminary*!"; Powell, "Look What Happened Here."

79. *Feminary*, 4.

80. For more on *Feminary*, see chapter 2.

81. Pratt, *Rebellion*, 162.

82. Anyda Marchant to Barbara Grier, 20 March 1974. Barbara Grier–Naiad Press Collection.

83. Barbara Grier to Anyda Marchant, 26 March 1974. Barbara Grier–Naiad Press Collection.

84. Barbara Grier to Sandy Boucher, 21 July 1976. Barbara Grier–Naiad Press Collection.

85. Barbara Grier to Anyda Marchant, 16 December 1975. Barbara Grier–Naiad Press Collection. Author's ellipses in brackets.

86. Barbara Grier to Anyda Marchant, 29 April 1977. Barbara Grier–Naiad Press Collection.

87. Barbara Grier to Elsa Gidlow, 26 November 1977. Barbara Grier–Naiad Press Collection.

88. Ortiz Taylor, *Faultline*, back cover.

89. Ortiz Taylor, back cover.

90. Passet *Indomitable*, 179, 180.

91. Passet, 182.

92. For more on this controversy, see Passet, chap. 12 (191–208).

93. Bertha Harris to Barbara Grier, 18 June 1989. Barbara Grier–Naiad Press Collection. Emphasis in the original.

94. Barbara Grier, interview by Pokey Anderson. Barbara Grier–Naiad Press Collection.

95. Dorothy Allison to Barbara Kerr, 22 January 1988. Correspondence, Box 37, Dorothy Allison Papers.

96. Pratt, "Watching the Door," in *Rebellion*, 187–88.

97. Pratt, 188–89.

98. Minnie Bruce Pratt, interview by Kelly Anderson. 78.

99. Pratt interview.

100. Dorothy Allison to Nancy Bereano, 24 October 1991. Correspondence, Dorothy Allison Papers.

101. Dorothy Allison to Carole DeSanti, 24 October 1991. Correspondence, Dorothy Allison Papers.

102. Dorothy Allison to Sybil and Jay, 13 December 1987. Dorothy Allison Papers.

103. Dorothy Allison to Carole DeSanti, 24 October 1991. Dorothy Allison Papers.

104. Boyd, "Dorothy Allison," 17.

Chapter Two

1. Payne, "Human Rights Campaign."

2. Daniels, "Same-Sex Marriage Licenses."

3. Lavers, "Mississippi Governor's Son."

4. For more on SNCC, see Zinn, *SNCC*; Carson, *In Struggle*; Morgan and Davies, *From Sit-Ins to SNCC*; Cohen and Snyder, *Rebellion in Black and White*. For more on the roots of the civil rights movement, see Gilmore, *Defying Dixie*.

5. McGuire, *At the Dark End of the Street*.

6. Jeffries, *Bloody Lowndes*.

7. Evans, *Personal Politics*.

8. For more information, see Dent, *Free Southern Theater*; Smethurst, *Black Arts Movement*; Hale, *Freedom Schools*.

9. For more information, see Price, *Maroon Societies* and Diouf, *Slavery's Exiles*.

10. For more information, see Aptheker, *American Negro Slave Revolts*; Rasmussen, *American Uprising*; Hoffer, *Cry Liberty*; Oates, *Fires of Jubilee*; Walters, *American Slave Revolts and Conspiracies*.

11. See Huggins, *Slave and Citizen* and Yellin, *Harriet Jacobs: A Life*.

12. Lerner, *Grimke Sisters from South Carolina*.

13. Hurt, *Agriculture and the Confederacy*.

14. Du Bois, *Black Reconstruction in America*; Foner, *Reconstruction: America's Unfinished Revolution*; Egerton, *Wars of Reconstruction*; Guelzo, *Fateful Lightning*.

15. Kelley, *Hammer and Hoe*; Miller, *Remembering Scottsboro*; Tyson, *Radio Free Dixie*; Segrest, *Memoir of a Race Traitor*.

16. Sitkof, *A New Deal for Blacks*; Korstad, *Civil Rights Unionism*; Gilmore, *Defying Dixie*; Honey, *Southern Labor and Black Civil Rights*; Hall and Murphy, *Like a Family*.

17. Norman, "And So It Begins," 15; hereafter cited parenthetically in text by page number.

18. For more on the varied roots of feminist activism, see Evans, *Personal Politics*; McGuire, *At the Dark End of the Street*; McDuffie, *Sojourning for Freedom*.

19. See Valk, *Radical Sisters*; Gilmore, "Dynamics of Second-Wave Feminist Activism"; Wilkerson, "Company Owns the Mine"; Blair, *Revolutionizing Expectations*.

20. Boyd, *Terminal Velocity*, 53.

21. For more on Minnie Bruce Pratt, see Farley, "'Dirt She Ate'"; Peckham, "Reconstructing Self"; Hunt, "Interview with Minnie Bruce Pratt."

22. Pratt, *Rebellion*, 56. Emphasis in the original.

23. Pratt, 156.

24. Brown, *Hand that Cradles the Rock*, 12; hereafter cited parenthetically in text by page number.

25. Reid, introduction.

26. For more on Pat Parker, see Clarke and Enszer, "Introduction"; Washburn, "Unpacking Pat Parker"; Green, "'Anything that Gets Me'"; and Van Ausdall, "'Day All of the Different Parts.'"

27. Parker, *Pit Stop*, 13.

28. Parker, 30.

29. For one example, see Chen's *Animacies*.

30. For a classic example, see Berlant and Warner, "Sex in Public."

31. Parker, *Pit Stop*, 2–4.

32. Parker, 28.

33. Parker, *Womanslaughter*, 43–44.

34. Parker, 14.

35. For two popular examples, see John T. Edge's *Potlikker Papers* and Michael Twitty's *Cooking Gene*.

36. Parker, *Womanslaughter*, 54.

37. Parker, 61.

38. Parker, 62. Emphasis in the original.

39. Brown, *Plain Brown Wrapper*, 60.

40. Brown, 55

41. Brown, 13.

42. Walker, *In Search*, 160–61.

43. South, *Clenched Fists*, epigraph.

44. South, 16. Emphasis in the original.

45. South, 29.

46. South, 180.

47. Mays, "Delta, a Story."

48. Cornwall, "Backward Journey."

49. Pratt, "Reading Maps: Two," 121.

50. Pratt, 121.

51. Pratt, 125–26.

52. Segrest, *Memoir of a Race Traitor*, 80. Emphasis in the original.

53. Segrest, 150.

54. Pratt, *Rebellion*, 23. Emphasis in the original.

55. Pratt, 45–46.

56. Pratt, 113. Emphasis in the original.

57. Pratt, *Crime against Nature*, 57. Emphasis in the original.

58. Arnold, *Sister Gin*, 210–15.

59. Pratt, *Crime against Nature*, 114–15.

60. Maureen Brady to Minnie Bruce Pratt, 14 October 1979. Minnie Bruce Pratt Papers.

61. Maureen Brady to Minnie Bruce Pratt, 26 February 1980. Minnie Bruce Pratt Papers.

62. Minnie Bruce Pratt to Maureen Brady, 4 June 1980. Minnie Bruce Pratt Papers.

63. Brady, *Folly*, 27.

64. Brady, 28.

65. Enszer, "'Black and White of It.'"

66. Segrest, *Memoir of a Race Traitor*, 42. Emphasis in the original.

67. Enszer, "'Fighting to Create.'"

68. Enzser, 162.

69. Enzser, 169.

70. For more on *Say Jesus and Come to Me*, see Tuttle, "'Best Stuff God Did'"; Green, "'What the Eyes'"; Tomeio, "Marginal Black Feminist Religiosity"; Krantz, "Political Power."

71. Shockley, *Say Jesus and Come to Me*, 129; hereafter cited parenthetically in text by page number. All emphases in the original.

72. Bibler, *Cotton's Queer Relations*.

73. Ennis, *South of the Line*, 9.

74. Ennis, 30.

75. Ennis, 132.

76. See Bynum, *Free State of Jones*.

77. Ennis, 156.

78. Flagg, *I Still Dream about You*, back cover.

79. Flagg, *I Still Dream about You*, 59; hereafter cited parenthetically in text by page number.

Chapter Three

1. See Duck, *Nation's Region*; Grierson, *Our South*.

2. Anderson, Hagood, and Turner, *Undead Souths*, 4. Emphasis in original. See also Jones and Donaldson's *Haunted Bodies*.

3. Gleeson-White, introduction to *Strange Bodies*. 6, 10.

4. McCullers, "Notes on Writing."

5. Lillian Smith's 1947 essay collection *Killers of the Dream* also critiqued the role of sex, especially transgressions like miscegenation, in southern racism and segregation; published after *Reflections in a Golden Eye* but before *Other Voices, Other Rooms* and *Ballad of the Sad Café*, the collection emphasizes the decadent

lure of "forbidden" sexuality, even as public pronouncements condemn them. Her own novel *Strange Fruit*, though it avoided same-sex homoerotics, investigated the sexual taboo to critique segregation; not quite part of the southern gothic, her writing on the South and sexuality is an important fellow traveler.

6. Segrest, *My Mama's Dead Squirrel*, 34; hereafter cited parenthetically in text by page number.

7. Dorothy Allison to Mab Segrest, 18 June 1985, Mab Segrest Papers.

8. Allison to Segrest. Emphasis in the original.

9. Harris, *Confessions of Cherubino*, back cover. Author's ellipses in brackets.

10. Harris, 166–67. Author's ellipses in brackets.

11. Allison, *Trash*, 90.

12. Allison, 92.

13. For more on Florence King, see Pugh, *Precious Perversions*, 68–90.

14. King, *Southern Ladies and Gentlemen*, 32; hereafter cited parenthetically in text by page number.

15. Harris, *Lover*, xxi.

16. Gerhard, *Desiring Revolution*, 82.

17. Harris, *Lover*, xx–xxi.

18. Cordova, *When We Were Outlaws*, 106.

19. Jay, *Tales of the Lavender Menace*.

20. Boyd, *Terminal Velocity*, 41.

21. For more on this controversy, see Vance, *Pleasure and Danger*, and Duggan and Hunter, *Sex Wars*.

22. See Halperin and Traub, *Gay Shame*.

23. See Warner, *Trouble with Normal*.

24. Jagose, *Orgasmology*.

25. Bersani, "Is the Rectum a Grave?," 215; hereafter cited parenthetically in text by page number

26. Muñoz, *Cruising Utopia*, 1.

27. Puar, *Terrorist Assemblages*, xxvii.

28. Puar, xxvii.

29. For one version of this debate, see Schulman's *Israel/Palestine and the Queer International*.

30. Bertha Harris to Barbara Grier, 17 March 1975, Barbara Grier–Naiad Press Collection.

31. Harris, *Lover*, 123–24; hereafter cited parenthetically in text by page number.

32. Arnold, *Cook and the Carpenter*, 24–25. Author's ellipses in brackets. Arnold experiments with gender neutral pronouns in the novel. For more on this strategy, see chap. four, note 29.

33. Shockley, *Say Jesus and Come to Me*, 156–57.

34. Brown, *Rubyfruit Jungle*, 165; hereafter cited parenthetically in text by page number.

35. For more on *Six of One*, see Martindale, "Rita Mae Brown's *Six of One*," and Ward, *Rita Mae Brown*, 76–109.

36. Brown, *Six of One*, 108.

37. Brown, 110.

38. Walker, *In Search*, 355.

39. Abbandonato, "View from 'Elsewhere,'" 1109.

40. Walker, *Color Purple*, 84.

41. Walker, 267.

42. Walker, 275–76.

43. Chauncey, *Gay New York*.

44. Arnold, *Sister Gin*, 129–30.

45. Boyd, *Mourning the Death of Magic*, 208.

46. Boyd, 205.

47. Walker, *Color Purple*, 118. Emphasis in the original.

48. Walker, 123.

49. Arnold, *Baby Houston*, 233. Emphasis in the original.

50. Freeman, *Time Binds*, 37–38.

51. For more on Bertha Harris's queer critique in *Lover*, see Gable, "Bertha Harris's *Lover*."

52. Desmoines and Nicholson, "Sinister Wisdom." Catherine Nicholson Papers.

53. Desmoines and Nicholson, 1. Author's ellipses in brackets. Emphasis in the original.

54. Desmoines and Nicholson, 6.

55. Desmoines and Nicholson, 13.

56. For more on *Southern Discomfort*, see Levine, "Uses of Classical Mythology"; Irwin, "Freedoms as Value"; Ward, *Rita Mae Brown*, 110–21.

57. Brown, *Southern Discomfort*, prologue, n.p.; hereafter cited parenthetically in text by page number.

58. *Southern Discomfort* was published a year after the film *The Best Little Whorehouse in Texas* was released, and while there is no evidence that the film directly influenced the novel, the focus on transgressive sexuality as central to southern life is common to both.

59. Shockley, *Say Jesus and Come to Me*, 92.

60. Shockley, 93.

61. Shockley, 97.

62. Yaeger, *Dirt and Desire*, xiii.

63. Barker, *Reconstructing Violence*, 1.

64. Walker, *Color Purple*, 1–2.

65. Field, "Alice Walker's Revisionary Politics of Rape," 160. Emphasis in the original.

66. South, *Clenched Fists*, 83.

67. South, 83–84. Emphasis in the original.

68. Allison, *Bastard out of Carolina*, 284–86.

69. Cvetkovich, *Archive of Feelings*, 100–101.

Chapter Four

1. For more, see Janney, *Burying the Dead* and McElya, *Clinging to Mammy: The Faithful Slave in Twentieth-Century America*.

2. Howard, *Men Like That*, 14.

3. Howard, 15.

4. Herring, *Another Country*, 9.

5. Giesking, "A Queer Geographer's Life," 14.

6. Rose, Mushroom, and Ellison, introduction to *Feminist Geographies*, 9.

7. Rose, Mushroom, and Ellison, 9.

8. Massey, *For Space*, 140–41.

9. Massey, 13.

10. Gieseking, "A Queer Geographer's Life," 15.

11. Gieseking, 15.

12. Rensenbrink, "Parthenogenesis and Lesbian Separatism," 291.

13. Bell and Valentine, "Introduction: Orientations," 8.

14. Sine, Anahita. "Nestled into Niches," 724.

15. Norman et al., "Notes for a Special Issue," 8.

16. Norman et al., 5.

17. Mosbacher, *Radical Harmonies*.

18. Resenbrink, "Parthenogenesis and Lesbian Separatism," 292.

19. Fougère, *Lesbiana*.

20. Newton, *Margaret Mead Made Me Gay*, 277n6.

21. Sears, *Rebels, Rubyfruit, and Rhinestones*.

22. For more information, see Daniels, "Pagoda, Temple of Love."

23. "Copper Fountains Bring Ponchatoula."

24. A 2009 *New York Times* article discusses the Alabama community—see Kershaw, "My Sister's Keeper." For more on Camp Sister Spirit, see "Controversial Camp Sister Spirit."

25. For more on Sally Gearhart, see http://sallymillergearhart.net/sallys-story/.

26. Gearhart, *Wanderground*, 186; hereafter cited parenthetically in text by page number.

27. Arnold, *Cook and the Carpenter*, 3–4; hereafter cited parenthetically in text by page number.

28. Smith and Cohn, *Look Away!*; Smollett et al., *Plantation Kingdom*.

29. To match Arnold's linguistic experiment, I use "they" and "them" to refer to characters from *Cook and the Carpenter*, consistent with contemporary usage for those who identify as nonbinary. Though this term was not in usage when Arnold wrote the novel, it is consistent with her vision of a society free from hegemony of gender.

30. King, *When Sisterhood Was in Flower*; hereafter cited parenthetically in text by page number.

31. Boyd, *Terminal Velocity*, 3.

32. Boyd, 68.

33. Boyd, 100.

34. Boyd, 84. Emphasis in the original.

35. Faludi, "Death of a Revolutionary."

36. Boyd, *Terminal Velocity*, 89.

37. Boyd, 158.

38. Boyd, "Bitter Harvest."

39. Castells, *City and the Grassroots*, 170.

40. Bell and Valentine, "Introduction: Orientations," 6.

41. Gray, *Out in the Country*, 88.

42. Gray, 92–93. Emphasis in the original.

43. Gray, 103.

44. Gray, 116.

45. Pratt, "Arts of the Contact Zone," 34.

46. Harker, "'And You Too, Sister, Sister?,'" 52.

47. Allison, *Bastard out of Carolina*, 178–79; hereafter cited parenthetically in text by page number.

48. Flagg, *Fried Green Tomatoes*, 191; hereafter cited parenthetically in text by page number.

49. Russell, "Homeward Bound," 197.

50. Walker, *Color Purple*, 30; hereafter cited parenthetically in text by page number.

51. Russell, "Homeward Bound," 203.

52. Ortiz Taylor, *Outrageous*, 2; hereafter cited parenthetically in text by page number. Emphasis in the original.

Conclusion

1. Ortiz Taylor, *Outrageous*, 73.

2. Ortiz Taylor, 73.

3. Passet, *Indomitable*, 245.

4. See Barot, "Where Art Meets Craft."

5. Passet, *Indomitable*, 245.

Bibliography

Manuscript Collections

Dorothy Allison Papers, Sallie Bingham Center for Women's History and Culture, Duke University Special Collections Library

Barbara Grier–Naiad Press Collection, San Francisco Public Library

Catherine Nicholson Papers, Sallie Bingham Center for Women's History and Culture, Duke University Special Collections Library

Minnie Bruce Pratt Papers, Sallie Bingham Center for Women's History and Culture, Duke University Special Collections Library

Mab Segrest Papers, Sallie Bingham Center for Women's History and Culture, Duke University Special Collections Library

Sophia Smith Collection, Voices of Feminism Oral History Project, Smith College

Books and Articles

Abbandonato, Linda. "A View from 'Elsewhere': Subversive Sexuality and the Rewriting of the Heroine's Story in *The Color Purple*." *PMLA* 106, no. 5 (October 1991): 1106–15.

Adams, Kathryn. "Paper Lesbians: Alternative Publishing and the Politics of Lesbian Representation in the United States, 1950–1990." PhD diss., University of Texas at Austin, 1994. ProQuest (9505939).

Allison, Dorothy. *Bastard out of Carolina*. New York: Plume, 1992.

———. "Public Silence, Private Terror." In *Pleasure and Danger: Exploring Female Sexuality*, edited by Carole S. Vance, 103–14. Boston: Routledge and Kegan Paul, 1984.

———. *Trash*. Ithaca, NY: Firebrand Books, 1988.

Allured, Janet. *Remapping Second-Wave Feminism: The Long Women's Rights Movement in Louisiana, 1950–1997*. Athens: University of Georgia Press, 2016.

Anahita, Sine. "Nestled into Niches: Prefigurative Communities on Lesbian Land." *Journal of Homosexuality* 56, no. 6 (August/September 2009): 719–37.

Anderson, Eric G., Taylor Hagood, and Daniel Cross Turner, eds. *Undead Souths: The Gothic and Beyond in Southern Literatures and Cultures*. Baton Rouge: Louisiana State University Press, 2015.

Anzaldua, Gloria. *Borderlands/La Frontera: The New Mestiza*. San Francisco: Aunt Lute Books, 1999. First published 1987.

Aptheker, Herbert. *American Negro Slave Revolts*. New York: Periodicals Service, 1978.

Arnold, June. *Applesauce*. Plainfield, VT: Daughters, Inc, 1977. First published 1966.

———. *Baby Houston*. Austin, TX: Texas Monthly Press, 1987.

———. "Consciousness-Raising." In *Women's Liberation: Blueprint for the Future*, edited by Sookie Stambler, 155–60. New York: Ace Books, 1970.

———. *The Cook and the Carpenter*. New York: New York University Press, 1995. First published 1973.

———. "The Cook and the Carpenter (from the Novel)." *Amazon Quarterly: A Lesbian-Feminist Arts Journal* 2, no. 2 (1973): 44–45.

———. "Feminist Presses and Feminist Politics." *Quest* 3, no. 1 (Summer 1976): 18–26.

———. *Sister Gin*. New York: Feminist Press, 1989. First published 1975.

Arnold, June, and Bertha Harris. "Lesbian Fiction." *Sinister Wisdom* 1, no. 2 (Fall 1976): 42–51.

Arnold, Roberta, and Fairfax Arnold. "Art *Is* Politics." *Sinister Wisdom* 89 (Summer 2013): 34–48.

Baker, Houston. *I Don't Hate the South: Reflections on Faulkner, Family, and the South*. Oxford: Oxford University Press, 2007.

Barker, Deborah E. *Reconstructing Violence: The Southern Rape Complex in Film and Literature*. Baton Rouge: Louisiana State University Press, 2015.

Barot, Len. "Where Art Meets Craft." Flax Mill Creek Writers Retreat. 2014. http://flaxmillcreek.com/.

Bell, David, and Gill Valentine. "Introduction: Orientations." In *Mapping Desire: Geographies of Sexualities*, edited by David Bell and Gill Valentine, 1–27. New York: Routledge, 1995.

Berlant, Lauren, and Michael Warner. "Sex in Public." *Critical Inquiry* 24, no. 2 (Winter 1998): 547–66.

Bersani, Leo. "Is the Rectum a Grave?" *October* 43 (Winter 1987): 197–222.

Bibler, Michael. *Cotton's Queer Relations: Same-Sex Intimacy and the Literature of the Southern Plantation, 1936–1968*. Charlottesville: University of Virginia Press, 2009.

Blair, Melissa Estes. *Revolutionizing Expectations: Women's Organizations, Feminism, and American Politics, 1965–1980*. Athens: University of Georgia Press, 2014.

Bone, Martyn. *The Postsouthern Sense of Place in Contemporary Fiction*. Baton Rouge: Louisiana State University Press, 2005.

Boyd, Blanche McCrary. "Bitter Harvest." *Village Voice* 38, no. 41 (12 October 1993): SS19.

———. "Dorothy Allison, Crossover Blues." In *Conversations with Dorothy Allison*, edited by Mae Miller Claxton, 17–22. Jackson: University Press of Mississippi, 2012.

———. *Mourning the Death of Magic*. New York: Macmillan, 1977.

———. *The Redneck Way of Knowledge*. New York: Vintage, 1995.

———. *The Revolution of Little Girls*. New York: Vintage, 1992.

———. *Terminal Velocity*. New York: Vintage Contemporaries, 1997.

Brady, Maureen. *Folly*. Trumansburg, NY: Crossing Press, 1982.

Brown, Rita Mae. *The Hand that Cradles the Rock*. Baltimore, MD: Diana Press, 1974. First published 1971.

———. *A Plain Brown Rapper*. Oakland, CA: Diana Press, 1976.

———. *Rubyfruit Jungle*. New York: Bantam Books, 1977. First published 1973.

———. *Six of One*. New York: Bantam Books, 1978.

———. *Southern Discomfort*. New York: Bantam Books, 1982.

———. "'Violet Hill Elementary School' and 'Fort Lauderdale High,' from the novel *Rubyfruit Jungle*." *Amazon Quarterly: A Lesbian-Feminist Arts Journal* 1, no. 2 (1973): 6–17.

Bynum, Victoria E. *The Free State of Jones: Mississippi's Longest Civil War*. Chapel Hill: University of North Carolina Press, 2016. First published 2003.

Cantrell, Jaime. "Subscribe to *Feminary*! Producing Community, Region, and Archive." In *Out of the Closet, into the Archives: Researching Sexual Histories*, edited by Amy L. Stone and Jaime Cantrell, 311–36. Albany: State University of New York Press, 2015.

Capote, Truman. *Other Voices, Other Rooms*. New York: Penguin, 2004. First published 1948.

Carson, Clayborne. *In Struggle: SNCC and the Black Awakening of the 1960s*. Cambridge, MA: Harvard University Press, 1981.

Castells, Manuel. *The City and the Grassroots: A Cross-Cultural Theory of Urban Social Movements*. Berkeley: University of California Press, 1983.

Chauncey, George. *Gay New York: Gender, Culture, and the Making of the Gay Male World, 1890–1940*. New York: Basic Books, 1995.

Chen, Mel Y. *Animacies: Biopolitics, Racial Mattering, and Queer Affect*. Durham, NC: Duke University Press, 2012.

Cheney, Joyce, editor. *Lesbian Land*. Minneapolis, MN: Word Weavers, a Lesbian Publishing Company, 1985.

Clarke, Cheryl, and Julie R. Enszer. "Introduction: Where Would I Be without You." *Journal of Lesbian Studies* 19, no. 3 (July–September 2015): 275–89.

Clausen, Jan. "The Politics of Publishing." *Sinister Wisdom* 1, no. 2 (Fall 1976): 95–116.

Cohen, Robert, and David J. Snyder, eds. *Rebellion in Black and White: Southern Student Activism in the 1960s*. Baltimore, MD: Johns Hopkins University Press, 2013.

Combahee River Collective. "The Combahee River Collective Statement." In *Home Girls: A Black Feminist Anthology*, edited by Barbara Smith, 272–82. New York: Kitchen Table: Women of Color Press, 1983.

"Controversial Camp Sister Spirit Celebrates 10 Years." *WLOX News*. n.d. http://www.wlox.com/story/1451559/controversial-camp-sister-spirit-celebrates-10-years.

"Copper Fountains Bring Ponchatoula Artisans Fame." *Ponchatoula Times*,
    31 July 1986. http://ptl.stparchive.com/page_image.php?paper=PTL&year
    =1986&month=7&day=31&page=1&mode=F&base=PTL07311986P01&title
    =The%20Ponchatoula%20Times.

Cordova, Jeanne. *When We Were Outlaws: A Memoir of Love and Revolution*.
    Midway, FL: Spinsters Ink, 2011.

Cornwall, Anita. "Backward Journey." *Feminary* 12, no. 1 (1982): 86–105.

Cvetcovich, Ann. *An Archive of Feelings: Trauma, Sexuality, and Lesbian Public
    Cultures*. Durham, NC: Duke University Press, 2003.

Daly, Mary. *Beyond God the Father: Toward a Philosophy of Women's Liberation*.
    Boston: Beacon Press, 1985. First published 1973.

Daniels, Callie. "Same-Sex Marriage Licenses Filed at Lafayette Chancery Court."
    HottyToddy.com. 15 August 2014. http://hottytoddy.com/2014/08/15/same-sex
    -marriage-licenses-filed-at-lafayette-chancery-court/.

Daniels, Lin. "Pagoda, Temple of Love: Practice Ground for the Matriarchy." 1977.
    http://kongress-matriarchatspolitik.ch/upload/Lin-Daniels.pdf.

Davis, Thadious. *Southscapes: Geographies of Race, Region, and Literature*.
    Chapel Hill: University of North Carolina Press, 2011.

Dent, Thomas, ed. *The Free Southern Theater, by the Free Southern Theater:
    A Documentary of the South's Radical Black Theater, with Journals, Letters,
    Poetry, Essays*. New York: Bobbs-Merrill, 1969.

Desmoines, Harriet. "Notes for a Magazine." *Sinister Wisdom* 1, no. 1 (July 1976): 3–27.

———. "Notes for a Magazine." *Sinister Wisdom* 1, no. 3 (Spring 1977): 99–101.

———. "Retrieved from Silence." *Sinister Wisdom* 5 (1978): 62–71.

Desmoines, Harriet, and Catherine Nicholson. "Letter to Beth." *Sinister Wisdom* 1,
    no. 2 (Fall 1976): 126–30.

Diouf, Sylviane A. *Slavery's Exiles: The Story of the American Maroons*. New York:
    New York University Press, 2014.

Du Bois, W. E. B. *Black Reconstruction in America, 1860–1880*. New York: Free
    Press, 1998. First published 1935.

Duck, Leigh Anne. *The Nation's Region: Southern Modernism, Segregation, and
    U.S. Nationalism*. Athens: University of Georgia Press, 2006.

———. "Southern Nonidentity." *Safundi: The Journal of South African and
    American Studies* 9, no. 3 (July 2008): 319–30.

———. "What Was the 'New Southern Studies?'" *Society for the Study of Southern
    Literature Newsletter* 47, no. 1 (Spring 2013). http://southernlit.org/society-for
    -the-study-of-southern-literature-newsletter-47-1-spring-2013.

Duggan, Lisa. "The New Homonormativity: The Sexual Politics of Neoliberalism."
    In *Materializing Democracy: Toward a Revitalized Cultural Politics*, edited by
    Russ Castronovo and Dana D. Nelson, 175–94. Durham, NC: Duke University
    Press, 2002.

Duggan, Lisa, and Nan D. Hunter, eds. *Sex Wars: Sexual Dissent and Political
    Culture*. New York: Routledge, 2006.

Dykewomon, Elena. *Riverfinger Women*. Tallahasee: Naiad Press, 1992.
First published 1974.

Echols, Alice. *Daring to Be Bad: Radical Feminism in America, 1967–1975*.
Minneapolis: University of Minnesota Press, 1989.

Edge, John T. *The Potlikker Papers: A Food History of the Modern South*. New York:
Penguin Books, 2018.

Egerton, Douglas. *The Wars of Reconstruction: The Brief, Violent History of
America's Most Progressive Era*. New York: Bloomsbury, 2015.

Ennis, Catherine. *South of the Line*. Tallahassee, FL: Naiad Press, 1989.

Enszer, Julie. "'The Black and White of It': Barbara Grier Editing and Publishing
Women of Color." *Journal of Lesbian Studies*, 18, no. 4 (2014): 346–71.

———. "'Fighting to Create and Maintain Our Own Black Women's Culture':
Conditions Magazine 1970–1990." *American Periodicals: A Journal of History,
Criticism, and Bibliography* 25, no. 2 (2015): 160–76.

———. "The Whole Naked Truth of Our Lives: Lesbian-Feminist Print Culture from
1969–1989." PhD diss., University of Maryland, College Park, 2013. ProQuest
3590787.

Estes, Clarissa Pinkola. *Women Who Run with the Wolves: Myths and Stories of the
Wild Woman Archetype*. New York: Ballantine Books, 1996. First published 1992.

Evans, Sara. *Personal Politics: The Roots of Women's Liberation in the Civil Rights
Movement and the New Left*. New York: Random House, 1979.

Faludi, Susan. "Death of a Revolutionary." *New Yorker*, 15 April 2013. http://www
.newyorker.com/magazine/2013/04/15/death-of-a-revolutionary.

Farley, Tucker Pamella. "'The Dirt She Ate': Minnie Bruce Pratt 'Acting Contrary
Somehow.'" *Lesbian Review of Books* 8, no. 1 (Fall 2001): 3–4.

Faulkner, William. *The Sound and the Fury*. New York: Vintage, 1990.
First published 1929.

Feminary: A Feminist Journal for the South, Emphasizing the Lesbian Vision 10,
no. 1 (1979).

"The Feminist Press: An Annotated Bibliography." *Amazon Quarterly: A Lesbian-
Feminist Arts Journal* 2, no. 4 (1973): 65–70.

Field, Robin E. "Alice Walker's Revisionary Politics of Rape." In *Alice Walker's
"The Color Purple,"* edited by Kheven LaGrone, 149–71. New York: Rodopi, 2009.

Flagg, Fannie. *Fried Green Tomatoes at the Whistle Stop Café*. New York: Random
House, 1987.

———. *I Still Dream about You*. New York: Ballantine Books, 2011.

Flannery, Kathryn. *Feminist Literacies, 1968–1975*. Urbana: University of Illinois
Press, 2005.

Foner, Eric. *Reconstruction: America's Unfinished Revolution, 1863–1877*. New York:
HarperCollins, 1988.

Foote, Stephanie. "Deviant Classics: Pulps and the Making of Lesbian Print
Culture." *Signs: Journal of Women in Culture and Society* 31, no. 1 (Fall 2005):
169–90.

Forest, Katherine. *Curious Wine.* Tallahasee, FL: Naiad Press, 1983.

Foster, Jeannette. *Sex Variant Women in Literature.* Tallahassee, FL: Naiad Press, 1985. First published 1956.

Fougère, Myriam, dir. *Lesbiana: A Parallel Revolution.* Women Make Movies, 2012.

Freeman, Elizabeth. *Time Binds: Queer Temporalities, Queer Histories.* Durham, NC: Duke University Press, 2010.

"Frontiers." *Amazon Quarterly: A Lesbian-Feminist Arts Journal* 1, no. 1 (1972): 5.

Gable, Amanda. "Bertha Harris's *Lover*: Lesbian *and* Postmodern." In *Gay and Lesbian Literature since World War II: History and Memory,* edited by Sonya L. Jones, 143–54. New York: Harrington Park Press, 1998.

Galana, Laurel. "How to Make a Magazine." *Amazon Quarterly: A Lesbian–Feminist Arts Journal* 2, no. 3 (1973): 66–69.

Gallo, Marcia M. *Different Daughters: A History of the Daughters of Bilitis and the Rise of the Lesbian Rights Movement.* Emeryville, CA: Seal Press, 2007.

Gearhart, Sally. *The Wanderground: Stories of the Hill Women.* Watertown, MA: Persephone Press, 1979.

Gerhard, Jane. *Desiring Revolution: Second-Wave Feminism and the Rewriting of American Sexual Thought, 1920–1982.* New York: Columbia University Press, 2001.

Giesking, Jen Jack. "A Queer Geographer's Life as an Introduction to Queer Theory, Space, and Time." In *Queer Geographies: Beirut, Tijuana, Copenhagen,* edited by Lasse Lau, Mirene Arsanios, Felipe Zuniga-Gonzalez, Mathia Kryger, and Omar Mismar, 14–19. Roskilde, Denmark: Museet for Samtidskunst, 2014.

Gilmore, Glenda Elizabeth. *Defying Dixie: The Radical Roots of Civil Rights, 1919–1950.* New York: W. W. Norton, 2008.

Gilmore, Stephanie. "The Dynamics of Second-Wave Feminist Activism in Memphis, 1971–1982: Rethinking the Liberal/Radical Divide." *NWSA Journal* 15, no. 1 (Spring 2003): 94–117.

———, ed. *Feminist Coalitions: Historical Perspectives on Second Wave Feminism in the United States.* Urbana: University of Illinois Press, 2008.

Gleeson-White, Sarah. *Strange Bodies: Gender and Identity in the Novels of Carson McCullers.* Tuscaloosa: University of Alabama Press, 2003.

Gould, Lois. "Creating a Women's World." *New York Times Magazine,* 2 January 1977.

Grahn, Judy. *A Simple Revolution: The Making of an Activist Poet.* San Francisco: Aunt Lute Books, 2012.

———, ed. *True to Life Adventure Stories, Volume 2.* Trumansburg, NY: Crossing Press and Diana Press, 1984.

Gray, Mary L. *Out in the Country: Youth, Media, and Queer Visibility in Rural America.* New York: New York University Press, 2009.

Green, David B. "'Anything that Gets Me in My Heart': Pat Parker's Poetry of Justice." *Journal of Lesbian Studies* 19, no. 3 (July–September 2015): 317–55.

Green, Kai M. *Lesbiana: Book Reviews from* The Ladder, *1966–1972.* Tallahassee, FL: Naiad Books, 1976.

———. "'What the Eyes Did Not Wish to Behold': Lessons from Ann Allen Shockley's *Say Jesus and Come to Me*." *South Atlantic Quarterly* 112, no. 2 (Spring 2013): 285–302.

Grierson, Jennifer. *Our South: Geographic Fantasy and the Rise of National Literature*. Cambridge, MA: Harvard University Press, 2010.

Guelzo, Allen C. *Fateful Lightning: A New History of the Civil War and Reconstruction*. Oxford: Oxford University Press, 2012.

Gunn, Drewey Wayne, ed. *The Golden Age of Gay Fiction*. Albion, NY: MLR Press, 2009.

Gunn, Drewey Wayne, and Jaime Harker, eds. *1960s Gay Pulp Fiction: The Misplaced Heritage*. Amherst: University of Massachusetts Press, 2013.

Halberstam, J. Jack. *Gaga Feminism: Sex, Gender, and the End of Normal*. Boston: Beacon Press, 2012.

Hale, Jon N. *The Freedom Schools: Student Activists in the Mississippi Civil Rights Movement*. New York: Columbia University Press, 2016.

Hall, Jacqueline Dowd, and Mary Murphy. *Like a Family: The Making of a Southern Cotton World*. Chapel Hill: University of North Carolina Press, 2012.

Halperin, David M., and Valerie Traub, eds. *Gay Shame*. Chicago: University of Chicago Press, 2016.

Harker, Jaime. "'And You Too, Sister, Sister?' Lesbian Sexuality, *Absalom, Absalom!*, and the Reconstruction of the Southern Family." In *Faulkner's Sexualities*, edited by Annette Trefzer and Ann J. Abadie, 38–53. Jackson: University of Mississippi Press, 2010.

———. *Middlebrow Queer: Christopher Isherwood in America*. Minneapolis: University of Minnesota Press, 2013.

Harker, Jaime, and Cecilia Konchar Farr, eds. *This Book Is an Action: Feminist Print Culture and Activist Aesthetics*. Urbana: University of Illinois Press, 2016.

Harris, Bertha. *Catching Saradove*. New York: Harcourt, Brace, and World, Inc., 1969.

———. *Confessions of Cherubino*. New York: Daughters, Inc., 1978. First published 1972.

———. *Lover*. New York: New York University Press, 1993. First published 1976.

———. "The More Profound Nationality of Their Lesbianism: Lesbian Society in Paris in the 1920s." In *Amazon Expedition: A Lesbian Feminist Anthology*, edited by Phyllis Birkby, Bertha Harris, Jill Johnston, Ester Newton, and Jan O'Wyatt, 77–88. Cedar Rapids, IA: Times Change Press, 1973.

———. "What We Mean to Say: Notes toward Defining the Nature of Lesbian Literature." *Heresies* 1, no. 3 (Fall 1977): 5–8.

Hemmings, Clare. *Why Stories Matter: The Political Grammar of Feminist Theory*. Durham, NC: Duke University Press, 2011.

Herring, Scott. *Another Country: Queer Anti-Urbanism*. New York: New York University Press, 2010.

Hesford, Victoria. *Feeling Women's Liberation*. Durham, NC: Duke University Press, 2013.

Hewitt, Nancy A., ed. *No Permanent Waves: Recasting Histories of U.S. Feminism*. New Brunswick, NJ: Rutgers University Press, 2010.

Hodges, Beth, ed. "Lesbian Writing and Publishing." Special issue, *Sinister Wisdom* 1, no. 2 (Fall 1976).

——. "Letter from the Editor." *Sinister Wisdom* 1, no. 2 (Fall 1976): 122–25.

Hoffer, Peter Charles. *Cry Liberty: The Great Stono River Slave Rebellion of 1739*. Oxford: Oxford University Press, 2010.

Hogan, Kristen. *The Feminist Bookstore Movement: Lesbian Antiracism and Feminist Accountability*. Durham, NC: Duke University Press, 2016.

Honey, Michael K. *Southern Labor and Black Civil Rights: Organizing Memphis Workers*. Urbana: University of Illinois Press, 1993.

Howard, John. *Men Like That: A Southern Queer History*. Chicago: University of Chicago Press, 1999.

Huggins, Nathan Irvin. *Slave and Citizen: The Life of Frederick Douglass*. New York: Pearson, 1980.

Hull (Akasha) Gloria T., Patricia Bell-Scott, and Barbara Smith, eds. *But Some of Us Are Brave: Black Women's Studies*. New York: The Feminist Press, 1993.

Hunt, V. "An Interview with Minnie Bruce Pratt." *Southern Quarterly* 35, no. 3 (Spring 1997): 97–108.

Hurt, R. Douglas. *Agriculture and the Confederacy: Policy, Productivity, and Power in the Civil War South*. Chapel Hill: University of North Carolina Press, 2015.

Irwin, Edward E. "Freedoms as Value in Three Popular Southern Novels." *Proteus: A Journal of Ideas* 6, no. 1 (Spring 1989): 37–41.

Jagose, Annamarie. *Orgasmology*. Durham, NC: Duke University Press, 2013.

Janney, Caroline E. *Burying the Dead but Not the Past: Ladies' Memorial Associations and the Lost Cause*. Chapel Hill: University of North Carolina Press, 2008.

Jay, Karla. *Tales of the Lavender Menace: A Memoir of Liberation*. New York: Basic Books, 2000.

Jeffries, Hasan Kwame. *Bloody Lowndes: Civil Rights and Black Power in Alabama's Black Belt*. New York: New York University Press, 2010.

Jones, Ann Goodwyn, and Susan V. Donaldson, ed. *Haunted Bodies: Gender and Southern Texts*. Charlottesville: University of Virginia Press, 1997.

Keller, Yvonne. "'Was It Right to Love Her Brother's Wife So Passionately?' Lesbian Pulp Novels and U.S. Lesbian Identity, 1950–1965." *American Quarterly* 57, no. 2 (June 2005): 385–410.

Kelley, Robin D. G. *Hammer and Hoe: Alabama Communists during the Great Depression*. Chapel Hill: University of North Carolina Press, 2015.

Kershaw, Sarah. "My Sister's Keeper." *New York Times*, 30 January 2009. http://www.nytimes.com/2009/02/01/fashion/01womyn.html.

King, Florence. *Confessions of a Failed Southern Lady*. New York: St. Martins, 1990.

———. *Southern Ladies and Gentlemen*. New York: Bantam Books, 1976. First published 1975.

———. *When Sisterhood Was in Flower*. New York: Viking Press, 1982.

Korstad, Robert Rodgers. *Civil Rights Unionism: Tobacco Workers and the Struggle for Democracy in the Mid-Twentieth-Century South*. Chapel Hill: University of North Carolina Press, 2003.

Krantz, Carrie. "Political Power in Reverend Black's Sermons." *MAWA Review* 4, no. 2 (December 1989): 42–44.

Kreyling, Michael. *Inventing Southern Literature*. Jackson: University Press of Mississippi, 1998.

Lavers, Michael K. "Mississippi Governor's Son Reportedly Vicitim of Anti-Gay Attack." *Washington Blade*, 12 April 2016. http://www.washingtonblade.com /2016/04/12/source-mississippi-governors-son-victim-of-anti-gay-attack/.

Lerner, Gerda. *The Grimke Sisters from South Carolina: Pioneers for Women's Rights and Abolition*. Chapel Hill: University of North Carolina Press, 2004.

"Lesbians and Literature." *Sinister Wisdom* 1, no. 2 (1976): 20–33.

Levine, Daniel B. "Uses of Classical Mythology in Rita Mae Brown's *Southern Discomfort*." *Classical and Modern Literature: A Quarterly* 10, no. 1 (Fall 1989): 63–70.

Martindale, Kathleen. "Rita Mae Brown's *Six of One* and Anne Cameron's *The Journey:* Fictional Contributions to the Ethics of Feminist Nonviolence." *Atlantis: A Women's Studies Review* 12, no. 1 (Fall 1986): 102–10.

Massey, Doreen. *For Space*. London: Sage Publications, 2005.

Mays, Raymina. "Delta, a Story." *Feminary* 12, no. 1 (1982): 7–13.

McCullers, Carson. *Ballad of the Safe Café*. New York: Mariner Books, 2005. First published 1951.

———. "Notes on Writing: The Flowering Dream." *Esquire*, December 1959. http://www.sisabianovenia.com/LoLeido/Ficcion/Carson-Flowering.htm.

———. *Reflections in a Golden Eye*. New York: Mariner Books, 2000. First published 1941.

McDuffie, Erik S. *Sojourning for Freedom: Black Women, American Communism, and the Making of Black Left Feminism*. Durham, NC: Duke University Press, 2011.

McElya, Micki. *Clinging to Mammy: The Faithful Slave in Twentieth-Century America*. Cambridge, MA: Harvard University Press, 2007.

McGuire, Danielle L. *At the Dark End of the Street: Black Women, Rape, and Resistance: A New History of the Civil Rights Movement from Rosa Parks to the Rise of Black Power*. New York: Knopf, 2010.

McKee, Kathryn, and Annette Trefzer, eds. Introduction. "The U.S. South in Global Contexts: A Collection of Position Statements." *American Literature: A Journal of Literary History, Criticism, and Bibliography* 78, no. 4 (December 2006): 689–739.

Miller, James A. *Remembering Scottsboro: The Legacy of an Infamous Trial*. Princeton, NJ: Princeton University Press, 2009.

Moraga, Cherrie, and Gloria Anzaldua, eds. *This Bridge Called My Back: Writings By Radical Women of Color*. Albany, NY: SUNY University Press, 2014. First published 1981.

Morgan, Iwan, and Philip Davies, eds. *From Sit-Ins to SNCC: The Student Civil Rights Movement in the 1960s*. Gainesville: University Press of Florida, 2012.

Morris, Bonnie J. *The Disappearing L: Erasure of Lesbian Spaces and Culture*. Albany: State University of New York Press, 2016.

Mosbacher, Dee, Director. *Radical Harmonies: Woodstock Meets Women's Liberation in a Film about a Movement that Exploded the Gender Barriers in Music*. Wolfe Video, 2004.

Muñoz, José. *Cruising Utopia: The Then and There of Queer Futurity*. New York: New York University Press, 2009.

Nealon, Christopher. *Foundlings: Lesbian and Gay Historical Emotion before Stonewall*. Durham, NC: Duke University Press, 2001.

Newton, Esther. *Margaret Mead Made Me Gay: Person Essays, Public Ideas*. Durham, NC: Duke University Press, 2000.

Norman, Rose. "And So It Begins: Gainesville, Florida, Home of the First Women's Liberation Group in the South." *Sinister Wisdom* 93 (Summer 2014): 15–16.

Norman, Rose, Merril Mushroom, and Kate Ellison. "Notes for a Special Issue, Landykes of the South: Women's Land Groups and Lesbian Communities in the South." *Sinister Wisdom* 98 (Fall 2015): 5–12.

Oates, Stephen B. *The Fires of Jubilee: Nat Turner's Fierce Rebellion*. New York: Harper Perennial, 2014.

Onosaka, Junko. *Feminist Revolution in Literacy: Women's Bookstores in the United States*. New York: Routledge, 2006.

Ortiz Taylor, Sheila. *Faultline*. Tallahassee, FL: Naiad Press, 1982.

———. *Outrageous*. Midway, FL: Spinsters Ink, 2006.

Parker, Pat. *Pit Stop*. Oakland, CA: Women's Press Collective, 1973.

———. *Womanslaughter*. Oakland, CA: Diana Press, 1978.

Passet, Joanne. *Indomitable: The Life of Barbara Grier*. Tallahassee, FL: Bella Books, 2016.

Payne, Steven. "Human Rights Campaign Launches New Effort to Bring Equality to Our Southern States." *Daily Kos*. 26 April 2014. http://www.dailykos.com /stories/2014/4/26/1294882/-Top-Comments-Human-Rights-Campaign -launches-new-effort-to-bring-equality-to-our-Southern-states.

Peckham, Joel. "Reconstructing Self, Sex, and the South: Minnie Bruce Pratt's Walking Back Up Depot Street." *Texas Studies in Literature and Language* 55, no. 2 (Summer 2013): 207–33.

Powell, Tamara M. "Look What Happened Here: North Carolina's Feminary Collective." *North Carolina Literary Review* 9 (2000): 91–102.

Pratt, Mary Louise. "Arts of the Contact Zone." *Profession* (1991): 33–40.

Pratt, Minnie Bruce. *Crime against Nature*. Ithaca, NY: Firebrand Books, 1990.

———. "Reading Maps: Two." *Feminary* 12, no. 1 (1982): 121–28.

———. *Rebellion: Essays, 1980–1991*. Ithaca, NY: Firebrand Books, 1991.

Price, Richard, ed. *Maroon Societies: Rebel Slave Communities in the Americas*. Baltimore, MD: Johns Hopkins University Press, 1979.

Puar, Jasbir K. *Terrorist Assemblages: Homonationalism in Queer Times*. Durham, NC: Duke University Press, 2007.

Pugh, Tison. *Precious Perversions: Humor, Homosexuality, and the Southern Literary Canon*. Baton Rouge: Louisiana University Press, 2016.

radicallesbians. "The Woman-Identified Woman." 1970. http://www.glbtqarchive .com/ssh/woman_identified_woman_S.pdf.

Rasmussen, Daniel. *American Uprising: The Untold Story of America's Largest Slave Revolt*. New York: Harper Perennial, 2012.

Reid, Coletta. Introduction to *The Hand that Cradles the Rock*, by Rita Mae Brown, n.p. Baltimore, MD: Diana Press, 1974.

Rensenbrink, Greta. "Parthenogenesis and Lesbian Separatism: Regenerating Women's Community through Virgin Birth in the United States in the 1970s and 1980s." *Journal of the History of Sexuality* 19, no. 2 (May 2010): 288–316.

Rich, Adrienne. "Compulsory Heterosexuality and Lesbian Existence." *Signs* 5, no. 4 (Summer 1980): 631–60.

———. "Diving Into the Wreck." https://www.poets.org/poetsorg/poem/diving -wreck.

Richards, Gary. *Lovers and Beloveds: Sexual Otherness in Southern Fiction, 1931–1961*. Baton Rouge: Louisiana State University Press, 2007.

Robinson, Zandria. *This Ain't Chicago: Race, Class, and Regional Identity in the Post-Soul South*. Chapel Hill: University of North Carolina Press, 2014.

Romine, Scott. "Southern Affects: Field and Feeling in a Skeptical Age." In *The Oxford Handbook of the Literature of the U.S. South*, edited by Fred Hobson and Barbara Ladd, 161–79. New York: Oxford University Press, 2016.

Rose, Gillian, Nicky Gregson, Jo Foord, et al. Introduction to *Feminist Geographies: Explorations in Diversity and Difference*, edited by Women and Geography Study Group, 1–12. Essex, UK: Longman, 1997.

Rule, Jane. *Desert of the Heart*. Tallahassee, FL: Naiad Press, 1993. First published 1964.

———. "For 'Writer/Publisher Relationships: Feminist and Traditional." In *A Hot-Eyed Moderate*, 47–53. Tallahassee, FL: Naiad Press, 1985.

Russ, Joanna. *The Female Man*. Boston: Beacon Press, 2000. First published 1975.

Russell, Danielle. "Homeward Bound: Transformative Spaces in *The Color Purple*." *Dialogue* 5 (2009): 195–207.

Schulman, Sarah. *Israel/Palestine and the Queer International*. Durham, NC: Duke University Press, 2012.

Sears, James T. *Rebels, Rubyfruit, and Rhinestones: Queering Space in the Stonewall South*. New Brunswick, NJ: Rutgers University Press, 2001.

Sedgwick, Eve. *Epistemology of the Closet*. Berkeley: University of California Press, 2008.

Segrest, Mab. *Memoir of a Race Traitor.* Boston: South End Press, 1994.

———. *My Mama's Dead Squirrel: Lesbian Essays on Southern Culture.* Ithaca, NY: Firebrand Books, 1985.

Shockley, Ann Allen. *Loving Her.* Chicago: Northeastern University Press, 1978. First published 1974.

———. *Say Jesus and Come to Me.* Tallahassee, FL: Naiad Press, 1987. First published 1982.

Sisley, Emily, and Bertha Harris. *The Joy of Lesbian Sex.* New York: Simon and Schuster, 1978.

Sitkof, Harvard. *A New Deal for Blacks: The Emergence of Civil Rights as a National Issue: The Depression Decade.* Oxford: Oxford University Press, 2008.

Smethurst, James Edward. *The Black Arts Movement: Literary Nationalism in the 1960s and 1970s.* Chapel Hill: University of North Carolina Press, 2005.

Smith, Barbara, ed. *Home Girls: A Black Feminist Anthology.* New York: Kitchen Table Women of Color Press, 1983.

Smith, Jon. *Finding Purple America: The South and the Future of American Cultural Studies.* Athens: Georgia University Press, 2013.

Smith, Jon, and Deborah Cohn, eds. *Look Away! The U.S. South in New World Studies.* Durham, NC: Duke University Press, 2004.

Smith, Lillian. *Killers of the Dream.* New York: W. W. Norton and Co., 1994. First published 1949.

———. *Strange Fruit.* New York: Harvest Books, 1992. First published 1944.

Smollett, Richard, Sven Beckert, Peter Coclanis, and Barbara Hahn. *Plantation Kingdom: The American South and Its Global Commodities.* Baltimore, MD: Johns Hopkins University Press, 2016.

South, Cris. *Clenched Fists, Burning Crosses: A Novel of Resistance.* Trumansburg, NY: Crossing Press, 1984.

Stone, Amy L., and Jaime Cantrell, eds. *Out of the Closet, into the Archives: Researching Sexual Histories.* Albany: State University of New York Press, 2015.

Tomeio, Ashford. "Marginal Black Feminist Religiosity: Ann Shockley's Construction of the Divine Heroine in *Say Jesus and Come to Me.*" *CLA Journal* 48, no. 3 (March 2005): 290–307.

Town Bloody Hall. Documentary. Panel of feminist advocates for women's liberation and Norman Mailer, filmed April 30, 1971, in New York City Town Hall. Consulted online at Pennebaker Hegebus Films, https://phfilms.com/films/town-bloody-hall.

Traub, Valerie. "The New Unhistoricism in Queer Studies." *PMLA* 128, no. 1 (January 2013): 21–39.

Travis, Trysh. "The Women in Print Movement: History and Implications." *Book History* 11 (2008): 285–300.

Tuttle, Tara. "'The Best Stuff God Did': The Rhetoric of Same Sex Intimacy and Egalitarian Christianity in Alice Walker's *The Color Purple* and Ann Allen Shockley's *Say Jesus and Come to Me.*" In *Constructing the Literary Self: Race and Gender in Twentieth-Century Literature*, edited by Patsy J. Daniels, 151–66. Newcastle upon Tyne, UK: Cambridge Scholars, 2013.

Twitty, Michael. *The Cooking Gene: A Journey through African American Culinary History in the Old South*. New York: Amistad, 2017.

Tyson, Timothy B. *Radio Free Dixie: Robert F. Williams and the Roots of Black Power*. Chapel Hill: University of North Carolina Press, 2001.

Valk, Anne. *Radical Sisters: Second-Wave Feminism and Black Liberation in Washington, D.C.* Urbana: University of Illinois Press, 2008.

Van Ausdall, Mimi Jimuro. "'The Day All of the Different Parts of Me Can Come Along': Intersectionality and U.S. Third World Feminism in the Poetry of Pat Parker and Wilyce Kim." *Journal of Lesbian Studies* 19, no. 3 (July–September 2015): 336–56.

Vance, Carole S., ed. *Pleasure and Danger: Exploring Female Sexuality*. Boston: Routledge and Kegan Paul, 1984.

Walker, Alice. *The Color Purple*. New York: Pocket Books, 1982.

———. *In Search of Our Mothers' Gardens: Womanist Prose*. London: Women's Press, 1985. First published 1983.

Walters, Kerry. *American Slave Revolts and Conspiracies: A Reference Guide*. New York: ABC-CLIO, 2015.

Ward, Carol M. *Rita Mae Brown*. New York: Twayne Publishers, 1993.

Warner, Michael. "Queer and Then." *Chronicle of Higher Education*, 1 January 2012. http://chronicle.com/article/QueerThen-/130161/.

———. *The Trouble with Normal: Sex, Politics, and the Ethics of Queer Life*. Cambridge, MA: Harvard University Press, 1999.

Washburn, Amy. "Unpacking Pat Parker: Intersections and Revolutions in 'Movement in Black.'" *Journal of Lesbian Studies* 19, no. 3 (July–September 2015): 305–16.

Whitehead, Kim. *The Feminist Poetry Movement*. Jackson: University Press of Mississippi. 2012.

Wilkerson, Jessica. "The Company Owns the Mine but They Don't Own Us: Feminist Critiques of Capitalism in the Coalfields of Kentucky in the 1970s." *Gender and History* 28, no. 1 (April 2016): 199–220.

Winterson, Jeannette. *Written on the Body*. New York: Vintage, 1993.

Wittig, Monique. *Les Guerilleres*. Urbana, IL: University of Illinois Press, 2007. First published 1969.

"Writer's Conference to Discuss Woman as Artist in a Sexist Society: Conference to Feature Millett, Kizer, Harris, and Whisnant." *The Ridgerunner* 7, no. 10 (13 January 1972): 1–4.

Yaeger, Patricia. *Dirt and Desire: Reconstructing Southern Women's Writing*. Chicago: University of Chicago Press, 2000.

Yellin, Jean Fagan. *Harriet Jacobs: A Life*. New York: Basic Civitas Books, 2005.

Zinn, Howard. *SNCC: The New Abolitionists*. Cambridge, MA: South End Press, 2002. First published 1965.

For Further Research

This section offers a selected list of major publications by the writers discussed in this book. The aim of this bibliography is to give readers a centralized list of the key works that southern lesbian feminists contributed to the women in print movement, with the further aim of facilitating additional research. I list the authors alphabetically; I list each author's works chronologically. This is neither an exhaustive list of each writer's publications nor a comprehensive list of all the writers who published during this time. (Rita Mae Brown, Fannie Flagg, and Alice Walker, in particular, have many more publications than I have listed here.) When useful, I have included either the original publication information or the first publication by a feminist press. If the text has been reprinted more recently, I also include that information to help readers find more accessible copies. I have also included a list of the major feminist periodicals that many of these authors either edited or published in, or both. This list is not comprehensive, but it gives readers a sense of when the periodical was published and the southern writers and editors involved with the publication. Finally, I have listed the archival collections I used, all of which have more information to discover and new authors to investigate.

Allison, Dorothy. *The Women Who Hate Me*. Ithaca, NY: Firebrand Books, 1983.
———. *Trash*. Ithaca, NY: Firebrand Books, 1988.
———. *Skin: Talking about Sex, Class, Literature*. Ithaca, NY: Firebrand Books, 1988.
———. *Bastard out of Carolina*. New York: Plume, 1992.
———. *Two or Three Things I Know for Sure*. New York: Plume, 1995.
———. *Cavedweller*. New York: Dutton, 1998.
Arnold, June. *Applesauce*. New York: McGraw-Hill, 1966.
———. "Consciousness-Raising." In *Women's Liberation: Blueprint for the Future*, edited by Sookie Stambler, 155–60. New York: Ace Books, 1970.
———. *The Cook and the Carpenter*. New York: New York University Press, 1995. First published 1973 by Daughters, Inc.
———. *Sister Gin*. New York: Feminist Press, 1989. First published 1975 by Daughters, Inc.
———. "Feminist Presses and Feminist Politics." *Quest* 3, no. 1 (Summer 1976): 18–26.
———. *Baby Houston*. Austin, TX: Texas Monthly Press, 1987.

Arnold, June, and Bertha Harris. "Lesbian Fiction." *Sinister Wisdom* 1, no. 2 (Fall 1976): 42–51.

Boyd, Blanche McCrary. *Nerves*. Plainfield, VT: Daughters, Inc., 1973.

———. *Mourning the Death of Magic*. New York: Macmillan, 1977.

———. *The Redneck Way of Knowledge: Down-Home Tales*. New York: Vintage, 1995. First published 1982.

———. *The Revolution of Little Girls*. New York: Vintage, 1991.

———. *Terminal Velocity*. New York: Vintage Contemporaries, 1997.

———. "Dorothy Allison, Crossover Blues." In *Conversations with Dorothy Allison*, edited by Mae Miller Claxton, 17–22. Jackson: University Press of Mississippi, 2012.

Brady, Maureen. *Give Me Your Good Ear*. Trumansburg, NY: Crossing Press, 1981.

———. *Folly*. Trumansburg, NY: Crossing Press, 1982.

———. *The Question She Put to Herself*. Freedom, CA: Crossing Press, 1987.

———. *Ginger's Fire*. New York: Harrington Park Press, 2003.

Brown, Rita Mae. *The Hand that Cradles the Rock*. Baltimore, MD: Diana Press, 1974. First published 1971.

———. "'Violet Hill Elementary School' and 'Fort Lauderdale High,' from the Novel *Rubyfruit Jungle*." *Amazon Quarterly: A Lesbian-Feminist Arts Journal* 1, no. 2 (1973): 6–17.

———. *Rubyfruit Jungle*. Plainfield, VT: Daughters, Inc.: 1973.

———. *Songs to a Handsome Woman*. Baltimore, MD: Diana Press, 1973.

———. *In Her Day*. New York: Bantam Books, 1988. First published 1976.

———. *A Plain Brown Rapper*. Oakland, CA: Diana Press, 1976.

———. *Six of One*. New York: Bantam Books, 1978.

———. *Southern Discomfort*. New York: Bantam Books, 1982.

———. *Sudden Death*. New York: Bantam Books, 1984.

———. *Bingo*. New York: Bantam Books, 1989.

———. *Venus Envy*. New York: Bantam Books, 1994.

———. *Alma Mater*. New York: Ballantine Books, 2002.

Ennis, Catherine. *To the Lightning*. Tallahassee, FL: Naiad Press, 1988.

———. *South of the Line*. Tallahassee, FL: Naiad Press, 1989.

———. *Chautauqua*. Tallahassee, FL: Naiad Press, 1991.

———. *Clearwater*. Tallahassee, FL: Naiad Press, 1991.

———. *Up, Up and Away*. Tallahassee, FL: Naiad Press, 1994.

———. *Time and Time Again*. Tallahassee, FL: Naiad Press, 1996.

———. *The Naked Eye*. Tallahassee, FL: Naiad Press, 1998.

Flagg, Fannie. *Fried Green Tomatoes at the Whistle Stop Café*. New York: Random House, 1987.

———. *I Still Dream about You*. New York: Ballantine Books, 2011.

Gearhart, Sally Miller. *The Wanderground*. Watertown, MA: Persephone Press, 1979.

———. *The Kanshou (Earthkeep)*. Denver, CO: Spinsters Ink, 2002.

———. *The Magister (Earthkeep)*. Denver, CO: Spinsters Ink, 2003.

Grier, Barbara. *Lesbiana: Book Reviews from* The Ladder, *1966–1972*. Tallahassee, FL: Naiad Books, 1976.

Harris, Bertha. *Catching Saradove*. New York: Harcourt Brace, 1969.

———. *Confessions of Cherubino*. New York: Daughters, Inc., 1978. First published 1972.

———. "The More Profound Nationality of Their Lesbianism: Lesbian Society in Paris in the 1920s." In *Amazon Expedition: A Lesbian Feminist Anthology*, edited by Phyllis Birkby, Bertha Harris, Jill Johnston, Ester Newton, and Jan O'Wyatt, 77–88. Cedar Rapids, IA: Times Change Press, 1973.

———. *Lover*. New York: New York University Press, 1993. First published 1976.

———. "What We Mean to Say: Notes toward Defining the Nature of Lesbian Literature." *Heresies* 1, no. 3 (Fall 1977): 5–8.

King, Florence. *Southern Ladies and Gentlemen*. New York: St. Martins, 1993. First published 1975.

———. *When Sisterhood Was in Flower*. New York: Viking Press, 1982.

———. *Confessions of a Failed Southern Lady*. New York: St. Martins, 1990.

Ortiz Taylor, Sheila. *Faultline*. Tallahassee, FL: Naiad Press, 1982.

———. *Southbound*. Midway, FL: Spinsters Ink, 1990.

———. *OutRageous*. Midway, FL: Spinsters Ink, 2006.

Parker, Pat. *Pit Stop*. Oakland, CA: Women's Press Collective, 1973.

———. *Child of Myself*. Oakland, CA: Women's Press Collective, 1974.

———. *Womanslaughter*. Oakland, CA: Diana Press, 1978.

———. *Jonestown and Other Madness*. Ithaca, NY: Firebrand Books, 1985.

———. *The Complete Works of Pat Parker*. Brookville, NY: A Midsummer Nights Press, 2016.

Pratt, Minnie Bruce. *The Sound of One Fork*. Durham, NC: Night Heron Press, 1981.

———. "Reading Maps: Two." *Feminary* 12, no. 1 (1982): 121–28.

———. *We Say We Love Each Other*. San Francisco: Spinsters/Aunt Lute, 1985.

———. *Crime against Nature*. Ithaca, NY: Firebrand Books, 1990.

———. *Rebellion: Essays, 1980–1991*. Ithaca, NY: Firebrand Books, 1991.

———. *S/He*. Ithaca, NY: Firebrand Books, 1995.

Segrest, Mab. *My Mama's Dead Squirrel: Lesbian Essays on Southern Culture*. Ithaca, NY: Firebrand Books, 1985.

———. *Memoir of a Race Traitor*. Boston: South End Press, 1994.

Shockley, Ann Allen. *Loving Her*. Indianapolis, IN: Bobbs-Merrill, 1974.

———. *The Black and White of It*. Tallahassee, FL: Naiad Press, 1980.

———. *Say Jesus and Come to Me*. New York: Avon Books, 1982.

———. *Celebrating Hotchclaw*. Rehoboth Beach, DE: A&M Books, 2005.

South, Cris. *Clenched Fists, Burning Crosses: A Novel of Resistance*. Trumansburg, NY: Crossing Press, 1984.

Walker, Alice. *The Color Purple*. New York: Harcourt, 1982.

———. *In Search of Our Mothers' Gardens: Womanist Prose*. London: Women's Press, 1985. First published 1983.

———. *The Temple of My Familiar.* New York: Harcourt, 1989.
———. *Possessing the Secret of Joy.* New York: Harcourt, 1991.

Selected Periodicals

The Ladder, 1956–1972 (especially 1966–72). Contributors include Barbara Grier,
     Lorraine Hansberry, and Rita Mae Brown.
Quest: A Feminist Quarterly, 1970–85. Contributors include Charlotte Bunch,
     June Arnold, Bertha Harris, and Dorothy Allison.
Amazon Quarterly, 1972–75. Contributors include Rita Mae Brown and
     June Arnold.
Sinister Wisdom, 1976–present. Contributors include Audre Lorde, Adrienne Rich,
     Minnie Bruce Pratt, and many more.
Conditions, 1976–90. Contributors include Dorothy Allison, Jewelle Gomez,
     Cheryl Clarke, and Barbara Smith.
Heresies, 1977–93. Contributors include Bertha Harris and Louise Fischman.
Feminary: A Feminist Journal for the South, Emphasizing the Lesbian Vision,
     1978–1982. Contributors include Cris South, Minnie Bruce Pratt, Mab Segrest,
     and Barbara Smith.

Archival Holdings

The San Francisco Public Library. Collections include the Naiad Press archives
(which includes individual author files for a number of southern writers, and the
correspondence of a wide range of lesbian and feminist writers) and the James C.
Hormel LGBTQIA Center (which includes Barbara Grier's lesbian literature
collection).

     The Sallie Bingham Center for Women's History and Culture, Duke's
Rubenstein Library. Collections include the manuscripts of Dorothy Allison,
Catherine Nicholson, Minnie Bruce Pratt, Mab Segrest, and Blanche McCrary Boyd,
the Atlanta Lesbian Feminist Collective, and Feminist Movements, 1880s to the
present.

Index

Allison, Dorothy, 52, 56, 162, 189, 193; attendance at Sagaris Feminist Institute, 26, 53; attitude toward incest, 125–26; as author of S/M erotica, 56; *Bastard out of Carolina*, 55–57, 136–39, 169–70; Bone's rape in *Bastard Out of Carolina*, 136–39; correspondence with Mab Segrest, 102; early feminism of, 3, 4, 27–28, 38, 65, 90, 110, 146; as employee of *Conditions* magazine, 47, 53, 90; grotesque (southern gothic) writer, 102–4, 106–7; involvement with *Quest* magazine, 47, 53; involvement with WIP Movement, 57; as member of Lesbian Sex Mafia, 110; and Cherrie Moraga, 11, 89; relationship with Bertha Harris, 34, 35, 53, 56, 106; relationship with Barbara Smith, 11, 47, 89; *Trash*, 47, 53, 55, 80, 106; *The Women Who Hate Me*, 53; as a writer of southern identity, 5, 6
Amazon Quarterly, 15, 28, 30–31, 40, 44
anti-Klan activism, 61, 65, 76–77, 80, 135
antiracist coalitions, 15, 75–83, 90, 96, 174
Antoniou, Laura, 192–93
Anzaldua, Gloria, 182; *Borderlands/La Frontera*, 182; *This Bridge Called My Back*, 89
Applesauce (Arnold), 21
archive of southern lesbian feminism, 3, 6, 7, 11, 13, 15, 16, 39, 57, 63–64, 75, 83, 86, 88, 98, 103–4, 107, 113–17, 118, 121, 133–34, 136, 139, 143–47, 148–51, 157, 179, 195

archives, 1, 2, 8, 10, 14, 89, 110, 141; feminist, 9. *See also* archive of southern lesbian feminism
Arnold, June, 43, 44, 158, 162, 165, 191, 194; *Applesauce*, 21; association with avant-garde, 33–34, 42; *Baby Houston*, 39, 125; *The Cook and the Carpenter*, 25, 31, 32, 40, 115–16, 150–57; early childhood of, 17; founding of Daughters, Inc., 3, 15, 17, 30, 31–33, 35–39, 48–49; involvement in early women's liberation, 18, 24–25, 26, 64; involvement in Women in Print Conference, 17; involvement with *Sinister Wisdom*, 39, 40, 41, 44; move to Greenwich Village, 17, 40; published in *Amazon Quarterly*, 31, 40; *Sister Gin*, 84–85, 120–21
avant-garde, 15, 18, 25, 31, 33, 37, 42, 49, 51, 52, 56, 194. *See also* esoteric fiction; feminist avant-garde

Baby Houston (Arnold), 39, 125
Bastard out of Carolina (Allison), 55–57, 169–70; Bone's rape in, 136–39
Bella Books, 190, 191, 193
Bereano, Nancy, 47, 55; role as publisher at Crossing Press, 47; role as publisher at Firebrand Press, 55, 80
Bold Strokes Books, 191, 193
Bone, Martyn, 4
boundary publics, 167–68, 171, 174
Bowman, Parke, 24, 38, 39, 44

Boyd, Blanche McCrary, 6, 11, 56, 57, 126, 129, 163; attendance at Sagaris Feminist Institute, 65; and Daughters, Inc., 3, 32; early feminism of, 26, 32, 65, 110, 123; *Mourning the Death of Magic*, 55, 123–24; *Nerves*, 32, 40, 55, 165; *The Redneck Way of Knowledge*, 55, 162; relationship with June Arnold, 26, 110; *The Revolution of Little Girls*, 55, 162, 182; *Terminal Velocity*, 63, 109–10, 146, 161–64

Brady, Maureen, 26; contributor to *Sinister Wisdom*, 86; and Feminary collective, 80, 86; *Folly*, 47, 83, 86–88; Spinsters Ink, 26, 86

Brown, Rita Mae, 4, 6, 15, 33, 39, 50, 81, 83, 126, 128, 129–32, 148, 189; and *Amazon Quarterly*, 31; and Daughters, Inc., 3; early activism with Radicalesbians, 25, 26, 27, 65, 94; early activism as Lavender Menace, 25, 65; early childhood, 25; and *Feminary*, 47; *The Hand that Cradles the Rock*, 65–67; and *The Ladder*, 24, 27; *A Plain Brown Rapper*, 67; relationship with Charlotte Bunch, 25, 110; relationship with Fannie Flagg, 110; relationship with Martina Navratilova, 110; *Rubyfruit Jungle*, 32, 35, 117–20, 122, 146–47; and *Sinister Wisdom*, 44; *Six of One*, 118; *Southern Discomfort*, 132

Bunch, Charlotte, 25, 38, 47, 110
Butler, Judith, 107
But Some of Us Are Brave, 89
Bywater Books, 191, 193, 194

Campaign for Southern Equality, 195
Catching Saradove (Harris), 21
Charis Books, 1, 190
civil rights, 15, 26, 65, 71, 75–76, 78, 80, 89, 96, 174. *See also* civil rights movement
civil rights movement, 60–61, 135, 194. *See also* civil rights

Clarke, Cheryl, 47, 89, 90
Clausen, Jan, 44
Clenched Fists, Burning Crosses (South), 47, 76, 80, 135, 138
communes, 16, 17, 26, 32, 47, 53, 62, 65, 143–47, 148–65, 165–70
Confessions of a Failed Southern Lady (King), 157, 189
Confessions of Cherubino (Harris), 104–47, 165
consciousness raising, 24, 34, 62–67, 110, 146
Cook and the Carpenter, The (Arnold), 25, 31, 32, 40, 115–16, 150–57
Crime against Nature (Pratt), 8, 53–54, 83–86
Cvetkovich, Ann, 138

Daughters of Bilitis, 19, 23
Desmoines, Harriet, 26, 38, 40, 41, 44–47, 128, 146
Diana Press, 27, 33, 49, 66; lawsuit against, 50; *Sex Variant Women* reprint, 50
Duck, Leigh Anne, 4–5

Enchanted Clitoris, The (King), 158–61
Ennis, Catherine, 146; member of artist collective, 92; *South of the Line*, 92–94
Enszer, Julie, 11, 31, 37, 89, 90, 190
esoteric fiction, 20–21, 31, 35, 38, 49

Farr, Cecilia Konchar, 18
Feminary, 3, 15, 38, 45, 80, 89, 147; early life as a newsletter, 45; key themes and writers for, 78–80, 86, 90, 98; reinvention as southern lesbian journal, 46–47, 78. *See also* Pratt, Minnie Bruce; Segrest, Mab; South, Cris
feminist avant-garde, 18, 30–31, 32, 34, 35. *See also* esoteric fiction

feminist bookstores, 1, 2, 3, 12, 15, 16, 18, 26–27, 31, 33, 38, 52–55, 57, 65, 185, 190–92

feminist poetry, 65

feminist presses, 1–3, 11, 31, 33, 35, 41, 42, 49, 50, 56, 90. *See also* Bella Books; Bold Strokes Books; Bywater Books; Diana Press; Kitchen Table Press; Naiad Press; Persephone Press; Women's Press Collective

Fifth Street Takeover, 24, 31, 64, 151. See also *The Cook and the Carpenter*

Firebrand Press, 3, 47, 55, 80

Flagg, Fannie, 3, 6, 65; *Fried Green Tomatoes at the Whistle Stop Café*, 94, 170–76, 189; *I Still Dream about You*, 94–98, 189; life in California, 26; relationship with Rita Mae Brown, 110

Folly (Brady), 47, 83, 86–88

Forrest, Katherine: *Curious Wine*, 51, 191; editing for Naiad Press, 51, 191

Foster, Jeannette, 19, 50

Fried Green Tomatoes at the Whistle Stop Café (Flagg), 94, 170–76, 189

Friedan, Betty, 75, 109

Fugitives, 6, 47, 64

Garden of Eden, queer, 116, 178, 179, 187

gay pulp, 21–22, 37, 113, 119, 126, 192

Gearheart, Sally, 147, 149, 150; *The Wanderground*, 147–48, 150

Gidlow, Elsa, 50

Gittings, Barbara, 19, 23

Golden Crown Literary Society, 193–94

Gomez, Jewelle, 47, 56, 90

Grahn, Judy, 24, 25, 27, 31, 37

Gray, Mary, 5; boundary publics, 167–68; *Out in the Country*, 141, 167–68

Grier, Barbara, 18, 37, 56, 158, 190, 191, 193–94; as bibliophile, 17, 19–23; fictional appearance in *Outrageous*, 185–89; founding of Naiad Press, 1, 3, 7, 15, 48–52, 89, 190, 191; relationship with Bertha Harris, 36, 38, 114; relationship with June Arnold, 40, 49; relationship with Rita Mae Brown, 50; tributes to Granny Grier, 41–42, 189; work for *The Ladder*, 15, 19, 23–24, 27, 36, 41–42, 48, 50

Grove Press, 21

Hand that Cradles the Rock, The (Brown), 65–67

Harris, Bertha, 3, 15, 25, 28, 29, 38, 41, 44, 47, 49, 50, 52, 82, 83, 102, 104, 115, 126, 190, 191, 194; *Catching Saradove*, 21; *Confessions of Cherubino*, 104–47, 165; and early women's liberation, 12, 26, 41, 53, 108–10; *Joy of Lesbian Sex*, 37; love for *The Ladder*, 36–37; *Lover*, 12, 37, 38, 51, 52, 55, 114, 122–24, 126–29, 146, 147, 165; relationship with June Arnold, 21, 25, 30, 32–35, 37, 39, 42–43, 44, 49, 52

HB 1523 (Mississippi legislation), 59, 188

Hemmings, Clare, 7–8, 10

Herring, Scott, 5, 142

Hesford, Victoria, 13

heteropatriarchy, 66, 116, 131, 164

Highsmith, Patricia, 50; *The Price of Salt*, 50, 119

Hodges, Beth, 41, 44

Hogan, Kristen, 38

Howard, John, 2, 141

HRC Project One America, 58–59

incest, 16, 32, 55, 65, 104, 132; connection to lesbian stereotypes, 117, 121–29; connection to southern stereotypes, 99, 102, 105, 106, 117, 123, 124, 126; critique of, 128, 129, 138

intergenerational romance, 128, 146

intergenerational sex, 16, 104, 117, 119–21, 126

intersectionality, 9, 15, 60, 63, 64, 68, 73, 75–90, 156, 167, 187; class critique of, 5, 6, 7, 20, 28, 39, 46–47, 49, 63, 64, 71–75, 77, 83, 86, 88, 89, 92, 93, 102, 120, 129, 132, 133, 135, 152, 154, 156–57, 165, 167, 182, 188; creation of coalitions, 60, 75, 89, 92, 153, 167, 182, 186. *See also* antiracist coalitions

I Still Dream about You (Flagg), 94–98, 189

Johnston, Jill, 12–13; debate on feminism with Norman Mailer, 13; fictional appearance in *Lover*, 12, 146; friendship with Bertha Harris, 146; *Lesbian Nation*, 30; Town Bloody Hall, 13

Joy of Lesbian Sex (Harris), 37

King, Florence, 3, 6, 26, 104, 107–8, 159–60, 162, 165, 191; *Confessions of a Failed Southern Lady*, 157, 189; *The Enchanted Clitoris*, 158–61; "The Misanthrope's Corner" (*National Review* column), 189; *Southern Ladies and Gentlemen*, 157, 189; *When Sisterhood Was in Flower*, 157–58

Kitchen Table Press, 49, 78, 89

Kreyling, Michael, 4

Ladder, The, 17, 41; early history of, 15, 19, 23–24, 27, 50, 79; Bertha Harris's love of, 36; pilfered mailing list to Naiad Press, 23, 48, 190. *See also* Grier, Barbara

landykes, 16, 140–51, 157, 162, 170

Lavender Menace, 25, 65

lesbian desire, 37, 100, 128–29; depictions of, 88, 100, 104–11, 115, 122–25, 145, 154; "origins" of, 93

lesbian feminism, 12, 19, 26, 31, 35, 37, 39, 53, 76, 83, 86, 88, 107, 150, 157, 190, 194; historical reevaluation, 9, 11–14; history of, 12–14, 15–16, 110; role in lesbian sex wars, 12; and

southern lesbian feminists, 12–14, 45, 47, 57, 63–64, 89, 97–98, 103, 104, 113–16, 118, 121, 123, 133, 134, 136, 139, 142, 145, 147–48, 151, 195

lesbian modernism: Margaret Anderson, 31; Djuna Barnes, 29, 37; Natalie Barney, 29; Hogarth Press, 30, 32; Gertrude Stein, 29, 30, 37, 51; Renee Vivien, 30; Virginia Woolf, 30, 32, 37

lesbian mysteries, 51

lesbian pulp, 19–20, 36–37, 119, 194; Ann Bannon, 20, 36; Bertha Harris's parody of, 36–37; Valerie Taylor, 20. *See also* gay pulp; Highsmith, Patricia; pulp

lesbian romance, 32, 51, 92–93, 190, 191, 193; *Curious Wine* as example of, 51

lesbian sex wars, 11, 53, 111, 158

Lesbiana, 19–23, 52, 145. *See also* Grier, Barbara

lesfic, 189–95

Lethe Press, 192

LICE (Literary Industrial Corporate Establishment), 38, 51

literary works, 2, 14, 15, 16, 17, 20, 21, 24, 25, 37, 39, 51, 52–57, 64, 90, 100–3, 105, 121, 129, 139, 140, 158, 168, 169, 189–94; avant-garde versus popular, 56 (*see also* avant-garde); competing definitions of, 4–5, 7, 15, 18–19, 34–35, 47, 49–50; enmeshment with southern nostalgia, 7, 60, 96, 157, 168, 175, 182, 183, 191; feminist debate over, 18–19, 22–23, 27–29, 31, 47; about lesbianism, 30–31, 35, 39, 42, 44, 45, 52–57, 113–14, 126, 193; traditional definitions of, 15, 28, 103, 106, 126. *See also* esoteric fiction; LICE

Lorde, Audre, 13, 31, 44, 45

Lover (Harris), 12, 37, 38, 51, 52, 55, 114, 122–24, 126–29, 146, 147, 165

Loving Her (Shockley), 26

Marchant, Anyda, 48–49

Memoir of a Race Traitor (Segrest), 55, 80, 81

Millett, Kate, 13, 24, 25, 32, 75

Moraga, Cherríe, 11, 89; *This Bridge Called My Back*, 89

Movement in Black (Parker), 80

Mourning the Death of Magic (Boyd), 55, 123–24

Ms. Magazine, 3, 26, 76

My Mama's Dead Squirrel (Segrest), 47, 80, 102

Naiad Press, 1, 2, 3, 7, 11, 15, 17, 24, 28, 48–53, 56, 89, 92, 116–17, 179, 190–91; founding of, 17, 48–50; funding by Anyda Marchant, 48; Naiad Press novelists: Pat Califia, 50; Katherine Forrest, 51; Patricia Highsmith, 50; Jane Rule, 50; Gertrude Stein, 30; Renee Vivien, 30. *See also* Grier, Barbara; lesbian mysteries; lesbian romances; Shockley, Ann Allen; Taylor, Sheila Ortiz

National Review, 189

Nerves (Boyd), 32, 40, 55, 165

new southern studies, 4

Nicholson, Catherine, 11, 46; attendance at first Women in Print Conference, 38, 41; founding of *Sinister Wisdom*, 25, 39, 40, 41, 44, 45, 128; relationship with Bertha Harris, 25, 38, 47, 52; relationship with Harriet Desmoines, 26, 38, 40, 41, 45, 47, 128, 146; relationship with June Arnold, 39, 40, 44, 47, 52

nonbinary identity, 127

NOW, 25, 65, 123

Olivia Records, 25

Out in the Country (Gray), 141, 167–68

Paperback originals, 15, 17, 18, 19–23, 31, 35–36, 48, 91. *See also* pulp

Parker, Pat, 15, 65, 76, 89, 90, 110; *Movement in Black*, 80; *Pit Stop*, 67–71; relationship with Judy Grahn and Women's Press collective, 25, 27, 67; *Where Would I Be without You*, 25; *Womanslaughter*, 72–75

Pensacola Pride, 166–68

Persephone Press, 49, 148

Pit Stop (Parker), 67–71

Plain Brown Rapper, A (Brown), 67

Polyamory, 9, 104, 110, 117–19

Pratt, Minnie Bruce, 3, 4, 9, 11, 63–64, 65, 79, 88, 189; association with Feminary Collective, 15, 45, 47, 78–80, 89, 90; *Crime against Nature*, 48, 53–54, 83–86; loss of children, 26, 53, 84; *Rebellion*, 55, 81–83; relationship with Cris South, 3, 15, 45, 90, 110; relationship with Leslie Feinberg, 81; relationship with Mab Segrest, 3, 11, 15, 26, 45, 80, 86, 89, 90; winner of Lamont Poetry Prize, 53–54, 84

Price of Salt, The (Highsmith), 50, 119

prostitution, 91, 104, 117, 129–33

pulp, 15, 18, 36, 37, 192, 194. *See also* gay pulp

queer contact zone, 140–47, 166–88

queer sexuality, 6, 14, 15, 20, 99–100, 129–30, 143–44; complicity with conservative power structure, 104, 119, 126, 135, 139, 150, 152; depictions of, 106; liberatory potential of, 3, 33, 59, 103–4, 108–11, 176

queer South, 10, 14, 15–16, 59, 129, 166, 182, 185, 195

queer space, 6–7, 14, 16, 140–53, 159, 166–71, 175, 178, 187

queer theory, 3, 8, 12, 14, 16, 102, 104, 108, 111–13, 139

Quest magazine, 47, 53

radical feminism, 24, 26, 55, 129, 164. *See also* second-wave feminism; women's liberation

radicalism in the South, 6, 15, 47, 61, 65, 83, 58–98, 129

rape, 4, 16, 62, 63, 73, 74, 77, 78, 99, 101, 102, 104, 105, 117, 133–39, 149, 150, 161, 169, 175, 176; critique of, 73, 74, 133–39; depictions of in archive of southern lesbian feminism, 16, 73–74, 77–78, 99, 101, 105–7, 117, 134–39, 149–50, 161, 169, 175–76; as tool of patriarchal control, 73, 77, 78, 133–39, 150, 176

rape crisis centers, 62

Rebellion (Pratt), 55, 81–83

Redneck Way of Knowledge, The (Boyd), 55, 162

Revolution of Little Girls, The (Boyd), 55, 162, 182

Rich, Adrienne, 12–13, 31, 45, 53, 65, 128

Romine, Scott, 7

Rubin, Gayle, 23, 100

Rubyfruit Jungle (Brown), 32, 35, 117–20, 122, 146–47

Rule, Jane, 1, 44, 48, 50

Sagaris Feminist Institute, 26, 53, 65

Say Jesus and Come to Me (Shockley), 91–92, 116–17, 132–33

Schulman, Sarah, 56, 194

Seajay, Carol, 38

second-wave feminism, 109, 144. *See also* radical feminism; women's liberation

SEC Women's Basketball Tournament, 140

Segrest, Mab, 3, 11, 15, 65, 81, 86, 88, 189; association with Feminary Collective, 45, 80, 89–90; early life, 26; *Memoir of a Race Traitor*, 55, 80, 81; *My Mama's Dead Squirrel*, 47, 80, 102

Shelley, Martha, 23

Shockley, Ann Allen, 3, 89; *Loving Her*, 26; *Say Jesus and Come to Me*, 91–92, 116–17, 132–33

Sinister Wisdom, 3, 15, 25, 39, 40–45, 62, 86, 128, 144, 146, 190

Sister Gin (Arnold), 84–85, 120–21

Six of One (Brown), 118

Smith, Barbara, 11, 47, 78, 89

South, Cris, 3, 81; *Clenched Fists, Burning Crosses*, 47, 76, 80, 135, 138; membership in Feminary, 15, 45, 78, 90; relationship with Dorothy Allison, 90; relationship with Minnie Bruce Pratt, 110

southern agrarians, 4; *Feminary's* revision of "the southern tradition," 46, 47

Southern Discomfort (Brown), 132

southern gothic, 16, 99, 100–4, 105–8, 113, 121, 126, 129, 139, 159, 160

southern grotesque, 16, 99–104, 113–14, 122, 134, 139; grotesque camp form of, 104–8

southern history, 81, 94; Confederate distortion of, 61, 140–41, 165, 180, 183; revisionist versions of, 10, 61, 92, 180, 195

Southern Ladies and Gentlemen (King), 157, 189

southern lesbian feminism. *See* lesbian feminism

South of the Line (Ennis), 92–94

Taylor, Sheila Ortiz, 50, 89; *Faultline*, 50, 51; and Naiad Press, 50; *Outrageous*, 179, 180–87, 189; relationship with Barbara Grier, 189

Terminal Velocity (Boyd), 63, 109–10, 146, 161–64

This Bridge Called My Back, 89

Trash (Allison), 47, 53, 55, 80, 106

"trash" fiction, 19, 20, 35, 48–52, 56, 193. *See also* Grier, Barbara; lesbian pulp; paperback originals

Walker, Alice, 125, 189; early civil rights activism, 26, 65, 76; *In Search of Our Mother's Gardens*, 76; *The*

Color Purple, 26, 51, 55, 76, 118, 119, 124, 129, 134, 135, 175, 176; work for *Ms.* Magazine, 26
Wanderground, The (Gearheart), 147–48, 150
Warner, Michael, 14
Wittig, Monique, 35, 45
When Sisterhood Was in Flower (King), 157–58
Where Would I Be without You (Parker), 25
Womanslaughter (Parker), 72–75
Women in Print Movement (WIP), 2–3, 15–19, 26, 28, 31–35, 38, 41, 54, 57, 185, 189–94
women of color feminism, 7, 11, 78, 89, 90
women's culture, 3, 12, 149

women's liberation, 12, 13, 26, 32, 34, 46, 54, 75, 103, 104, 108, 109, 111, 113, 119, 121, 129, 133, 143, 146, 157, 158, 162, 167; histories of, 7–11, 63; misconceptions about, 91; role of southern lesbian feminists in, 11, 17–19, 23–27, 62–65, 113, 129; role of print culture within, 17–19, 23–27, 30, 32, 34, 46, 54, 67, 158, 161–63. *See also* lesbian feminism; radical feminism; second-wave feminism
Women's Press Collective, 27, 33, 67, 146
Women Who Hate Me, The (Allison), 53

Yaeger, Patricia, 100, 133; *Dirt and Desire*, 100